Romance Writer's Sourcebook

Where to sell your manuscripts

FIRST EDITION

Edited by
DAVID H. BORCHERDING

WRITER'S DIGEST BOOKS
CINCINNATI, OHIO

Romance Writer's Sourcebook. Copyright © 1996 by Writer's Digest Books. Printed and bound in the United States of America. All rights reserved. No part of this book may be reproduced in any form or by any electronic or mechanical means including information storage and retrieval systems without permission in writing from the publisher, except by a reviewer, who may quote brief passages in a review. Published by Writer's Digest Books, an imprint of F&W Publications, Inc., 1507 Dana Avenue, Cincinnati, Ohio 45207. 1-800-289-0963. First edition.

This hardcover edition of *Romance Writer's Sourcebook* features a "self-jacket" that eliminates the need for a separate dust jacket. It provides sturdy protection for your book while it saves paper, trees and energy.

97 96   5   4   3   2   1

International Standard Serial Number
ISSN 1081-6739
International Standard Book Number
ISBN 0-89879-726-8

Cover Design: Lamson Design
Cover illustration: Chris O'Leary
Interior Design: Sandy Kent

Attention Booksellers: This directory is published every two years by F&W Publications. Return deadline for this edition is April 30, 1998.

TABLE OF CONTENTS

SECTION III

Markets

❤ ❤

SECTION IV

Agents

❤ ❤

From the Editor

I read romance. That's right, me. A guy.

I didn't always read romance; it is, in fact, a rather recent development. Okay, okay—I didn't read romance until they told me I'd be editing this sourcebook for romance writers, so I'd better get on the stick and start learning about the genre.

That's when I called my mother.

"They want me to edit a romance writer's sourcebook," I told her. "You've been reading these things for years. Tell me some good ones."

Two hours, ten pages and half a pencil later, she said I probably had enough to get me *started*.

Like any good son, I ignored it all and struck out on my own. Upon a co-worker's recommendation, I picked up Jenny Crusie's *Strange Bedpersons*, and—surprise, surprise—I loved it! Funny and well-written, it was not at all what I had expected. I quickly bought her *Getting Rid of Bradley*, which was even better, and then *What the Lady Wants*. When I started interviewing the **Success Stories** authors, I of course had to read *their* books, as well as the **Craft & Technique** authors' novels; I was only being polite.

But then my wife caught me in bed with Margot Early's *The Third Christmas*.

On our honeymoon.

I told her it didn't mean anything, that I was just catching up on my research. I said I could quit any time I wanted. But even as I said it, I knew the awful truth.

I was hooked.

As I worked on this sourcebook, I talked to authors, editors, agents. I gathered information about publishers, organizations and resources. I enlisted the aid of my co-workers, and got a few of them hooked, too. I even went to a romance conference, and although I wasn't the only guy there, I'm sure I was the only guy not accompanying his wife.

I learned some very surprising things. For one, romance is a huge business. Earning almost one billion dollars per year, it accounts for nearly 50% of all mass market fiction sold. Harlequin Enterprises, the largest romance publisher, annually sells more than 190 million romances worldwide. The average romance reader is a college-educated career woman in the 30- to 50-year-old range who works outside the home. Several are trying their hand at writing romance, as well; Romance Writers of America boasts more than 7,600 members.

Even books *about* romance are popular. *Dangerous Men and Adventurous Women: Romance Writers on the Appeal of the Romance*, edited by Jayne Ann Krentz, has been one of the University of Pennsylvania Press's bestsellers. It is one of the first academic books published on the subject, indicating a change in attitude toward romance fiction.

The genre has attracted attention from the media, too. In August of 1995, *The Wall Street Journal* ran an article by Ellen Graham called "Romances, Long Denied Reviews, Get Some Respect." Earlier that year, *Library Journal* began reviewing romance novels, and *Publishers Weekly* and *USA Today* started giving the books more favorable reviews than in the past. The television news show *48 Hours* devoted an entire hour to "Isn't It Romantic?"—a report (albeit a poor one) on the popularity of romance novels. Even *U.S. News and World Report* published a special report on romance in its November 6, 1995, issue.

What it all means is that romance no longer fits the image many people have assigned it. It is not formulaic, it does not depend on cliché and it is much harder to write than most people assume. It is a legitimate form of literature, demanding all the study, review and respect that any other genre deserves.

Therefore, it is my pleasure to give you this *Romance Writer's Sourcebook*. Part directory and part how-to, this book is a hybrid of the two kinds of resources Writer's Digest Books has been publishing for years. In the **Craft & Technique** section, established romance authors share their tips on writing dialogue, creating characters, handling love scenes, using humor and exploring new subgenres in romance fiction.

In the **Markets** section, you'll find interviews with editors at the major publishing houses, telling you what they look for in a manuscript. And later, two of those editors—Shauna Summers at Bantam and Malle Vallik at Harlequin—each examine a recently published first novel and tell what made them decide to buy. Excerpts from those novels, plus six First Sale stories of new writers, can be found in **Success Stories**.

Authors' representative Denise Marcil tells you how to find and work with an agent, and attorney Stephen Gillen gives you excellent advice to keep in mind when negotiating a book deal and signing a contract. All of that plus listings of agents can be found in the **Agents** section. And, in **Resources**, we have lists of organizations, conferences, contests, online resources and references all geared toward the romance writer.

In short, we've tried to give you everything you need to make your dream of getting published come true, including the most up-to-date information on writing and marketing your romance novel. But everything changes, and that is especially true in the publishing industry. Therefore, you should continue to read widely both romance novels and periodicals about romance, such as *Romance Writer's Report, Affaire de Coeur, Romantic Times* and, of course, *Writer's Digest Magazine.* Query publishers before sending them your work, and request tips sheets if they offer them. And, if you find some information in this book that has changed, help us keep you and other romance writers updated by letting us know.

Likewise, we would like to hear about your successes. When you sell that first or next novel, drop us a note. Our address is:

The Marketplace Series
Writer's Digest Books
1507 Dana Avenue
Cincinnati, Ohio 45207
Email: Wdigest@aol.com

Good luck!

David H. Borcherding

New Ground:
The Evolution of Romance

NORA ROBERTS

What is a romance novel? It's a love story. That's the simplicity that remains the base for plot, for character, for setting. It is a relationship book that deals with people, their problems and joys, their hearts and minds and goals. That's the complexity that offers a rich trove to mine.

Today's romance novels evolve and change as people evolve and change, but the elemental premise that women have explored so well remains constant. Tell me a story, a wonderful story about people I'd like to meet, about a heroine I can admire, a hero I could fall in love with. Give me atmosphere, give me emotion. Above all, give me hope.

Romance novels are books about hope, the hope that love will find a way, whatever the odds, whatever the obstacles. That core of hope is the foundation for a rich and exciting genre that continues to reinvent itself.

One of the finest things about romance novels, and those who write them, is the willingness and the determination to grow, to reflect the reader's needs; to concentrate on reader expectation. They are, primarily, books written by women for women. This is something to celebrate, just as the power of love and commitment is something to celebrate. What a joy it is to open a book and experience, to remember, that awesome rush of plunging headlong into love for the first time. Or more importantly, the last time. The time that counted.

The women I've met through my work, both writers and readers, are a fascinating, entertaining and generous group. The books we share bond us, not only in our choice of entertainment, but in our belief that love matters most.

Yes, that happy ending means that the hero and heroine will walk off into the sunset at the book's end. This is a constant of romance, and it's reader expectation. Just as in a mystery, the villain will be revealed and good will overcome evil. Love is, after all, the grandest mystery. Why this man and this woman are attracted to each other, why they find each other, why they struggle to reach common ground to become a couple is a puzzle the human race will never completely solve.

It's chemistry and timing, it's effort and it's luck. It's frustrating and it's painful. And it's great, glorious fun.

What could be more entertaining than reading the tale of two people who are fighting their way through that complex and baffling puzzle?

There are innumerable ways to tell a love story. Just as there are, with 88 keys to work with on a piano, innumerable love songs to compose.

EARLY CATEGORY ROMANCES

Once upon a time, Harlequin offered the readers a different play on the theme of boy meets girl. Short, quick reads for busy times, books that provided a one man-one woman love story, with conflict, sexual tension, emotional commitment and a happy ending. These were category romances, published as a line under the Harlequin imprint, and written for the most part by British authors in British style.

In Harlequins, we were treated to romances set in exotic places, taken into the lives and loves of people created by writers such as Violet Winspear, Anne Mather, Charlotte Lamb and that brash new American Janet Daily. New doors opened. There were contemporary stories with contemporary characters packaged and priced to sell.

And sell they did.

These books, these love stories, epitomized romance. They showed values; the commitment of a man and woman to each other and to overcoming problems and conflict in order to marry and live happily ever after. What is a romance if not a celebration of the heart, and the basic human need to find a mate?

The Harlequins of the 60s and early 70s often boasted wealthy, brooding heros and innocent, virginal heroines. She would be young, usually orphaned and engaged in a traditionally female profession. They were written from the heroine's point of view only—the poor guy never got to think—but these were, after all, women's books. There was plenty of sexual tension, but no consummation without marriage. Even then, the bedroom door stayed firmly closed. And by the end, though the hero had remained cynical, aloof, brooding and often enigmatic, our plucky heroine brought him to his knees.

The readers loved them. And again, these stories inspired many of us to try our hand at writing.

IN DAYS OF OLD

On the historical romance front, Kathleen Woodiwiss and Rosemary Rodgers were breaking new ground. Sex. What a concept in romance. Men and women actually had sex—hot, steamy, page-burning sex. Bodices were ripped, chests gleamed and virgins gave up their innocence. Heros seduced, abducted or plundered, but, by the end, were once more on their knees, desperately in love.

Readers responded to the idea by flocking to the bookstores in droves. *The Flame and the Flower* and *Sweet, Savage Love* pushed the boundaries of romance with their hot-blooded characters, their adult relationships, and their frank and imaginative love scenes. We, the readers, were fascinated. And we wanted more.

Romance grew with its variety. The innocence of the Harlequin, the fire of the sexy historical, the charm of the Regency. Let's not forget one of my favorites: the Gothic. I haunted bookstores searching for covers that showed a beautiful woman, in obvious fear and distress, fleeing from a castle/manor house/cliff-side mansion where a light was always burning in the topmost window. I adored them, the eerie atmosphere, the intangible danger, the heroine's courage. Even when it meant she wandered into the dark in her nightgown, with only a flickering candle to light the way, her restless sleep disturbed by a suspicious noise downstairs.

Everyone had their favorite types, favorite authors. I was a Gothic junkie who broadened her habit with Harlequin Presents, a series that offered exotic locales and comtemporary people, adventurous historicals ranging from medievals to pirates to cowboys, and Regency drawing room comedies that celebrated a brief, delightful era where everyone went to Almack's. I, like other readers, picked and chose according to my mood. They were fun to read, compelling, interesting, sexy and, above all, entertaining.

But there were still changes to come.

LOVE, AMERICAN STYLE

In 1980, Silhouette launched its category romance line, using the monstrously successful Harlequin framework and giving it an American spin.

The constants remained, but the stories were written by American writers, using American characters, American settings. New stars erupted. Sandra Brown, Jayne Anne Krentz, Dixie Browning. The early '80s were a fertile time for romance. Silhouette and Harlequin added more lines and more variety with such innovations as Desire, Intrigue and Special Editions. The opportunity for writers and readers boomed.

The sex was modern, too. The bedroom door burst open. We, ah, thrust into the physicality of romance in contemporary category with great enthusiasm. Men began to think, allowing the reader to understand the hero's motivations, his heart, his mind. Heroines no longer had to be—hold onto your hats—virgins. A modern heroine wasn't required to be 18 and innocent any longer. The hero was no longer burdened with the responsibility of being the richest man in the free world, with all the arrogance and cynicism this required. The relationship between hero and heroine became equal, a partnership, and the problems writers chose reflected the problems in contemporary society. Wrenching divorce, single parenthood, demanding careers—yes, our heroine might have a career. She could be a CEO, a small businesswoman, a cop, a recording star. She could be anything.

In contemporary romance fiction there were now short, sexy romances, longer more intricately plotted stories and the more gentle, innocent romances that had cemented the theme. Publishers, impressed with the explosion of popularity, rushed to create their own category line. Most faded, but Bantam's Loveswept, using the twist of humor with romance, remains, along with Silhouette and Harlequin, a solid force in romance publishing.

Changes happened quickly in the 1980s. What did the reader want, and how could publishers provide it? The answer, to me, was always simple: Tell me a story. Writers who did, and did it well, blossomed: Jude Devereaux, Johanna Lindsay, Julie Garwood, Catherine Coulter and more in historical fiction; Sandra Brown, Jayne Anne Krentz, Dixie Browning, Elizabeth Lowell and more in contemporary. These women continue to write and sell today, earning reader loyalty because, while they've never forgotten their roots, they're willing to risk new ground.

STRANGE NEW WORLDS

New ground is what it's all about today. Because writers of romance are readers first, they understand the need for variety, for challenge, for a fresh way of playing the theme. Since the early Mary Stewart and Victoria Holt, romance novels have combined elements from other genres. Subgenres have always existed in romance publishing, but today they seem to require labels. Contemporary and historical are apparent, of course, but now you might mix either of these into a time travel. The enormous popularity of the time travel romance provides writers an opportunity to yank a character out of her own time and place, plunging her into the unexplored. Take a modern career-oriented, independent woman, toss her back into the eighteenth century and see how she copes, not only with the time shift, but with a hero who doesn't have a twentieth century sensibility. Or take an eighteenth century hero, the Earl of Arrogance, and zap him into modern times. There are enormous possibilities for fun, for fantasy and romance when we use time warps and culture shocks.

Paranormal romance is another subgenre that can be found in either historical or contemporary. Set in any time, these books can weave spells along with the passion and adventure. Here we touch on the otherworld, the occult, the powerful element of fairy tale or horror. Again, the mystery of it, the hint of danger and the unknown make a perfect match with the excitement of a developing relationship.

And a hero who grows fangs or can walk through walls makes a pretty exciting love interest.

Paranormal romance has opened wide, as have the time travel, fantasy and science fiction subgenres because, I believe, romance is the single genre that can and does embrace elements of all other areas of fiction. This is one of the reasons for its success, its popularity and its endurance.

Another personal favorite is romantic suspense. It was from the very beginning my choice of pleasure reading. It was from the very beginning what I wanted most to write. Blending the mystery, intrigue, external risk and conflict of murder with the mystery, intrigue, internal risk and conflict of falling in love seems like a natural mix to me. Certainly, finding the right mix, convincing the reader to be equally invested in the resolution of the mystery and the resolution of the love story, is vital. The writer must be equally invested to make it work well. There should probably be a connection between the two levels, their progress and their resolution for a smooth plot and full reader satisfaction. The thrill of the chase, the hunt, the analyzing of clues dropped works on both levels in this dual subgenre. The added punch of a good juicy murder sure keeps me turning the pages.

NO LIMITS

In romance we venture anywhere from small town to small planet, from Celtic mysticism to futuristic fantasies. We've got vampires, werewolves, space travelers, cowboys, CEOs, knights and dragons, mermaids, cops and robbers, pirates, truck drivers and witches. Our cynical hero might fall for the Sunday school teacher, or our no-nonsense heroine could lose her heart to a ghost.

There are no limits. Romance is everywhere, in everyone, and occasionally, in everything.

Anne McCaffrey's *Restoree* was a blend of science fiction and romance. Her Pern series is ripe with the elements that make a romance novel hum. Dean Koontz's *Watchers* was a thriller, with horror overtones, but it sure had a heck of a love story blooming through it. Steven King's *The Dead Zone*, has one of the most haunting and effective love scenes I've ever read. No one would ever call King a romance writer, but he certainly touched the chords.

As romance readers embrace other genres, romance writers include the elements of those genres in their work. Of all popular fiction, romance is the most flexible and open to pushing its boundaries. We've benefited from this freedom to explore. I can't be Mary Stewart, but I can write romantic suspense. Or time travel, or police procedurals or horror. Whatever the story, the *love* story, demands.

As readers, we've benefited as well. It's such a thrill to go into a bookstore and come out loaded with books, knowing the romances I've chosen will provide me with sex, murder, an exotic setting, a new planet, a trip to eighteenth century Scotland or a weekend in pastoral Virginia. I might find myself being held hostage by a pirate, or rocketing through space with my hands on the controls, solving a murder or being rescued from a dragon. My hero might be wearing buckskins, a brocade waistcoat or Savile Row. Wherever the story takes me, I know I'll fall in love, and, more than likely, have terrific sex. That's a pretty good deal.

THE NEWEST GROUND

New genres are popping up faster than they can be labeled, as writers and readers continue to explore. And books become more difficult to tag. Under the name J.D. Robb I'm doing what could be called romantic suspense/mystery/police procedural/futuristics. I don't like to worry about trends, and certainly wouldn't attempt to predict them. In romance, we're always dipping our toes into something new. Certainly paranormal, futuristics and time travel stories are gaining a larger audience. Books that deal with different planets and times, or feature the unexplainable are ripe territory for plucking new stories. These are just a few of the places romances will take us as we zip into the next millennium. But there will always be a place on the shelves and in the readers' hearts for the classic. I have no doubt that when some young woman looking for a book to wile away an evening picks up *Airs Above the Ground*, as I once did, she'll be just as delighted, just as hooked, as I was. Once she falls for Mary Stewart, she'll likely go roaming those shelves for more.

THE EVOLUTION CONTINUES

Romance novels will never stand still. There will always to more elements to blend and mix and shuffle into that core love story. You may still find that book with the 18-year-old virgin on the shelf—sandwiched between one about the 40-plus widow and one about the single father with triplets. You'll find adventurous women hitching up their wagons and heading west—or commanding their own starships. The reader can look forward to more excitement, more variety, more surprises without losing what attracted her to romance to begin with: the emotion, the atmosphere, the heart of a solid relationship book.

A new generation of writers is crafting stories, and their books are sharing shelf space with the familiar and favorite. With romance novels in their many forms garnering 50 percent of the paperback market, the reader has more choices than ever before. Spin the wheel, and take your pick. Then be prepared to be seduced and abducted, to run from the law or hunt down a villain, to fall in love with the white knight or a man who just dropped in from another galaxy.

Just remember, whatever place, whatever time, whatever problems the story provides, you're about to live happily ever after.

THE GROUNDBREAKERS

Mary Stewart, Victoria Holt, Phyllis Whitney, Georgette Heyer. These names are magic to me. These women introduced me, and millions of other readers, to the wonderful and varied world of romance novels. Very often when I'm talking with a group of writers and readers discussing which authors hooked us on the romance genre, which books we remember most fondly through the years, these names are mentioned time and time again.

Nine Coaches Waiting, The Devil's Cub, Mistress of Mellyn are personal favorites of mine, and lovers of the genre will find these books and others by these authors a common ground of delight. Characters you never forget, stories that play through the heart and head years after the first sampling. The romance, the danger, the atmosphere were brought to life so vividly by these talented writers in such a timeless fashion that their books are read over and over, generation after generation, and remain as fresh and vital as the day they were first published.

I cut my teeth on them, and am continually grateful for the places their stories took me. To Greece in Ms. Stewart's *My Brother Michael*, to fashionable Regency England through Ms. Heyer's *The Grand Sophie*. I'm delighted to have fallen in love with the strong, mysterious heros who strode through Ms. Whitney's and Ms. Holt's works, to have admired and empathized with their marvelous and courageous heroines. The hours I've spent with one of their books in my hand haven't been just entertainment. They have been an adventure.

Their books remain on my shelf, continue to give me pleasure, and always take me into that exciting and special reality the best storytellers create with words. Mary Stewart's incomparable talent for blending suspense and romance, Ms. Heyer's wit and charm, Ms. Holt's glorious Gothics and Ms. Whitney's skillful play on atmosphere have provided endless hours of reading pleasure, transporting the reader to fabulous places and fascinating times. That is, after all, the purpose of a novel.

But these women provided even more. They inspired others, myself included, to pick up a pen and challenged admirers to reach for excellence in storytelling. So many of us who write today took that first hesitant step into the business because we simply fell in love with the words these women wrote, and the worlds they created.

It's impossible to count the number of times I've read their work. Over and over. Each time I've wept and laughed and sighed and shuddered. I will confess that Mary Stewart was, and is, my hero. No, she is my goddess. In fact, I wanted to *be* Mary Stewart. That certainly wasn't possible, but without the influence of her books, I might never have written the first word. So I, and everyone who writes romance today, owe these talented women an enormous debt. Their books paved the way, showed us what could be done with the basic premise of boy meets girl. The rich variety of their work is a sterling example of the romance novel at its best. The popularity of their books broke the ground for those of us who came after.

—*Nora Roberts*

Craft & Technique

Mind, Body, Heart and Soul: Creating Fully-Developed Characters in Romance Fiction

SUZANNE SIMMONS

ardboard. Two-dimensional. All the depth of a wading pool. Cookie-cutter characters.

How many times have you picked up a novel and halfway through the story decided not to finish reading it because you didn't care what happened to the people? They were dull, uninteresting, cardboard cut-outs. They were strictly two-dimensional. They had all the depth of a wading pool, and they seemed to be made of the same stuff as a hundred, a thousand, other fictional characters.

The greatest sin in fiction writing is creating characters that no one gives a fig about.

A clever plot will carry a writer only so far. The same is true for exhaustive research, an exciting or exotic backdrop, sparkling wit or brilliant prose. All is for naught if you haven't created compelling characters that make the reader laugh, that make the reader cry, that make the reader give a tinker's damn.

It's true for any novel, but it's especially true for a romance novel.

For the sake of this discussion I'm going to divide characters into two categories: primary and secondary. Primary and secondary characters are, of course, developed differently.

In the romance novel there should be two, *and only two*, primary characters: the male and female lead, usually referred to in the genre as the hero and the heroine. As a romance writer, you must like—nay, must love— your hero and heroine. If you don't care passionately about the man and woman that you've chosen to write about, how can you expect anyone else to?

I believe that the fully-realized hero or heroine must possess *seven* characteristics:

1. a strong sense of personal honor and integrity
2. intelligence
3. attractiveness
4. an interesting background
5. an internal source of conflict
6. flaws or weaknesses
7. the ability (or at least the potential) to experience the full range of human emotions, especially, in the end, love.

Now let's look at each of these seven characteristics, one at a time.

HONOR AND INTEGRITY

Perhaps Shakespeare said it best when he penned in *Richard II*: "Mine honour is my life; both grow in one/Take honour from me, and my life is done."

There is nothing left for the hero or the heroine if they are not a man or a woman of honor. Honor above all else. Honor first and foremost. Without a strong sense of personal integrity and personal honor, the hero ceases to be a hero, the heroine is no longer a heroine. This doesn't mean, naturally, that they don't make mistakes and plenty of them. (See characteristic number 6: flaws and weaknesses.)

If the hero or heroine tells a lie or practices any form of deception in your story—romance writer, be warned—you'd better have a darned good reason. Otherwise, your character will appear sneaky, untrustworthy, perhaps even deceitful; all unattractive characteristics best saved for the villain/villains of the piece.

INTELLIGENCE

Your hero or heroine may occasionally do or say something stupid, but they must never actually *be* stupid. And, please, don't confuse naivete or inexperience with stupidity.

Both your hero and heroine must possess some form of underlying intelligence, whether it be academic learning, plain old common sense, an understanding of human nature that comes from the heart, or personal experience.

ATTRACTIVENESS

By attractiveness I don't necessarily mean physical beauty or physical perfection, but there must be something that initially attracts the hero to the heroine and vice versa. It may be his confidence, his demeanor or his incredibly broad shoulders. It may be her kindness, her goodness or her lovely long legs.

AN INTERESTING BACKGROUND

Since the hero and the heroine are the only two primary characters in your romance novel, since they dominate your story, you need to create a man and a woman of sustaining interest to the reader.

Another warning: You can always tell when a writer hasn't done her homework in this respect. She tends to bring in more and more secondary characters and perhaps even introduce an additional storyline or two. This only results in padding. Extraneous padding should be avoided at every opportunity. Don't kid yourself: all that froufrou detracts from the story you originally set out to tell.

AN INTERNAL SOURCE OF CONFLICT

The hero is fighting against something within himself. The same is true for the heroine. Whether it is the inability to trust, or to express love, or perhaps to even believe in love, the internal conflict keeps the hero and heroine apart until it is resolved.

Meanwhile, the external source of conflict may initially keep the hero and heroine apart, but what ultimately unites them in a partnership is the "it's-the-two-of-us-against-the-world" ploy.

An additional word here about conflict. The essential, built-in conflict of the romance novel is the eternal struggle between *male* and *female*. Make the most of it! It started with Adam and Eve, progressed through Samson and Delilah, continued with King Kong and Fay Wray, and ended up on the modern movie screen as Harry and Sally. It has endured because it works. Make it work to your advantage.

FLAWS AND WEAKNESSES

You, the romance writer, must show that a character flaw has developed logically from your hero or heroine's background, experiences or personality. A character flaw must make sense. It cannot be thrown in without a bit of explanation.

A flaw or weakness in one lead character is often counterbalanced by a strength in the other. She redeems him. He redeems her. The strength of their love redeems them both.

Yet another warning: Tread softly, or at least cautiously, when endowing your hero and heroine with flaws and weaknesses. They need not be perfect—after all, they're only human—but if you create characters that are too flawed, then they can't be fully redeemed in the reader's eyes by the end of the book.

THE FULL-RANGE OF EMOTIONS

In a successful romance novel the reader should know how the hero and heroine feel about love, sex, men and women, children, physical passion and a myriad of other subjects. Therefore, you must know how you, the writer, feel about all of the above.

"Know thyself." That was the inscription at the Delphic Oracle, according to Plato and attributed to the Seven Sages.

Alexander Pope expressed it in these words: "Know then thyself, presume not God to scan; the proper study of mankind is man."

Indeed, to create fully-developed characters in any genre you must know, first, yourself, and then your characters, inside and out. What is your heroine's favorite color? Her favorite book? What music does she prefer? Where was your hero born? What was his family like when he was growing up? What is his educational background? What are her interests? Her passions? Has either been in love before? Has his/her heart been broken? What, if any, is their level of sexual experience?

You must know everything. Then the hero and heroine become real to you, and you, the omnipotent creator of your own world, can breathe life into *people* you care about, into *people* the reader will care about, not simply characters in a book.

Yet another word of warning: Don't tell your reader everything. As a writer, you will use common sense and restraint, and convey only the bits and pieces that enhance your story.

SECONDARY CHARACTERS

Secondary characters always take a backseat to the primary characters. They are second in importance, in rank and in value, serving only in a subordinate or auxiliary position to the hero and heroine.

Romance writers everywhere would do well to remember this.

Secondary characters in the romance novel are generally either good (serving in a true supporting role to the hero or heroine) or evil (you dastardly villain, you!).

Cardinal rule: Whether good or evil, no secondary character should be of greater interest to you, the writer, or to your reader than the hero and heroine.

Cardinal sin: Creating a villain or villainess who is more fascinating, more intriguing, more downright mesmerizing than either the hero or the heroine of your story.

If you do err, may I recommend you go back to the drawingboard and begin again?

A few other thoughts about secondary characters. They must always serve a purpose in your story; to give the reader another view of people, places and events, or to serve as a foil or challenge for the hero or heroine.

Not all secondary characters are created equal. Some are drawn with a broader brush stroke than others. Some may enter a scene, do their bit and quickly exit. This type of secondary character makes a *cameo* appearance.

CHARACTERS IN GENERAL

I recently finished reading (okay, I admit to skimming the last third of the book) a highly-acclaimed, bestselling, hardcover, literary novel and, being thoroughly disgusted, chucked it into the trashbin.

Why?

Because every character in the novel spoke with the same voice and used the same vocabulary, especially the identical four- letter words. The list of characters included: a common thug, a twelve-year-old boy, his mother, a policeman and a cold-blooded assassin.

Whether hero or heroine, secondary character or merely cameo, each person in your book should have his own voice. It also helps if each person has his own agenda, his individual speech patterns, language, actions and thoughts.

A final word of warning: You may wish to reserve truly distinctive speech patterns for a character making a cameo appearance because most readers have difficulty, or lack patience, with dialect. In other words, a little goes a long way.

An example is Galsworthy, the head gardener, in my 1995 historical romance, *Bed Of Roses*.

"Beggin' yer pardon, my lady."

"Do come in, Galsworthy."

"It's one o' the lads, my lady."

"Yes," Alyssa prompted.

"Ian McKennitt, it is."

"What about Ian McKennitt?"

"Not so much somethin' about the lad as somethin' he saw in the woods."

"Which woods?"

"The Old Woods. Well, not so much somethin' he saw in the Old Woods as somethin' he saw in the Monk's Cave. . . . "

As I said: A little goes a long way.

VIEWPOINT

One of the leading and certainly most talented romance writers of our day has deliberately chosen to tell her stories using only the hero and heroine's points of view. Her success using this technique—and her continual bestselling status—speaks for itself.

Personally, I like to use multiple points of view in my romance novels (the variety of experience for the writer is downright seductive), but I must warn you of the problems involved.

First, the more viewpoints you employ, the more diluted your story becomes emotionally.

Second, if not clearly written, there is always the chance for confusion on the part of the reader, i.e. exactly whose head are we in during this scene?

Third, I don't recommend switching back and forth between points of view in the same scene. I've seen it done. I have *never* seen it done well. I avoid it like the plague.

Fourth, change viewpoints judiciously. I don't have a hard and fast rule on this, but I rarely allow myself inside the head of more than four or five characters in any single book. And I always stay in either the hero or heroine's head unless there is a valid reason to be inside someone else's.

For example, in *Desert Rogue* (1992) a sexual encounter between two secondary characters is witnessed by the villain of the story. The scene is seen through his eyes for several very good reasons. It keeps the primary characters pure and untainted. (It's all right for a villain to be a Peeping Tom, but not the hero or heroine.) And because it tells the reader as much, if not more, about the villain as it does the two people involved in the illicit act.

Use any change in viewpoint wisely and well, and exercise caution!

Finally, the overall feeling of your book must be a reflection of the hero and heroine you have chosen to write about. They should dominate the story in a well-told romance novel—not the clever plot, not the heinous villain, not the time period nor the place, not historical detail, but their love story. That is the story you, as a romance writer, must feel compelled to tell: the story of one man, *this man*; one woman, *this woman*.

The Well-Chosen Words

EVAN MAXWELL

*O*ur offices are separated by a short hallway, so I didn't have to raise my voice.

"They want a piece on dialogue," I said.

The silence was very loud.

Finally, "Who is 'they'?"

"The Writer's Digest folks. They are doing a sourcebook for romance writers."

More silence.

"It doesn't have to be too long," I added.

"Good. They're on the right track."

Smart woman, my collaborator. I wish she were doing this piece because she is much the smarter of the two of us about writing technique. But I'm the one who agreed to do this piece, so I'm stuck.

I said it aloud. "I'm stuck. That's what you're saying. Right?"

Silence.

"Right, dear?" I called down the hallway.

No answer.

"Dear?"

"What makes them think writing dialogue for romance is different than writing dialogue for any other genre?"

Then the door to her office swung shut. Hard.

Oh, well. I'll use my usual technique, spout something really outrageous and entice her into coming along and bailing me out.

Here goes:

Dialogue is not speech. Speech, the words that come tumbling out from the mouths of real people in real situations, is messy.

I spent 20 years in the newspaper business. One of the best reporters I ever knew was Gordon Grant. Gordy was a short, handsome devil with one eye and a wicked, lopsided grin. He had shared a foxhole with, and studied, Ernie Pyle, the great human-interest writer of World War II.

Gordy was a feature writer who covered the outdoors beat. About twice a week, he would crank out a gem of a piece about some salt-water sailor or back-country cowboy, a slice of life that tasted like Mom's apple pie. Invariably, each piece would contain a brilliant and evocative string of words inside quotation marks, the kind of line that makes the subject of a feature come alive.

One day I happened to sit in on one of Gordy's interviews. When the piece ran in the paper a day later, I was amazed.

Shocked, even.

"Gordy," I hollered, pointing to a pithy quote. "I was there. I never heard him say that."

"He would have said it if he had thought of it," Gordy replied blandly.

A point well-taken, particularly since I know for a fact that not one of Gordy's subjects ever complained about being misquoted. All writers need to begin from the proposition that dialogue is not real speech. If you think it is, go down to the courthouse and pull out the transcript of a trial. Read it aloud. Listen to how inarticulate most people are, how the words come in fits and starts and incomplete sentences.

The door to her office opened. My collaborator stuck her head out.

"Tell them to keep it short," she said. "Short, short, short. It's dialogue, not monologue."

The door closed again.

Okay, she's right. That's a good thing to remember.

Monologue was once entirely permissible in fiction. You still see a lot of long, unbroken lines of words enclosed by quote marks, long intricate thoughts and verbose exposition that come tumbling out of the mouth of one character or the other, running on for half a page sometimes because a writer is too lazy or too limited to stop and think about what really makes sense and how it looks on the page or about the poor devil of a reader who is stumbling along in the verbal morass without a signpost or blaze mark or anything else to help him sort out the mud from the cow pies.

(Did everyone get the point, or should I let the above sentence go on for another ten lines without a period?)

We live in the age of the 15-second sound bite.

We also have had our tastes shaped by the visual media. Commercial fiction, particularly, has tightened up considerably. Nowadays, the best of it looks like a screenplay, with the reader being left to play the role of the camera.

For a good illustration, look at two of the current masters of mystery fiction, Robert Parker and Elmore Leonard. They write short, lightning dialogue. Like bursts from an automatic weapon. They are worth studying.

(So, too, are the first 18 paragraphs of this piece, which were written with brevity in mind.)

Communication between man and woman is usually freighted, but that effect is best conveyed with fewer, not more, words. Think of the conversation between lovers. Men and women communicate verbally, but lovers communicate in a dozen other ways, as well. The message passes in a few words, but it also passes in a glance, a touch, a smile, a gasp, a sigh.

My collaborator and I have written in all genres. We are convinced that some principles apply across the board and dialogue is one of them. Short and sharp is better, to the point. The difference between, say, mystery and romance is not in technique but in focus.

Mystery focuses on the crime and its solution; romance focuses on the relationship and its resolution. We don't try to create different characters in our mysteries than we do in our love stories. The story creates the characters and our job is to give those characters voices with which to speak.

Jayne Krentz, a *New York Times* bestseller under her own name and under the "Amanda Quick" byline, shares this view.

"Dialogue is the modern voice, pretty much across the genres," she says. "If anything, romance relies more heavily on it than other genres, and that's probably because romance is so much about communication. You have to do a lot of dialogue to get the relationship going and to keep it going."

I would only add that regardless of genre, the fewer the words, the better.

Sure, sometimes long passages of dialogue seem unavoidable. Exposition requires the imparting of crucial information. Complicated situations need to be spelled out.

But exposition can be approached in two different ways. You can get out several fresh sets of empty quotation marks and start batting the conversational ball back and forth between two characters until you have delivered the necessary information.

Or you can use the magician's trick of distraction. Give the reader something else to look at while you are feeding him or her information. For instance:

The door just opened again. My collaborator came out, thumbing through a large book on Celtic magic, one of the themes in her current novel.

"Did you tell them to break up the longer pieces of dialogue with some little piece of action?" she asked absently, her attention fixed on a full-page reproduction of King Arthur wresting the sword Excaliber from the rock.

"Yes, dear, I was just getting to that," I said.

"So tell them that any time a character has more than three uninterrupted lines, the writer should look for a way to break up those lines."

"Yes, dear."

She turned and moved back toward her own office. This time the door didn't slam. It closed more gently.

It swung open again almost instantly.

"And don't forget to tell them to make it reader-friendly," she added.

My collaborator, who has written 35 of her own novels as well as her portion of our 20 collaborations, has a theory that helps to make sense out of this penchant for shortness. It involves publishers and the cost of paper and while the theory is mechanical, it is also true.

In the last decade, the price of paper has gone out of sight. Publishers, particularly mass-market publishers, have cut every corner they could find.

Margins have shrunk.

Type has gotten smaller.

The publishers have even tried to get us to hit the space bar once after a period, rather than twice.

Anything to cram more words onto the page.

The result is books that are reader-unfriendly. The words and paragraphs squat on the page in one undifferentiated mass.

Unless we writers do something about it.

That's why both my collaborator and I write shorter paragraphs, just to inject more white space onto the page.

That's why we find ourselves using more dialogue, albeit short snatches rather than long ones. The reader's eye can move more easily through the story.

And that's why even our interior monologue, the conversation a character has with him- or herself, has gotten shorter and snappier.

This comment applies to popular fiction and should not be taken as advice for other forms of fiction. Literary fiction is an entirely different matter. Literary fiction relies for its power on inventive use of language and intricacy of thought. Popular fiction relies on its accessibility and its uncommon use of common language.

"That's my line," she said.

I jumped. She had come back into my office so quietly I didn't know she was there.

"Of course it's your line," I said without looking up from the keyboard. "Where do you think I learned almost everything I know about writing good?"

"Well," she said, correcting me.

"Well, good, whatever. I owe it all to you."

She put her hands on my shoulders and dug her thumbs gently into the muscles I use to hold my head up.

"I love you too," she said, "but I'm not going to finish this for you. Besides, you're doing great. Stay with it."

"Bollocks," I said.

That reminded me of another little rule to remember. Be very, very, very careful with strong words, particularly swear words.

"God DAMN it," is enormously more powerful when it is written then when it is spoken. The "f" word, as common as it is in the world today, still has more punch on the page than it does on the tongue.

Use profanity, epithets and blasphemy sparingly.

"And don't forget dialect," she suggested. "Remember the idiotic dialect in what's-her-name's second book?"

"Huh?" I asked, still trying to spell blasphemy.

"Damn stuff went on 15 pages, transliterated directly from a Scottish dictionary. It was embarrassing."

"Try 'mortifying,'" I said. "It taught lots of writers not to use any dialect they hadn't been raised with."

"But you can throw in a characteristic word, here and there, and achieve a foreign flavor, *verdad*?"

"Yes, dear," I said, typing along madly.

Then I stopped.

"You know," I said, thinking out loud. "I just realized something.

Men and women are different."

"We've been married nearly 30 years and you just noticed?"

"No, I mean in terms of dialogue. Men are fact creatures. They'll listen all day long to somebody talking about the tiny differences between a Remington Model 20 in .270 caliber and the Holland & Holland .300, even if they've never fired a sniper rifle from a bench rest in their lives."

"Uh, huh," she said, "and women will throw that kind of book across the room."

I winced. Women read 80% of the fiction that is sold.

"Feelings, though, are a different matter," she said. "Women are fascinated by emotion. They detect subtle differences in feeling and think about them."

"As though they really mattered," I added, finishing the sentence my way.

Her thumbs dug into my neck. Hard.

"Oink, oink," she said.

She headed out of my office.

"Wait!" I said. "I was just kidding."

"You know what Freud said about humor."

"No, what?"

"He said, 'Sometimes a cigar is just a cigar, but sometimes a cigar is something less useful.' "

Oops. She hates cigars.

She closed the door firmly, leaving me to think about men, women and dialogue.

Guys, have you ever noticed that the women we love always get the last word?

Sense and Sensuality: Sexual Tension and Love Scenes in Romance Fiction

STELLA CAMERON

*L*et's discuss sex.

Sex is used to sell everything from hot dogs to hot cars. And it sells an incredible number of books. For the romance writer, the most exquisite lesson lies in learning to "feel" the sexual/sensual content required by your story.

You need a sex antenna!

In your mind.

Sensuality and sexuality are truly facts of life and, therefore, facts of fiction. There is nothing more mysterious about learning to deal with your characters' sexual lives than with any other area of conflict in your story.

Fiction is about conflict—about trouble—about making decisions that change the lives of your characters. Regardless of genre, but for obvious reasons, most particularly in romance, sexual tension is a distinct conflict. That is, sexual tension is trouble all on its own, trouble that heightens all the other trouble in your story.

For me, sex and sensuality arise absolutely naturally from every thread of my stories. Without them, there would be huge holes in my books. In fact, as far as I'm concerned, no sex and sensuality equal no story—in my books.

There are many wonderful romances written without sex on the page. But there is sensuality and, often, absolutely magnetic sexual tension. If you are writing a "sweet" romance (the industry term for romances that do not include actual sex scenes) you draw on the same sensual stimuli used by the writer producing more explicit stories. Thus, for our purposes, we will assume that all romance writers expand sensual awareness through exploring and showing their characters' sexual responses to each other. The difference exists in several points: reader expectation, writer understanding of his/her market, and the writer knowing whether, when and how to cross the line between non-explicit and explicit material.

As writers we all have different strengths and these strengths arise out of who we are as people, and as people who write. I cherish the intensity I draw from my characters by entering into their sexuality and watching their battles to use, revel in, or try to resist desire, arousal, lust. Love is the most complex emotion of all. I believe love grows, sometimes in tiny increments, sometimes in great chunks. I also believe that except in rare instances, sexual attraction—in a relationship that is going to include sex—most frequently occurs before love. This is the premise I usually work on as I develop my stories.

I don't mean that I can't envision liking and friendship developing into sexual interest, and eventually love. However, I do have difficulty believing that, generally, the emotion we call love between a man and a woman exists in a vacuum where no thought of the physical enters. Again, this comes into play in my theory about sensual writing—from the subtlest hint of attraction to consummated encounters.

You're reading this segment of the *Romance Writer's Sourcebook* because you're involved with the sexual content in your own romance novels. If you didn't think this element was important, I assume you wouldn't read a discussion on sexuality in romance writing.

So we agree; sex is serious business. For obvious reasons, sex could very well be said to be the most serious business in the world.

Sex is also funny business. Or should I say, fun? Potentially?

Then sex is poignant, evocative, sweet, giving, demanding, utterly involving, engrossing—the ultimate losing of self—the ultimate acceptance.

Sex joins two human beings in the supreme act of intimacy.

Sex is only cheap when either exploited or viewed as cheap.

Sex is only perverted when selfishly performed or observed, rather than consensually experienced and shared. Well-handled, consensual sex, spiced by the chase, adds irresistible levels of intensity to the conflict in your stories.

Love and lust are definitely not created equal, but every single emotion and motive I've mentioned in relation to sensuality and sexuality can have its place in powerful, absolutely magnetic romance fiction.

AVOID AVOIDANCE

We often encounter people who snicker about sex. They snicker and make odd faces, and use even more odd body language. And have you noticed the absolutely weird codes some people use when they're talking about sex but trying to pretend they aren't talking about sex? "It," takes on huge significance in this context. "*You know*"—accompanied by violent twitches of the head and eye-popping emphasis—is only overshadowed in the realm of wonderful ridiculousness by "*thingie*."

And so we hop right into the most sinful of all sins when writing about sex: avoidance.

Avoidance kills sensuality in fiction at any level. Avoidance can turn a potentially marvelous scene into a farce. Naturally I'm talking about a scene where the writer has set the reader up to expect a show-don't-tell episode—a *feel*-don't-tell episode. Let go. Allow the vast array of evocative images and impressions you see in your mind to come down on the page.

An important piece of advice follows: *DON'T*. Print that word in huge letters on a sign. Each time you get ready to write a sensual interlude, whip the sign out and put it where you can see it at all times. *Don't* hold back. *Don't* allow every rule of good, effective writing to slip when you write a sex/sensual scene. *Don't* become a reporter rather than a participator.

Do you worry about the reactions of your relatives if you write a great love scene—or, perish the thought, a great sex scene?

Do you actually worry about this when you're writing?

You can't. You simply can't stutter and stumble through anything but a crippled love scene, if you're visualizing Auntie's red face if she should read it later. You can't be embarrassed and still manage to write a passage guaranteed to bruise readers' eyeballs and wring out their emotional and erotic responses.

FANTASIZE

A mystery writer can't put one hand over her eyes, kill off the victim with the other hand, and hope the reader won't notice that the writer's heart wasn't in the piece.

Which brings us to another important point. Just as in the mystery where the writer doesn't have to be a murderer to write as if she is one, and doesn't have to be a victim to write, and feel, and sweat as if she is one, the romance writer dealing with sex doesn't have to have had intercourse in a hammock woven from banyan tree air roots to get in the mood of the moment.

Get in touch with these feelings. Be free with your fantasies and you will enrich your stories immeasurably.

That hammock sways, or perhaps even swings. Eventually the contraption may flip over and dump you in a heap on wet, red earth. The air is warm and it doesn't cool your heated skin, but it moves your hair and carries night scents. And skin does have a particular feel, doesn't it? Skin against skin. A particular feel depending upon whose skin you touch, and when, and how you feel about the man or the woman.

Back to what you don't have to be or do to write a particular scene. I've flown planes in my mind and on paper, and so have many of you. I've never actually flown a plane—or a helicopter—or sailed completely alone—or dived into a storm-crazed ocean (I can't swim). I've never escaped from a sinking vessel, or hung by my fingers from the open end of the icy deck of a car ferry. I've never been chased down a deserted mountain, on skis, in the dark. I've never been in an avalanche.

I have *written* about all those things.

I haven't infiltrated a remote mountain pleasure club, or given massages to men who look like Mel Gibson, but I wrote about it in *Sheer Pleasures*. If I did live in the 1820s, I don't remember it; nevertheless, *His Magic Touch, Fascination, Charmed, Bride,* and most recently, *Beloved,* were all set in that time. I've *never* been inside a brothel or watched from behind a screen while an aging prostitute entertained a despicable old fornicator, and yet that happens in *Only By Your Touch*.

And just in case there's any doubt, I absolutely deny any incidents involving body painting . . . with red paint . . . and a wall-sized canvas. (You can read about *that* in *Pure Delights*.)

I wrote every one of those situations and hundreds more. So can you. How? You become part of the scene. You become your viewpoint character, which I'll cover in more detail later.

Never write boring sex. Nestled in any star-studded, firecracker-infested box of smoke and mirrors, boring sex is boring sex and *telling* the reader it's anything but boring, is a laughable waste of time.

In fact, don't *tell* the reader anything. I've already said, show them by feeling the scene for them and helping them to feel the scene for themselves. Feeling is a word that takes us to the heart of what we're dealing with in this topic. Feeling, both in the tangible and the intangible sense.

DON'T FORGET THE ROMANCE

I must inject an extremely important note here: At the core of every successful romance is an irresistible romance. No, that is not a confusing statement; it couldn't be more clear. Copy this insight, too, and pin it up somewhere, and each time you get carried away with the brilliance of your plot, ask yourself the following questions:

1. Is this plot a great vehicle for my irresistible romance?
2. Is this plot so great, that I've forgotten my irresistible romance?

A "yes" response to the first question is wonderful.

A "yes" response to the second question is death to any romance.

There are two kinds of people writing and attempting to write romance. There are those who absolutely love the genre and wouldn't write anything else—these people fall into the group for whom a plot is a vehicle for romance. Then there are those who suffer through the romance in order to deal with the other, and to them, the more important elements of their plots. For those who feel romance is a necessary nuisance, it makes absolutely no sense to pursue a career in this genre.

Always remember that the reader who wants pure mystery, reads mystery. The reader who wants romance (in its many forms) reads *romance*. This reader often loves some mystery mixed in with his romance, or some adventure, ghostly tension, elements of science fiction or fantasy—he may really enjoy stories that incorporate down-to-earth themes about everyday life, but first, and always, he reads for the romance.

DON'T BE CLINICAL

I do, of course, have another very important reason for bringing up the essence of our genre. Just as plot mustn't overwhelm the romance, neither must sex that becomes clinical and contrived ever, ever overshadow the marvelous poignancy of an otherwise strong romance.

What constitutes clinical sex? Not some of the things you immediately think of. The word penis isn't particularly elegant, but sometimes it has its place. It's certainly an improvement over "iron hard glory," or "giant granite monolith" (doesn't that create visions of Grant's Tomb and sound painful?). Then there's "proud beauty," "male masthead," and "finger of fate." How about "love tool?" You're getting the point, I know. Euphemisms can result in reader collapse, and not from complimentary awe.

Clinical sex isn't the use of correct words, within reason. There are words that seem borrowed from medical texts, e.g., vagina, anus, etc. These are probably best avoided. But clinical sex in our context is sex by the numbers. Well-written sensuality draws on the senses and is, therefore, sensual. The hero glimpses a little lace at the hem of a slip, or a bra strap. He is so aware of the heroine that he can hardly stop himself from touching her. The heroine reacts to the hero's face—not necessarily because he's stunning, but for those irresistible little touches you, the writer, point out. Intelligent eyes, the way he smiles, or doesn't smile, how his walk makes the heroine feel, the fit of his shirt over his shoulders, his jeans over his thighs. You visualize these and hundreds of other sensual triggers and you get them on the page.

Avoid running a parts-and-moves checklist that goes something like this:

The kiss. The bigger kiss. The even bigger, longer, deeper kiss. We've got tongues in this one—let me see, what do the tongues do? Duel might be innovative (always consider the potential mental images). Now let me see, where are his hands? Her neck, her shoulders, her back, her arms? Oops, where are *her* hands? Now he's got to touch her breasts and she's got to groan and feel herself falling into a black, swirling vortex. Let's not forget the legs. Where are their legs? Where are his hands on her legs? Her calf? Her thigh? *Between* her thighs?

Stop it. Feel. Know your characters and feel what they feel. Put yourself into the scene and live through them. Not just through the heroine if you're a woman, or through the hero if you're a man, but through both characters because you are both characters. You made them. They have no life without you. If they have no life on the page, it's because you don't have the courage to give them life. Loosen up. We know you're crazy about these people and that you want to burst upon the page with all the power of what they feel.

A notebook—always at hand—is the writer's emergency kit. Haul it everywhere. Watch couples, their mannerisms, the way they flirt with each other. Take lots of notes then take lots of time to process your feelings and store them away. They'll pop out when you need them again.

I've never met a writer who didn't admit to a ritualistic approach to writing sessions—any writing sessions. But when you get ready to write a love scene, you're preparing to take your characters into the most intimate moments of their strut upon the page. You may want to take exceptional measures! These are a few suggestions from the routine I employ:

1. Set aside enough time to complete a draft of the scene.
2. Dress comfortably (I'm not joking). Feathers may cause sneezing and all that satin stuff gets hot and slides around.
3. Make certain your work station is non-intrusive, something you don't have to think about. That's probably why I avoid writing these scenes in a bubble bath. I'd undoubtedly get carried away and drop the keyboard in the water.
4. Unless you deal well with interruptions, don't allow them. Hang a sign on the door. Mine says gently, PLEASE DO NOT DISTURB. However, be prepared to enforce. If blood runs under the door, open it. Otherwise . . .
5. I'm a music fan. For those of you who write to music, make sure you've chosen well—and this will mean so many different things. Remember, music creates mood.
6. Think about the time of day or night when you can best isolate yourself completely with the scene. For me it's my favorite writing time which is in the middle hours of the night when I feel the rest of the world is asleep. Choose your time well. You're selecting a time to enter into a love affair. You need to be able to relax and be assured that you are alone with your characters.
7. Very well. You're comfortable and ready. Go for it and don't stop until you've finished your draft.
8. Give yourself some space between the writing and the read-through. I hesitate to make a comparison with rising bread dough, but some things just work better if they're given time to "do their thing." When you've separated yourself from the scene enough to be somewhat objective, read it again and be prepared to say, "YUCK." Do some tuning, then be prepared to say, "This is boring." This is partly because you've read it a few times too many or, just possibly, because it's boring.
9. Back to the drawing board and literally write over the scene. Not, write it over, but write over. Work along with what feels great,

and truly let yourself go. Trust your instincts and completely flesh the scene out.

10. Move on and don't touch the piece again until you have finished the book, by which time you'll have considerably more than one love scene to deal with. At this point, you'll know so much about your characters that any inconsistency will leap out and be easily dealt with.

EXERCISE

We're going to work on shifting into the mood, shifting into the sensual mood as writers. Then we're going to see what we can get on paper while we're in this mood. Work with characters you already have in mind, or create some entirely new ones and, yet again, let yourself go. Trust me not to lead you where you'll be uncomfortable to go. Do what you can, what pleases you. Where you falter, let yourself falter. Where you race along, race and enjoy it. Remind yourself that this isn't cute or silly or grubby—this is a time to play with sensual feelings, and sensual feelings can be beautiful, funny, poignant—even frightening—but always real and definitely an inevitable part of being sexual human beings.

1. We're going to work with our senses. Play with them. *Feel* them. Think about scent, sight, smell, taste, touch.

2. We'll use an element. Perhaps water. Why not rain, heavy rain, tropical rain, warm rain—with the slightest roll of thunder somewhere very far away.

3. In the tropics, rain makes the earth slippery and shiny. If you run, your feet slide. The scents are of fallen, crushed fruit. Citrusy. Lemon, guava, passion fruit. Your nose wrinkles. The scents are pungent. All of your senses are wide open, almost raw.

4. You are on a trail above a beach where the sea roils over lava rocks. And you're running on that trail. Above you the crowns of palms whip wildly back and forth, and around you giant philodendron leaves shimmer wet and dark green, and flowers, purple and pink and white, hide their heads beneath those leaves.

5. A running woman becomes your character, your heroine. What does she look like? What color is her hair? How does it look wet and clinging—streaking across her face, resting against her lips? What is she wearing? A cotton dress hiked up her thighs and transparent over her breasts? Is her skin tanned and glistening?

6. She smells all those pungent scents. What does she taste? Salt in the air, carried from the sea? Salt from her skin? The half-eaten guava that sends juice coursing down her wrist while she laughs and wipes rain from her eyes?

7. Add the man. Actually he's not ahead, but on the beach below, watching the woman run—and he's aroused. Wet sand pushes between his toes. His belly and thighs tense and he leans into the wind. His hair is sodden and plastered to his neck. His clothes are soaked. He can't stand and watch the woman anymore. He starts to run after her. Silently, swiftly—lithe and powerful as he hunts, he pursues the woman until he stands just below the trail. She looks down and sees him—and stops.

8. They know each other, these two. They've never made love, but they've known that as sure as they breathe, one day there will come a moment when everything will clear away from the circle of intimacy that has enclosed them even when they were in a crowd. And they will become lovers.

9. That moment is now:

"I thought I'd find you out here," he said.

She fought for breath and said, "Did you?" and knew they'd imagined this same moment, this same coming together.

"Do you mind?" he asked, moving closer. "Do you mind that I came looking for you?"

She didn't mind. "No," she told him simply. "No, I don't mind."

He inhaled slowly. Muscles in his jaw flexed. "May I join you?" he asked, offering her his hand. "Pull me up."

As if she could. She leaned to lace her fingers through his. And she squeezed her eyes shut when he tugged, tugged her down and caught her.

Her knees rested against his thighs. He spanned her waist and looked up into her face.

He was warm and hard and wet. When he slowly let her slide down his length, she rested her cheek on his shoulder and tasted salt on his skin.

"You look so wonderful," he said over the wind.

"I'm a wreck. *You* look marvelous." And he *felt* marvelous. Her breast pressed his tensed flesh with nothing more than the soaked cotton of her dress between them.

Holding her tightly, resting his chin atop her head, he lifted her into his arms and carried her into the surf. When she turned her face up to his, he kissed her, let her feet swing down once more until she stood before him in the water, and pulled her arms around his neck.

The sea swirled about them. They were alone, utterly, perfectly alone . . .

Now write a love scene. Don't judge your efforts or fight for the only word that can fit—write without stopping until you finish at least an abbreviated scene.

Follow my earlier instructions. Set your work aside and let it settle before you read it through.

There is the promise of love in the scene I began to write, but there is also eroticism. As sensual writers it's our job to arouse the erotic response. Not in a lascivious way, not in a crude, lewd or pornographic way, but in a manner that awakens the readers' senses. We hear over and over again that people who read romance tend to have more fulfilling and happy love relationships. I believe this is because our readers are sensual people who love to give and receive love. I don't think we provide them with "how-to" manuals. I do think we reinforce and validate the power of learning to give and receive without reservation in a love/sexual relationship that's mutually satisfying.

Happily Ever Laughter: Writing Romantic Comedy for Women

JENNIFER CRUSIE SMITH

Women's humor is hot right now. As Birgit Davis-Todd, senior editor at Harlequin, says, funny romance writers are "laughing all the way to the bank." Harlequin's launch of the Love and Laughter line in fall of 1996 supports this; according to editor Malle Vallik, the line is in direct response to the growing demand by readers for laughter with their happily-ever-after. But along with the good news comes the bad: women's humor is hard to write. It's not that women aren't naturally funny. Women laugh loud and long when we're together. But we've been told by a traditional society that women's humor is non-existent and that our laughter is inappropriate, and so it's difficult for us to go beyond the traditional male humor, the joke and the put-down, to find the things that make women laugh and put them on the page.

The biggest barrier to writing women's humor is the intrinsic belief that Good Girls don't laugh. Ever hear a woman laugh out loud—really loud—in public? Chances are your first reaction was, "She's no lady." Although you can refer to women's humor and female humor, the term "ladies' humor" doesn't exist. It can't; it's an oxymoron because nice women don't laugh. Laughing out loud is powerful and sexual; it demands attention and announces knowledge, not innocence. As Regina Barreca notes in her outstanding work on women's humor, *They Used To Call Me Snow White . . . But I Drifted*, virgins don't laugh at small penis jokes. A woman's laughter not only tells the world She Knows, it also communicates strength and confidence. A woman must be very sure of herself to make the joke, to tell the story, and to laugh out loud knowing people will stare. She must be proud, strong and confident. No wonder modern romance readers love the heroine who can laugh and who invites them to laugh with her.

So how do you make that invitation? First you have to understand how women think, and how men's thinking—the thinking that fuels traditional humor—is different. One theory is that, generally speaking, most women think in patterns, using details and context, while most men think in straight lines, using cause and effect. This theory explains why women "can't" tell jokes; jokes are based on rigid, linear sequence. You can't tell the sentences of a joke out of order, and you can't add extra information to the joke or the clear line of cause and effect will be lost. To work, the joke must be told exactly the same every time. Women find this boring and ultimately frustrating because they're more interested in the experience and the context than they are in the trip to the punchline.

For example, a man may tell a woman, "There was a traveling salesman . . ." and she will ask "Traveling in what?" "It doesn't matter," he'll reply, exasperated, because it doesn't matter to the cause and effect of the joke. But it does matter to the woman because context creates understanding: is he selling condoms or Bibles, miracle cures or pots and pans? The man may go on, "And he meets a farmer's daughter . . ." only to be interrupted with "How old is she?" "It doesn't make any difference," he'll reply, even more exasperated, and it doesn't matter to the progression of the joke, but it does to the understanding of the context: is she 16 and naive or 40 and bitter; does she have experience with salesmen or is she going to be a victim? Women want to know the details, the world in which the story takes place, because that's where the humor lies for them.

MUCH ADO ABOUT NOTHING

But while many women find traditional male humor lacking, many traditionalists reject women's humor because "nothing happens" in it. An example of female humor is Gilda Radner's story of dining in a very expensive restaurant after she became famous. The restaurant had ornate tapestry-covered chairs ("Who cares about the chairs?" male humor would demand, "Get to the point") and sometime during the meal, she began to menstruate. When she stood up to go, she noticed the stain on the tapestry, and she knew that everyone in the room would know that Gilda Radner had started her period. So she switched chairs with another table.

"That's it?" the traditionalist asks while women everywhere laugh, not at Radner because female humor does not laugh down, but with her because women have been in the same place and know how she felt. If those of us who are female were in the same room with her (with no males around), we'd immediately begin to contribute our own menstrual-disaster stories because we'd all have one. But the humor in Radner's story also goes beyond the immediate familiar situation to the context of the world at large and the absurdity of the way that world regards menstruation. The vast majority of women between puberty and menopause menstruate every month; it's normal, healthy, and desirable. Yet the male world has such a phobia about menstruation that many traditional males would find Radner's story in bad taste (although finding Polish jokes and dumb blonde jokes perfectly acceptable). Women live in a world where men will take them to the movies to see heads ripped off and blood spurting but will refuse to buy tampons for them, even though the tampons are perfectly clean, wrapped in paper inside a cardboard box which is in turn wrapped in cellophane. It is this absurdity that makes women laugh at the contextual richness of Radner's tapestry chair story while men are lost, trying to make the humor work in terms of the joke, the punchline. In women's humor, if you're not part of the community, you're not part of the humor.

Which means that first and foremost in constructing women's humor, you need to understand women and women's communities. You need to understand how friendships between women work, how relationships between mothers and daughters work, and how absurd the male world often appears to women. If you're a woman, this isn't hard: it's your daily life. And that's what you need to draw on to write women's humor. Forget slapstick unless it's drawn naturally from women's experiences, such as putting on panty hose in a hurry immediately after a shower while talking on the phone and trying to keep the baby's finger out of the light socket. Forget wisecracks and put-downs unless they're aimed up at those in positions of power over women—bosses, rotten husbands and lovers, Martha Stewart-types—who richly deserve it. Stick with relationships and community, drawing on the things that make women laugh in real life.

So how do you write humor specifically for women?

BASE YOUR HUMOR ON SHARED FEMALE EXPERIENCES

If you can put your heroine in a situation that most women have experienced or can sympathize with (she gets her period unexpectedly; her child says the wrong thing at the wrong time; her shoulder pads come loose and move around her suit like small animals while she tries to make an impression) and have her deal with it using her sense of humor, women will laugh in recognition and support because they're part of her community of experiences. Think of the last time you were embarrassed, so embarrassed that you didn't know how you'd ever face the people around you again. There was the day I decided to become a blonde and bleached my hair out, changed my mind and dyed it black, and walked around with green hair for a month as the black washed out; I got a book called *Getting Rid of Bradley* out of that experience. Or there's my favorite moment of all time, the day I walked the entire length of the English Department at Ohio State University with my skirt caught in my pantyhose, wearing no underwear. And nobody I passed said a word.

I posted that on the GEnie computer bulletin board and within a day or so several other women had posted similar pantyhose exposure experiences caused by static cling and other insidious forces. Some day in some book, one of my heroines is going to walk around with her skirt caught in her pantyhose because that's something that happens to women, and my readers will sympathize and laugh with her because she's laughing, too. Nothing is a tragedy if you can laugh at it, and one of the things that women love most about their humor is that pointing out how ridiculous something is removes the sting. There's a lot of relief in "My God, you did that, too?" and it's not just comic relief.

LAUGHING WITH VS. LAUGHING AT

But please note, you and the heroine are laughing at the absurdity of the situation, not at the heroine herself. Never, ever, ever make the reader laugh at your heroine. She can laugh with the heroine at the heroine's mistakes, but she should never laugh down at the heroine, especially if it's because she's a cute little ditz. You want your reader to identify with your heroine, not sneer at her. This means no slapstick scenes where the heroine makes a fool of herself rolling around in the mud in a cat fight or trips on her dress and falls downstairs, spilling wine down her dress and breaking her nose. Women don't find misfortune funny. They will lose respect for the cat fighter and feel sorry for the tripper, and both of these are death to reader-heroine identification. On the other hand, you can use humor to show that your heroine is strong and confident in the face of disaster. If the heroine trips, spills the wine, picks herself up, and announces that for her next trick she intends to do the same thing backwards in high heels, then she's used humor to take control of the situation without demeaning herself and is therefore admirable. However, she's still not very funny to women because they're sympathizing with her fall. Recovery humor is endearing, but it's not laugh-out-loud funny.

A classic example of a heroine who takes the sting out of a terrible situation occurs in Jayne Ann Krentz's *Perfect Partners*. The heroine, Letty, is telling the hero, Joel, how she walked in on her now ex-fiance only to find him with his pants around his ankles and another woman on her knees in front of him. At this point, she drops her face into her hands, and her shoulders begin to shake, and Joel tries to comfort her, assuming she's crying. But when she lifts her head, she's laughing. "Oh, I was shocked at first," she tells Joel. "But then I realized I had never seen anything so ludicrous in my entire life." Once Letty has laughed at her cheating ex, even though he's not there to see it, he can't hurt her again, and the situation has lost its pain. And the reader laughs along with her, delighted that she's strong and feisty and refusing to be a victim.

ARM YOUR HEROINE WITH HUMOR AS A DEFENSIVE WEAPON

If you can show your heroine one-upping someone offensive (a mechanic patronizes her, her date is obnoxious, her boss treats her like a robot) with defensive humor, you can make women laugh out loud. One of the books I received the most oh-my-God-I've-been-there mail on was my first, *Manhunting*, because the heroine goes on a series of dates from hell and defeats them all physically, pushing one in a pool, stabbing another with a fork, and generally fighting the good fight for women everywhere against men who deserve it while retaining her sense of humor throughout. A heroine in situations like these can get angry and complain, she can be noble and suffer through, she can get huffy and leave, but it's a lot more fun for the reader if she stays to turn her razor-sharp wit on the man who thought he was going to use her because she was too dumb to defend herself.

However, it's important to remember that women's humor is never offensive; it never makes fun of people who don't deserve it or laughs down at people who are less powerful. A woman who makes fun of a man who's trying to patronize her is wonderful; a woman who makes fun of a perfectly nice man who's trying to talk to her is not. Women's humor as a weapon should only be unleashed against powerful people who try to patronize women or use them in some way. Give your heroine enemies in situations that women can relate to and let her defeat them using her wit, and your reader will laugh with her.

DEVELOP A COMMUNITY FOR YOUR HEROINE TO SHARE HER HUMOR WITH

The power of community-based humor is evident in the success of shows like *Cheers, Frazier, Seinfeld, Mad About You,* and *Friends.* Give your heroine an ensemble like these to work with, and your reader will feel part of that community the same way viewers feel that if they dropped by the *Cheers* bar, they'd be welcomed right in. Solidify that community by giving its members common enemies and problems, and develop in-jokes for your characters that make the reader feel part of the community.

I did this deliberately in *Charlie All Night. Charlie* is set in a radio station and stars a producer-heroine and a disk jockey-hero who are surrounded by an ensemble that includes the station accountant and two other disk jockeys. Outside the group is the station's owner, a chronically grouchy patriarch, and the station's star, an ambitious but not-too-with-it morning show host who has dumped the heroine for a younger woman. This set-up gave me all the dynamics I needed for women's humor: the in-group is a tight community that has shared experiences and problems; the boss and the arrogant host try to patronize and control the group which makes them acceptable targets for defensive humor; and the progress of the story gives me ample opportunity to create running jokes, the in-jokes of the community.

For example, as the hero's show gains in popularity, the morning show host panics and begins to make more and more ridiculous bids for the public's attention. By half-way through the book, all one of the characters has to say is, "Mark had a new idea this morning," and everyone in the in-group—including the reader— grins because everyone knows Mark has screwed up again. Community-based writing has several other advantages, not the least of which is that it's fun to write about a group of people who support and respect each other while having a very good time.

Georgette Heyer uses community-based humor beautifully in *The Grand Sophy*. Sophy comes to live with a large family of cousins, headed by her cousin Charles, a young man about to buckle under the weight of his familial responsibilities and his haughty fiancee, Eugenia. The rest of the cousins (and the reader) rally to Sophy who in the course of trying to bring some fun to the family, gives them a monkey that Eugenia loathes. In one scene the monkey becomes a symbol that the community of the family wants to retain and Eugenia wants to eject with Charles caught in the middle. Adding to the trauma is the fact that one of the brothers, Theodore, has just hit a ball through a neighbor's window and put the rest of the community in a weak position. As Eugenia runs down a list of reasons to get rid of the monkey, all of which Charles answers noncommittally, the rest of the family (and the reader) waits to see which side Charles will choose. Finally, Eugenia plays her trump card, "I believe a monkey's bite is poisonous," to which Charles says, "In that case, I hope he may bite Theodore." The rest of the family responds with relieved smiles—if Charles can joke about Theodore dying, he's not mad any more and he's not going to get rid of the monkey—but on a deeper level, their relief is really about saving Charles because he's with them, not Eugenia. And the entire scene is done without anyone "telling off" Eugenia or attacking her in any way. It's a wonderful example of women's humor.

Another community that is implicit in every romance novel is the community that the heroine and hero create by falling in love. One aspect that people find attractive in each other, placing high on wish lists compiled by both women and men, is a sense of humor. Everything listed above that works in ensemble humor can be applied to the community of the hero and heroine alone (the in-joke works especially well here: there's nothing more seductive than meeting someone's eyes across a room and sharing a joke that no one else in the room gets), but the hero and heroine can also share something that the larger community can't: intimate banter. By intimate, I don't mean sexual, although that certainly can come into play. I mean the trusting give-and-take of relaxed conversation with someone you're close to. Best friends often maintain this kind of mindless not-quite-arguing, and your heroine and hero should be nothing if not best friends by the time they've created a community or even while they're creating it. Their ability to respond to each other in a way that shows they're relating to each other without tension foreshadows their ability to establish the same kind of deeper relationship later. The scene below from my book, *Anyone But You*, foreshadows the relationship the heroine, Nina, and the hero, Alex, will have when they become lovers. In this scene, Nina has just rescued Alex from a Date From Hell:

> Nina took her wine over to the table and sat down. "What happened in the middle of the entree?"
>
> Alex sat down, too. "She smiled at me across the table, and said, 'I just want you to know where you stand.' Then she opened her purse and handed me two condoms."
>
> "Oh." Nina blinked. "Well, she was just being prepared."
>
> "Prepared?" Alex looked at her as if she were demented. "I wasn't even sure I wanted to yet, and she's handing me condoms. Don't you think that's a little presumptuous?"
>
> Nina frowned at him. "So what are you saying here? You're mad at her because you're not That Kind of Guy?" She snorted. "Of course, you're That Kind of Guy."
>
> "And two," Alex went on, ignoring her. "Two, for crissakes. Talk about pressure."
>
> "Oh, right." Nina nodded wisely over her wine. "You are pushing 30. I suppose the equipment is going soft."
>
> "The equipment is fine, thank you," Alex said, glaring at her. "But there is such a thing as performance anxiety."
>
> "You know, I've learned more about men in the past month with you than I did in 15 years with Guy," Nina said. "I thought men just dove in whenever they got the chance. I would have assumed that you'd take that as a compliment."
>
> "You would have assumed wrong," Alex said gloomily.

As in all other kinds of humor for women, however, the banter should never be insulting, hurtful, or patronizing. Think of it as a verbal ping-pong match, not handball. Even if one of the shots hits home, nobody gets hurt. Writing humor for women, then, is nothing more than creating a heroine with whom the reader can identify; putting that heroine into a context and community which the reader finds familiar and comfortable;

developing that community with in-jokes and relaxed, friendly banter; adding conflict that unites the community and provides a deserving outlet for the defensive humor of the in-group; and cementing the relationship between the heroine and her hero with a shared sense of humor. Do all this, and your reader will laugh with you all the way to the end of your story . . . and on to the beginning of your next one.

Magic, Myth and Metaphysics: Exploding the Boundaries of Romance

KRISTIN HANNAH

For years, brave and visionary authors have added magic, myth and metaphysics to their novels, giving traditional romances a fresh, exciting spin. In the past few years, however, the genre has exploded into these realms, spawning a growing list of subgenres. Time travelers, space travelers, aliens, wizards and sorceresses abound.

The sudden acceptability of these elements can easily be seen. Harlequin, Silhouette, Zebra, New American Library and Leisure—just to name a few—have launched whole series of books that focus on the brave new worlds of romance. The Romance Writers of America recently included a separate category in its prestigious RITA award for Futuristic/Fantasy/Paranormal romance.

There's an insatiable demand for these innovative stories, and publishers are scrambling to print more of these titles on their lists.

This tells us that the romance reader is a sophisticated, discriminating individual who doesn't necessarily believe that there is only one kind of "acceptable" romance novel. It also tells us that the idea that there are "boundaries" on the content of a romance novel is rubbish. There are no hard and fast edges on the envelope of romance. Our readers will accept a wide and varied spectrum of books.

THE IMPORTANCE OF BEING EARNEST

For paranormal and all other romance novels, the quality must remain high. Unfortunately, a sudden run on any market—and paranormal romance is no exception—can ultimately hurt the long-term quality of that market's products. A paranormal or supernatural romance can be innovative and exciting. However, it must also be, at its core, a good romance—a work of fiction that ultimately satisfies the reader.

Many first-time authors erroneously believe that the best way to break into the competitive romance market is to jump on a topic while that topic is hot. In other words, they write to a trend. While it's true that a publisher starting a new line or imprint may be quickly buying a number of books—possibly even books of lesser quality—it won't do *your* career any good to begin with inferior work. The romance field is so full of wonderfully written, carefully crafted books that a new author must be the very best he or she can be. You must come out of the gate strong, with a dynamite book, and then follow that up with another great book, and another, and still another.

This may make the future of paranormal and supernaturally-themed books seem dark, but nothing could be further from the truth. The future for these types of books is as unlimited as the future of the romance genre itself. Regardless of how long the current trend lasts—and I think it will last a long time—there will *always* be room in romance for a standout paranormal romance. Our readers love epic fantasies, dark Gothics with a supernatural twist, time travels, futuristics. The more of these that are written and published, the greater the demand. Therefore, you must keep your priorities straight. Don't write a paranormal romance because it's hot and you think it'll be an easy sell. By the time you finish your book, the trend could be stone cold. Write the book that's in your heart, the story cannot be contained within you. That way, no matter what happens with the manuscript after it leaves your loving hands, you'll know you wrote the right book at the right time for you.

CONTENT

There are as many types of paranormal romances as there are authors who write them, but as a springboard to understanding this subgenre, it may be helpful to identify some of the more visible story types. As with any kind of writing endeavor, it is critical to read and understand as much of your chosen genre as possible. If you want to write a ghost story, you should read as many ghost stories as possible. Read the good, the bad and the wonderful. The more you know, the better. Analyze and dissect the books you read, try to understand *why* one works and another fails. To get you started, I've compiled a short list of subgenres and identified a small sampling of authors you may find helpful to read.

Begin with this list, or make up one of your own. Subscribe to romance publications, haunt your bookstores and libraries. Do research and discover authors who truly move and inspire you.

1. *Time Travel.* In these stories, one or more of the main protagonists moves either backward or forward in time. Some prominent authors in this field are Jude Devereaux, Linda Lael Miller, Diana Gabaldon, June Lund Shiplett and Constance O'Day Flannery.

2. *Historical Fantasy Romance.* These are stories—often set in ancient or medieval times—in which key elements of the story are fantastic. Myth, magic, sorcery and ancient legends are often cornerstones of either characterization or plot. Authors to read include Amanda Glass (Jayne Ann Krentz), Kathleen Morgan, Jessica Bryan and Betina Lindsey.

3. *Futuristic Romance.* Included in this subgenre are books which are set in imaginary worlds, parallel universes, Earth in the distant future—the settings and time periods are limited only by the authors' imaginations. Authors in this field include Marilyn Campbell and Kathleen Morgan.

4. *Contemporary Fantasy Romance.* These romances include a wide range of themes and topics, from modern ghost and vampire stories to extraterrestrials and reincarnation. Again, the breadth of the stories is limited only by the authors' imaginations. Some authors to study are Linda Lael Miller, Anne Stuart, Antoinette Stockenberg and Patricia Simpson.

Once you have studied the paranormal market, expand your horizons. Read as many romances as you can and study the emerging new talents as well as the big-name authors. In this way, you will begin to truly understand the romance genre. Like any genre, romance is guided by certain prevailing concepts and formulas. Our best books are usually powerful, credible love stories built around strong-willed, ultimately honorable protagonists, with snappy dialogue, steady pacing and a happily-ever-after ending. Paranormal romances are no different. Above all, a good paranormal romance must be a good love story.

TAKE THE "UN" OUT OF "UNBELIEVABLE"

Many writers think it's easy to integrate paranormal elements into romance, but in truth it is very difficult to make magic believable. While a reader will suspend a certain amount of disbelief—all fiction is, after all, a fantasy on some level—he or she will not ultimately accept a world which has no discernable rules. A supernatural element, whether it be magic or time travel or the sudden appearance of a ghost, must be handled in a way that makes sense.

You make magic believable through lots of research. Yes, paranormal elements require as much research as does your setting, your characterization or your historical period. It is a different kind of research, but it is still just as necessary. Without research, you will almost surely ask too much of your reader; you will ask her to suspend disbelief one too many times. Quite simply, your story will not ring true or make sense. Even magic has to have a logical basis. Otherwise, you risk a reader— or an agent or editor—thinking that your book is just plain silly. Or worse: contrived.

Magic or other paranormal elements should be so pivotal that if they were eliminated, you would have no story. They should *not* be used in a sloppy, offhand manner to get out of a sticky point in a bad plot. They should *not* solve problems between the characters; in fact, they should *create* problems. They should not sugarcoat a coincidence.

Once again, your magical element should be like every other plot point in your story. It should create and/or exacerbate conflict between the characters and move the story forward.

I have found in writing metaphysical elements that hard and fast rules are essential. You must define the magic, give it parameters and then stick to those parameters. The more defined the magic, the more believable it becomes. Without hard rules, magic will decimate your conflict.

For example, in time travel, it is essential to clearly state and understand the mechanism that initiates the travel. The reader must be aware that there was only one way into the portal of time and therefore only one way out. This heightens the conflict: Can the characters find the eye of the needle that will take them home? If all they have to do is wish or hope or go back to the same spot and hog out there, where is the conflict? Where is the risk that the characters will be unable to return? No conflict should be solved by a magical snapping of the fingers.

In my book, *Waiting for the Moon*, I developed a psychic character, and one of the great challenges of that book was creating the parameters of his gift. At first, I gave him broad-based psychic talents—an amalgam of the research I had done on the subject. But in actually writing the book, I found that such a huge spectrum was unworkable. The character could be allowed to see the past or the present in another place or the future, or he could possess mental telepathy. But to have him possess all of these powers would have been a mess. Every time he walked into a room, he would have been brought to his knees by images in his head. Instead, I focused on a single gift—the ability to "see" certain truths about an individual he touches. Simple, straight-forward, easily defined. The reader then knew that whenever the hero touched another character there would be a vision. I further defined this gift by tying it to a pattern of concrete physical reactions—headache, burning fingers, nausea. All of these physical symptoms signaled to the reader that a psychic moment was about to occur. Thus, the character's paranormal ability was clearly defined, rooted in clinical research and consistent throughout the book. Hopefully, this made the "magic" believable.

The believability of paranormal elements is crucial, and if you ground your magic in science and logic, you will establish credibility for your reader. Once again, research is the cornerstone to creating believable magic.

RESEARCHING THE PARANORMAL

Begin with the obvious. Read as many of the fantasy, science fiction and historical fantasy books you can. Pick a single paranormal, supernatural or metaphysical element that interests you—time travel, Celtic legends and myths, ghosts. Read extensively about your chosen subject, beginning with non-fiction. Read scientific journals, first-hand accounts of "strange happenings," watch public broadcasting for shows about the paranormal. When you begin to build a strong non-fiction foundation, move on to fiction involving the element you've chosen. Study how other writers have handled the parameters of that element. For example, what was special about the resolution of time travel in Jude Devereaux's classic, *A Knight in Shining Armor*? How did Penelope Williamson use ancient Celtic myth to create a believable wizard in *Keeper of the Dream*? How did J.R.R. Tolkien make Middle Earth so believable? What were the limits to Patrick Swayze's abilities in *Ghost*? In what concrete ways did Anne Rice reshape the vampire legend?

Metaphysical and scientific theory can go along way toward making the improbable seem possible. Current quasi-scientific theory is rife with fictional possibilities: near-death experiences and "going into the light"; parallel universes; black holes; alien abductions; UFOs; religious "miracles"; angels; the power of "fringe" sciences such as astrology, numerology, channeling; and the concept of time travel.

The list goes on and on. As you look at it, you'll begin to see the possibilities for a skilled writer willing to explore the world with an open mind.

After you've done all the initial reading on your chosen subject, you will face the unique aspect of paranormal research; taking what seems like an impossible concept, grounding it in hard and fast rules that give it a sense of verisimilitude, then thinking it through again and again. Our job is to explore a world that most people can't even imagine, and then to open that world to disbelieving minds. It is an exhilarating challenge.

When I was plotting my time travel romance, *When Lightning Strikes*, I did a large amount of research on the historical setting, the Wild West, outlaws of the nineteenth century, etc. That was easy.

The thematic issues in that book were a struggle. I had to take the highly improbable concept of time travel and somehow make it a logical scenario. This required an inordinate amount of thought. I ended up linking several improbable elements—time travel, reincarnation and the genesis of legends. All of these I funneled through the single quasi-acceptable metaphysical theory that negative experiences in a past life ultimately affect subsequent lives. There was plenty of Eastern philosophy to give this theory at least a patina of believability. Within the rules of such a metaphysical theory, I created a solid theme and stuck to it.

Always remember to have as much respect for magic as you do for any other element of your story. Include the paranormal in your story only if they fascinate and compel you. Don't shove them into a standard plot and use them for a slight twist or a few moments of comic relief or to get out of an unworkable plot. Although magic will do all of those things nicely, it will do so much more, *be* so much more.

CAVEAT SCRIPTOR

A final word of caution: Once you've stepped into the world of the impossible, walked with dragons and sorcerers or explored twilight worlds that cannot possibly exist, you will be changed. The way you see the world will be altered. You will have allowed just a little bit of magic into your soul, and you will find yourself voraciously reading about angels and near-death experiences and ancient Ireland. Suddenly, every half-baked scientific theory will seem filled with fictional possibilities.

You'll find yourself wondering if alien abductions are possible, and if they are, what if . . .

Your friends will ask you if you're from California.

And when that happens, you'll know you've crossed over completely. You're destined to write romances with a paranormal twist.

Advice from the Heart: Romance Authors Share Their Secrets

KAREN MORRELL

Romance Writers of America, a national organization for both published and unpublished writers, currently has over 7,600 members. Chapters all across the country hold monthly meetings where members offer support and encouragement, discuss marketing strategies and industry news, and share knowledge of the writing profession.

Romance authors and their works represent 177 million paperbacks and a staggering $885 million in sales annually. Romance novels account for only 20% of the books published yet nearly 50% of the books sold.

What accounts for the popularity of romance novels? Vivian Thompson, who writes as Val Daniels for Harlequin and is a former publicity director for Romance Writers of America, says, "maybe the most logical reason for reading and writing romances is that they all hold to the 'formula'—although they are not formulaic."

In other words they are about 1) people, 2) who triumph over their own short-comings, 3) so they can make permanent connections with other people, 4) which leads to a satisfying personal life.

In 1994, 27 publishers printed 1,790 romances in 57 various lines. Many were written by the authors who contributed to this article. *(Editor's note: Titles listed are the authors' newest as of January 1996.)* And, now, here are their tips on . . .

A WRITER'S LIFE

Talent isn't enough. A writer needs the 3 D's as well: The *drive* to tell a story, the *discipline* to put in the time and effort to tell the story, and the *desire* to tell the story well.

> Nora Roberts
> *Born in Ice* (Berkley/Jove)
> Author of 97 novels

There is no such thing as a born writer. Anyone can write if they approach it with an open mind, dedication, and the willingness to work hard to succeed. Even the best loved writers must keep at it, and if they don't, their work will eventually suffer.

> Connie Mason
> AKA Cara Miles
> *The Lion's Bride* (Leisure)
> Author of 21 novels

When the germ of an idea takes root and begins to reach through the soil of your thoughts toward the sun, hold it tightly. While it's still young and tender, don't be quick to share it with others. Nurture its growth until you can see what kind of plant, or work, it will be. Like a good crop, if you share your seeds of excitement too soon, there won't be enough enthusiasm left for a good story.

> Rita Clay Estrada
> AKA Tira Lacy and Rita Clay
> *Twelve Gifts of Christmas* (Harlequin)
> Author of 29 novels

I can't emphasize enough the importance of preparing for a "professional" life as a writer. With today's increasingly competitive market, it isn't enough to learn how to be a good writer. To truly succeed, the wise author instructs him/herself in the "business" of writing as well.

> Sharon Ihle
> AKA Sharon MacIver and June Cameron
> *The Bride Wore Spurs* (HarperCollins)
> Author of 10 novels

A genre fiction writer has the obligation to fulfill the expectations of the reading audience.

> Theresa Di Benedetto
> AKA Raine Cantrell
> *Whisper My Name* (Topaz/Penguin)
> Author of 15 novels

Find a good critique group/partner. By good, I don't mean someone who tells you everything you write is wonderful. Neither do I mean someone who trashes your work in the name of "constructive criticism." Find people who work *with* you to make you the best writer *you* can be.

> Linda Shertzer
> AKA Melinda Pryce
> *Homeward Bound* (Berkley)
> Author of 13 novels

Never forget who you're writing this book for: not for an editor, not for yourself, but for all the people out there who trustingly plunk down their hard-earned money in the belief that they are getting the best darned story you can write. Give it to them.

> Susan Horton
> AKA Naomi Horton
> *What Are Friends For?* (Silhouette)
> Author of 23 novels

"I don't even like these characters; I don't care what happens to them, and I want to start something new!" Those are merely symptoms of the Middle of the Book Blues. Keep writing. This, too, shall pass.

> Pam Hart
> *Lies and Shadows* (Meteor)
> Author of 1 novel

The temptation to talk about a work in progress is sometimes almost overwhelming, but resist it. For a storyteller the drive to write comes from the need to tell the story. Once you've told it aloud, your enthusiasm for putting the same thing down on paper wanes considerably.

Pamela Morsi
Something Shady (Berkely/Jove)
Author of 8 novels

Give your characters fascinating lives and conflicts, but don't forget to live your own life while you're building your career. Families and friends last a lot longer than bestseller lists and royalty checks.

Myrna Temte
AKA Molly Thomas
Room for Annie (Silhouette)
Author of 10 novels

When you feel you have enough writing experience, volunteer to judge a writing contest. You'll recognize mistakes in others' writing that you've made in your own.

Heather MacAllister
AKA Heather Allison
Jilt Trip (Harlequin)
Author of 8 novels

Write to please yourself first. Remember why you wanted to be a writer and don't allow the business of writing to ruin the pleasure of writing. Otherwise, you'll lose the magic that makes your work more than work.

Geralyn Williams
AKA Geralyn Dawson
Tempting Morality (Bantam)
Author of 3 novels

Never *ever* be caught without pen (pencil) and paper. (That includes your car, a restaurant, the bedroom, etc.) You never know when a hot idea will strike—or the inner voice will whisper in your ear. If you don't write an idea down, you can lose it! Heaven forbid!

Binnie Syril Braunstein
AKA Binnie Syril
Kosher Christmas (Romantic Interludes)
Author of 3 novels

PRODUCTIVITY

Write every day. Writing takes practice just like any other talent. Don't stop with one book and wait for it to sell. Go on to another. Each book is a learning process. I wrote nine books before I finally sold one. Since then (1982) I've sold 40 books.

> Rosanne Bittner
> *The Forever Tree* (Bantam)
> Author of 40 novels

Self-discipline should be of vital importance from the very beginning of your career. The greatest talent in the world won't magically produce a novel. You must write!

> Joan Elliot Pickart
> AKA Robin Elliott
> *Mother at Heart* (Silhouette)
> Author of 67 novels

Push yourself. An athlete who achieves success tries a little harder the next time to reach a greater goal. If now you can write three pages a day, strive to produce four.

> Barbara Dawson Smith
> *A Glimpse of Heaven* (St. Martin's)
> Author of 10 novels

Persistence, persistence, persistence! Keep writing, keep rewriting, keep sending it out. Somewhere there is an editor who is going to like your work; all you have to do is find him. Never give up!

> Helen Playfair
> *Flying High* (Zebra)
> Author of 2 novels

Delete all computer games from your hard drive. Burn the diskettes.

> Heather MacAllister
> AKA Heather Allison
> *The Santa Sleuth* (Harlequin)
> Author of 8 novels

A partnership is one of the most productive ways to write. Partners must have a 100 percent commitment to their joint effort. We divide the work: one develops ideas, does the plotting, writes the synopsis and does final editing. The other handles the character development and dialogue.

> Pam Hanson
> AKA Jennifer Drew and Pam Rock
> *Turn Back the Night* (Silhouette)
> Author of 5 novels

Once you have begun a novel, finish it before you revise a word. Don't polish as you go. By finishing the book you will not only gain a sense of accomplishment, but you will really know your characters and spot the pitfalls in the plot. Make notes of changes as you go and when finished, rewrite.

> Jill Marie Landis
> *After All* (Berkley/Jove)
> Author of 8 novels

Don't self-edit. When you sit down to write, don't think of your mother or what some might say. Believe in yourself and your story.

> Christine Pacheco
> *Risky Business* (Silhouette)
> Author of 1 novel

Keep a fact sheet posted by your computer listing all pertinent information about your characters, such as the color of their eyes, ages, traits, names of their family members and pets. This will serve as a quick reference and eliminate wasting time scanning your text for details.

> Barbara Harrison
> AKA Leann Harris
> *Deep in the Heart* (Silhouette)
> Author of 4 novels

To keep my chapters organized for ready reference, while I'm writing I use a spiral binder of pocket folders (they come six or eight to a binder). I keep my synopsis in one, research material and notes in one or two. Each chapter then has its own pocket. A short book takes two binders, longer books take more.

> Jan Hudson
> *Rogue Fever* (Bantam)
> Author of 16 novels

I like to know the story and the characters before I sit down to write the manuscript. I jot down scenes, dialogue, plot twists, and characterization notes on index cards. I arrange the cards into an outline. *Then* I start writing.

> Cathy Gillen Thacker
> *Miss Charlotte's Surrender* (Harlequin)
> Author of 40 novels

Write your first draft in your head during long driving trips. Experience the characters, the action, the dialogue, as they appear in your mind. When you finally sit down at your keyboard, replay that mind-tape and let the story flow.

> Pamela Browning
> *Angel's Baby* (Harlequin)
> Author of 35 novels

Remember that you don't have to start with chapter one, paragraph one. It's okay to skip around. If a later scene is particularly vivid in your mind, even if it's the ending, write that first. It will get the juice flowing and inspire you to write more to catch up.

> Elizabeth Bevarly
> *The Honeymoon* (HarperCollins)
> Author of 15 novels

Writing is a job. You do so many pages every working day, at least five days a week. It doesn't matter what else is happening in your life. Everybody has crises. Everybody has distractions. Everybody has *blah* days. Everybody gets tired. Everybody experiences discouragement. Work through it. Do your job.

> Sally McCluskey
> AKA Bethany Campbell, Lisa Harris, and Beth Ann Campbell
> *Your Number Is Up* (Bantam)
> Author of 32 novels

Find a way to keep going when the trials and upsets inherent in this business threaten to drag you down—the rejections, long periods of waiting for a response. The only way to give yourself an edge is to keep writing, keep sending something out.

> Kitty Bentch
> AKA Dani Criss
> *Sheriff's Lady* (Silhouette)
> Author of 3 novels

Write. This is the crucial step, and too often the one overlooked by novices. Dreaming, researching, networking, plotting, thinking, and reading are all helpful, but they won't make you a writer. You have to apply the *derrière* to the chair and keep it there.

> Shelly Thacker
> *A Stranger's Kiss* (Avon)
> Author of 6 novels

Don't worry about whether you're the smartest writer or the most talented writer; just be the most determined. Sooner or later, you'll get there.

> Sally Steward
> AKA Sally Carleen
> *The Improbable Wife* (Silhouette)
> Author of 4 novels

Listen to music—Yanni, David Sanborn, Reba McEntire, Anita Baker—everything, including classical. Different music evokes different moods and emotions, and emotion is the fuel of any novel. I've found that a bit of a lyric often triggers an idea for a scene or becomes the basis for an entire book.

> Penny Richards
> AKA Bay Matthews
> *The Greatest Gift of All* (Silhouette)
> Author of 21 novels

When you have to be away from writing your book for several days, make sure you leave your hero or heroine in the lurch. It provides you with the motivation to come back to work. If your characters are safe and sound, it is more difficult to generate enthusiasm to get the manuscript completed.

> Connie Feddersen
> AKA Carol Finch, Gina Robbins, and Debra Falcon
> *Midnight's Lady* (Zebra)
> Author of 40 novels

Write anyway! Don't use the problems of daily life as excuses for not writing. Don't wait for inspiration; it's an overrated commodity. Don't rely upon your "feelings" to decide if your writing is good or bad. Believe in yourself and your talent. Study and perfect your craft. Persevere despite the odds.

> Robin Lee Hatcher
> *Liberty Blue* (Harper Monogram)
> Author of 21 novels

Finish the book! It's a necessity overlooked by many writers. Publishers only publish the unfinished works of writers who are famous and dead—and these people are usually famous for their *finished* works in the first place.

> Linda Cajio
> *Perfect Catch* (Bantam)
> Author of 22 novels

If I've been sidetracked by the obligations of everyday life, I take a nap before I begin writing. It's like erasing the blackboard from messy scribbles, leaving it ready for fresh creating.

> Curtiss Ann Matlock
> *White Gold* (Harlequin)
> Author of 18 novels

Being a writer involves an action verb—writing. Make yourself write almost every day, especially when you don't feel like it. The best ideas come while you're at the keyboard, working. One thought will lead to another, if not this time, then when you're revising. Just do it.

> Marie Rydzynski-Ferrarella
> AKA Marie Charles, Marie Rydzynski, Marie Michael, and Marie Nicole
> *Caitlin's Guardian Angel* (Silhouette)
> Author of 68 novels

Write something every day. Don't use the excuse that you can't find time. Wake up an hour early, go to bed an hour late, but write. Believe in yourself. Say aloud at least once a day, "I am going to finish this book." Don't give up. Ever.

> Julie Moffett Czechowski
> AKA Julie Moffett
> *A Touch of Fire* (Leisure)
> Author of 2 novels

GOALS

All writers should have a list of personal writing goals. Setting such goals, especially short term goals, and MEETING them helps a writer stay on track. It's like the childhood game of following the dots—only instead of dots you are following your goals. As soon as you reach one goal, you head automatically for the next.

> Rosalyn Alsobrook
> *Beyond Forever* (Zebra)
> Author of 22 novels

Set a goal of a number of pages per day, be it one or five or eight and stick with it. Give yourself a reward when it's done. If you do more, that doesn't mean you can skip the next day. One page a day means a completed or near-completed book at the end of the year. Don't base your schedule on time, but on accomplishment.

> Patricia Potter
> *Wanted* (Bantam)
> Author of 21 novels

Goal-setting is an important part of the discipline of writing. I set two goals—one I know I can achieve no matter what kind of day I'm having—and one I would like to achieve if I should be having the best day of my life. Usually I end up somewhere in between, but it means I can go to bed every night feeling good about writing, which makes me eager to return to the computer the next day.

> Judy Christenberry
> *Daddy on Demand* (Harlequin)
> Author of 16 novels

If there is just one thing I could say to everyone who yearns to publish a novel, it's this: DREAM BIG DREAMS. Don't stuff them into the future with justifications and apologies. Don't be afraid. Who knows where they might take you.

> Debbie Macomber
> *The Trouble with Angels* (Harper)
> Author of 52 novels

Write every day if possible. Set realistic goals for yourself. One page a day makes better sense for a new writer than five or ten. You'll build a calendar of "writing success" rather than feeling like a failure if you didn't reach your goal.

> LaRee Bryant
> *Forever, My Love* (Zebra)
> Author of 7 novels

The people who make it in this business are not the ones who find time to write when everything else is done. They're the ones who do everything else when the writing is done.

> Margaret Benson
> AKA Maggie Shayne
> *Wings in the Night* (Silhouette)
> Author of 11 novels

CREATIVITY

Give yourself permission to write badly. Fear of not being good enough often blocks creativity. Rewriting is easier than writing fresh.

> Karen Leabo
> *Into Thin Air* (Silhouette)
> Author of 19 novels

If you think you have to be inspired before you can write, you have it backwards. Inspiration comes *while* you're writing. Think about it. Breakthroughs in any field come to those who are working in the field, not just dabbling around the edges. The mere process of writing activates the imagination.

> Jean Hager
> AKA Jeanne Stephens
> *Dead and Buried* (Avon)
> Author of 47 novels

One of the first words you ever learned to read is one of the most important words you'll need for your writing: LOOK. Look around you. Look at everything. Look at the way a woman puts on lipstick. Look at the way a child holds a duckling in her hands. Look at a man's jaw as he drives a sports car. . . . You get the idea. Make a picture.

> Susan Wiggs
> *Vows Made in Wine* (HarperCollins)
> Author of 15 novels

Listing a scene's sensory details before writing it will jog your creativity. Do this the night before sitting down to the keyboard and it will speed you along the next day.

> Sonya Birmingham
> *Frost Flower* (Leisure)
> Author of 4 novels

Just before writing, when you are all set, computer turned on, pencil and paper at hand, read. Read something that turns on your imagination and makes your mind start clicking. And always read writing you consider better than your own.

> Curtiss Ann Matlock
> *White Gold* (Silhouette)
> Author of 18 novels

STYLE

The prospect of being drawn into an irresistible story is what motivates a reader to pick up a book. Learn to write a sentence properly, then tell a good story.

> Glenda Sanders
> *More Than Kisses* (Avon)
> Author of 26 novels

"Make me shiver." These words were spoken by a high-school teacher, and I've never forgotten. Make the reader see, hear, taste, smell, touch. Make the reader feel. Make the reader shiver.

> Ruth Ryan Langan
> *Angel* (Harlequin)
> Author of 36 novels

A book that stays in a reader's heart comes from the writer's heart. Draw on your own life experiences: the Sunday morning drives you took with Grandpa, the summers you spent at 4-H camp, the birthday parties you never went to because your mother couldn't afford a present for your friend. Like a fingerprint, these are the telling details that will give your story warmth, authenticity, and feeling.

> Inglath Cooper
> AKA Inglath Caulder
> *Truths and Roses* (Harlequin)
> Author of 1 novel

Don't try to work at some other writer's speed or style. It's hers. It was custom-made by fitting family, personal and business adjustments together to suit her wants and needs. Write at your own pace, according to *your* family, personal and business adjustments. Don't compare yourself to anyone but you. You're the only one who will receive the credit and rewards for that body of work.

> Rita Clay Estrada
> AKA Tira Lacy and Rita Clay
> *Twelve Gifts of Christmas* (Harlequin)
> Author of 29 novels

Take the time to develop your own writer's "voice" and while you're creating, remember the words of James Thurber: "Don't get it right, get it written." Be free, have fun, you can always go back and edit later.

> Cathie Linz
> *Bridal Blues* (Silhouette)
> Author of 28 novels

Writers are a diverse group. Don't try to mimic someone else's habits. If you're a fast writer, great. If you aren't, don't force yourself to write fast because someone else can. Find your own way. You'll do your best work if you allow yourself the luxury of being yourself.

> Deb Stover
> *Shades of Rose* (Pinnacle)
> Author of 3 novels

Details are everything—the craft, the art, the style of your work—but mainly, details form your particular voice. Details of sight, sound, smell;

details of word choice and rhythm; these are the markers that will make your voice distinct from all others. Find your detail patterns and use them.

> Barbara Samuel
> AKA Ruth Wind
> *Lucien's Fall* (Harper)
> Author of 12 novels

Take big risks—with your characters and with their story, but especially with yourself. Spew out your guts, bleed on the page. Go ahead and be mushy and sappy and sentimental and melodramatic. You can always tone it down later. But if you haven't suffered and rejoiced and *wallowed* in it with your characters, then you can't expect your reader will.

> Penelope Williamson
> *Heart of the West* (Simon & Schuster)
> Author of 6 novels

No one remembers how fast you write—only how well.

> Antoinette Stockenberg
> *Time After Time* (Dell)
> Author of 8 novels

The most important thing we have to offer in the marketplace is ourselves, our unique talent. Therefore we shouldn't try to write like anyone else, but find the ways in which our own unique gifts best weave into our chosen genre.

> Jo Beverley
> *Dangerous Joy* (Zebra)
> Author of 15 novels

Don't fool yourself. Never write what you wouldn't read for pleasure. If a story doesn't entertain you, why would it entertain anyone else?

> Nora Roberts
> *Born In Ice* (Jove)
> Author of 97 novels

Read. Read. Read—everything! But write what you love. Above all— be fearless!

> Bonnie Jean Perry
> *Twice in a Lifetime* (Zebra)
> Author of 5 novels

MARKETS AND AGENTS

No market is "closed" or "over-stocked" if the book you target specifically for it is *excellent*.

> Vivian A. Thompson
> AKA Val Daniels
> *Forever Isn't Long Enough* (Harlequin)
> Author of 3 novels

Target your market precisely; avoid stories that fall between the cracks. Understand the conventions and fantasies of your genre thoroughly, and fulfill them. Then *transcend* them. Your unique voice is what makes a story special.

> Mary Jo Putney
> *Dancing on the Wind* (Penguin/Topaz)
> Author of 14 novels

Know the market you're submitting to. Go to the bookstore and find out who is publishing the kind of story you're writing. Buy and read some debut books. They will show you what editors are buying from a new writer.

> Nancy Harwood Bulk
> AKA Dee Holmes
> *Dillion's Reckoning* (Silhouette)
> Author of 9 novels

Read the best of the genre in which you want to write. And then read everything else you can.

> Fayrene Preston
> *One Enchanted Autumn* (Bantam)
> Author of 43 novels

If you want to write the book of your dreams—go for it. But if you want to sell, read, study the market and learn the rules. Then remember rules can be broken.

> Sue Kearney
> *Tara's Child* (Harlequin)
> Author of 1 novel

Writing is a business; empower yourself by learning all its facets. You will then be in a position to judge which agent and which publisher will best suit your needs.

> Theresa Di Benedetto
> AKA Theresa Michaels
> *Once a Maverick* (Harlequin)
> Author of 15 novels

No agent is better than a bad agent. Do your research! Don't jump at the first agent you come across. You want someone whose philosophy and personality traits mesh well with your own, as well as someone qualified, experienced, and knowledgable in your particular market.

> LaRee Bryant
> *Forever, My Love* (Zebra)
> Author of 7 novels

CHARACTERIZATION

Before any writer starts any story, whether fiction or non-fiction, there is something important every writer has to know: who her characters are. Before a writer can decide motivation, conflicts (both major and minor), what type of dialogue to use, or even which character should be the main viewpoint character, that writer has to know who the characters are and what their lives have been like until then.

> Rosalyn Alsobrook
> *Beyond Forever* (Zebra)
> Author of 22 novels

Concentrate on learning to create sympathetic characters. Readers will forgive a weak plot if you give them characters to care about and root for.

> Pat Kay
> AKA Trisha Alexander
> *The Girl Next Door* (Silhouette)
> Author of 16 novels

To create memorable characters who feel real emotions, you aim for the heart, but always via the head. Rely on logic and your own common sense as the acid test for your characters' actions and reactions.

> Helen R. Myers
> *The Law Is No Lady* (Silhouette)
> Author of 26 novels

Create characters with integrity who are seeking worthy goals that mean everything to them—their physical survival, their emotional survival, the survival of their family members, the survival of the universe as they know it. If they fail to accomplish their goal, it will mean the destruction of everything that matters.

> Pat Tracy
> *Saddle the Wind* (Harlequin)
> Author of 7 novels

Characterization can make or break a book. Strive to create a strong bond between the main character and the reader, one so solid that the reader cares about the growth and the ultimate happiness of your character.

> Constance O'Day-Flannery
> *Seasons* (Zebra/Kensington)
> Author of 11 novels

Characters are motivated by deeper reasons than the obvious. A woman refusing to see her ex-husband needs more motivation than anger. List eight reasons. Cross out the first six. Remaining will be the REAL reasons and superb characterization.

> Nancy Harwood Bulk
> AKA Dee Holmes
> *Dillion's Reckoning* (Silhouette)
> Author of 9 novels

Create a psychic closeness with your characters through internal dialogue. The human mind is constantly reacting, evaluating, accepting and/or rejecting what is being felt or said. A part of our awareness stands back and carries on a silent dialogue no matter what we're doing. Let your characters talk to themselves and create an inner depth to their personalities.

> Leona Karr
> AKA Lee Karr
> *Bodyguard* (Harlequin)
> Author of 28 novels

When developing the heroine of your novel, the most important characteristic you can give her is a sense of humor and the ability to laugh at herself. Humorless people are not fun to be around, either in real life or in the pages of a book.

> Pat Kay
> AKA Trisha Alexander
> *The Girl Next Door* (Silhouette)
> Author of 16 novels

Beware of perfect characters. Always write as if the good have weaknesses and the evil have reasons.

> Mona Sizer
> AKA Deana James
> *Duchess* (Zebra)
> Author of 18 novels

Delve into your darker side to create your antagonists, but don't make him or her purely evil. *Every* character should be a mixture of good and bad, with the emphasis on the good for protagonists, and the bad for antagonists. Remember . . . complexity deepens characterization.

> Linda Lang Bartell
> *Tender Scoundrel* (Zebra)
> Author of 10 novels

Paint yourself into a corner by putting your protagonists into a situation that even you don't know how to resolve. Having your characters face an insurmountable challenge will make them more vivid and unexpectedly wonderful things can come from this test of your creativity.

> Deborah A. Cooke
> AKA Claire Delacroix
> *A Magician's Quest* (Harlequin)
> Author of 7 novels

Make sure your characters aren't too much alike. Put contrasting characters together and tap the differences for a lively story.

> Glenda Sanders
> *Not This Guy!* (Harlequin)
> Author of 26 novels

If you write a character-driven story, be sure to listen to your characters. Remember, it's *their* story, not yours.

> Cathie Linz
> *Bridal Blues* (Silhouette)
> Author of 28 novels

The reader "lives" inside the skin of the viewpoint character. We know what the character is thinking, feeling, seeing, and touching. A common mistake made by beginners is head-hopping, where the reader jumps from the thoughts and emotions of one character to another in the same scene. Stick to one viewpoint per scene.

> Barbara Dawson Smith
> *A Glimpse of Heaven* (St. Martin's)
> Author of 10 novels

Point of view isn't just a matter of which character's head you are in. It is also the careful choice of the details that characters would notice.

For example: A mechanic probably wouldn't notice the "lovely blue floral couch" when he walks into an elegant room. He would probably be more likely to notice whether or not the carpet was spotless so that if it was, he could stand hesitantly by the door, lest he mar the floor with his oil-stained shoes.

> Vivian A. Thompson
> AKA Val Daniels
> *Forever Isn't Long Enough* (Harlequin)
> Author of 3 novels

DIALOGUE

To create great dialogue, first you have to listen. Tape a conversation with a friend or a TV show. As you listen, concentrate on the rhythm, the contractions, the incomplete sentences your English teacher would have hated. That's how real people talk and how dialogue should read.

> Sherryl Woods
> *Finally a Bride* (Silhouette)
> Author of 55 novels

To find your distinctive writing voice, read authors you admire and catch the cadence of their work. Sit down and find rhythm within your own words. It's simple. Write the way you talk. Victory comes when a reader finishes your book and says: "It's like we've had a chat."

> Deborah Bedford
> *Chickadee* (HarperCollins)
> Author of 10 novels

Read your work aloud. It's a great way to catch clunky passages, especially in dialogue.

> Heather MacAllister
> AKA Heather Allison
> *Bedded Bliss* (Harlequin)
> Author of 8 novels

PLOTTING

In the opening of the novel, try to begin with an event that is unique, or that raises curiosity. The opening should involve a moment-by-moment, vivid portrayal of some kind of dramatic action taking place that involves a character with whom the reader can sympathize.

> Sara Orwig
> *Falcon's Lair* (Silhouette)
> Author of 45 novels

The best plots are driven equally by events and emotions. Alternate the scene/sequel pattern. Scene/events: Give the character a goal. Provide conflict. A disaster results. Sequel/emotions: The character reacts. A dilemma arises. A decision to go after the goal in a different manner must be made. Begin the pattern again.

> DeWanna Pace
> AKA Dee Pace
> *So Close to the Flame* (Crown)
> Author of 6 novels

When you get stuck and don't know what happens next, instead of stewing about it, make a list of everything that can't possibly happen next, and—this is important—*why* it can't happen. The process of elimination will lead you to the answer.

> Cathy Gillen Thacker
> *Guilty as Sin* (Harlequin)
> Author of 40 novels

This brainstorming technique revolutionized my writing: whenever I am about to begin a new project, I ask myself, "What are twenty things that could happen in this story?" I make myself come up with twenty answers and try not to judge the early ones which are usually stupid.

> Linda Lael Miller
> *Remember This Night* (Berkley)
> Author of 42 novels

Stir the emotions of the readers. Make them love, laugh, cry, and hate. Move your plot in such a way that readers will keep turning the pages to find out if the lovers live happily and the villain gets his just rewards.

> Dorothy Garlock
> *Yesteryear* (Warner)
> Author of 38 novels

In each scene, ask yourself what your heroine *wants*. This is the goal that motivates her to act, to overcome any obstacle in order to attain her heart's desire. By giving the hero a goal that opposes *her* goal, you sow the seeds for a powerful conflict.

>Barbara Dawson Smith
>*A Glimpse of Heaven* (St. Martin's)
>Author of 10 novels

The difference between *plot* and *conflict* can be difficult to understand. Remember that the *conflict* is the basic problem, the angst in the story that must be resolved. The *plot* is the framework upon which your story is built, the means by which the conflict is set up, intensified, and ultimately resolved.

>Anne Marie Rodgers
>AKA Anne Marie Winston
>*Rancher's Baby* (Silhouette)
>Author of 9 novels

If your plot runs out of steam too soon, you don't have enough conflict, either within the characters or between the characters: conflict within your characters will carry you farther than conflict between your characters.

>Eileen Dreyer
>AKA Kathleen Korbel
>*Don't Fence Me In* (Silhouette)
>Author of 21 novels

When creating internal conflict, remember these six words: The issue is not the issue.

>Renee Roszel
>*Make-Believe Marriage* (Harlequin)
>Author of 17 novels

While writing a scene, you should experience your characters' emotions. If they're crying, you should be crying. If they're laughing, you should be, too. And if they're sexually aroused, you should be squirming in your chair. If you don't feel what your characters feel, neither will the reader.

> Beverly Beaver
> AKA Beverly Barton
> *The Outcast* (Silhouette)
> Author of 13 novels

Emotion begets emotion. If your story is flat, take time to listen to moving music, watch an intensely emotional film, or call a dear friend with whom you can whip up enthusiasm for your project. Then go back to your writing, revived and refreshed.

> Jodi Raynor
> AKA Jodi O'Donnell
> *Daddy Was a Cowboy* (Silhouette)
> Author of 4 novels

Drawing the maximum amount of emotion out of a scene often has as much to do with what you leave out as it does with what you put in. Less is more.

> Vivian A. Thompson
> AKA Val Daniels
> *Forever Isn't Long Enough* (Harlequin)
> Author of 3 novels

When writing romance, emotions are the key. Focus on everyday events, explore them. Search your own heart for the emotions these events evoke. Capture these memories with the five senses, and express them vividly in your characters' lives.

> Laurie Moeller
> AKA Laura Anthony
> *Raleigh and the Wrangler* (Silhouette)
> Author of 2 novels

Help the reader visualize each scene by using specific details of action, the five senses, and dialogue. Rather than *tell* the reader, "She was angry," *show* the character's emotion by having her throw a plate at the wall or by getting into an argument with someone.

> Barbara Dawson Smith
> *A Glimpse of Heaven* (St. Martin's)
> Author of 10 novels

PACING

Pacing is an important element in fiction. Readers have too many demands on their time to stick with a book that doesn't hold their attention, intrigue them, and lead them to the next page. Use more dialogue and action to keep the reader's interest. Put every word to the test of necessity.

> Judy Christenberry
> *Daddy on Demand* (Harlequin)
> Author of 16 novels

Start fast—fill in the back story later. Grab your reader by the throat on the first page and don't let go.

> Rita Rainville
> *Bedazzled* (Silhouette)
> Author of 24 novels

Be aware of first impressions. Your readers are the most vulnerable in the early pages of your story. Don't bore them with descriptions, confuse them with careless word choices, or show an intended sympathetic character kicking a dog.

> Nancy Harwood Bulk
> AKA Dee Holmes
> *Dillion's Reckoning* (Silhouette)
> Author of 9 novels

Use narrative when you want to slow the pace of a story and dialogue when you want to accelerate the pace of a story.

> Michele Wyan
> *Night Singer* (Pinnacle)
> Author of 1 novel

Scenes highly charged with emotion or suspense work best when written with an economy of words. Short, clean sentences convey a sense of urgency. Overwriting can dilute tension.

> Elizabeth DeLancey
> *Meant to Be* (Berkley)
> Author of 3 novels

The best compliment a writer can receive is, "I couldn't put it down." A page-turner's characters harbor secrets; its reader is forced to wait for emotional and physical pay-offs; and must be permeated with a sense of urgency the writer creates by including a ticking time bomb deadline.

> Brenda Hamilton
> AKA Brenda Todd
> *The Locket* (Harlequin)
> Author of 3 novels

Foreshadow your book's climax so there is a buildup to your final big scene. Anticipation heightens suspense. You can give hints of what will happen by focusing on your character's goal, as well as by giving the villain's threats. Make this big scene the most dramatic moment of the story.

> Sara Orwig
> *Falcon's Lair* (Silhouette)
> Author of 45 novels

REJECTION AND REVISION

Allow the act of writing itself to provide you with joy. No number of rejection letters should have the power to diminish that joy.

> Pat Tracy
> *Saddle the Wind* (Harlequin)
> Author of 7 novels

Rejection isn't personal. A rejection means your product didn't fit the current needs of the buyer. To sell your writing, you must refine that product until it fits the buyer's needs.

> Laura Phillips
> *Beginnings* (Meteor)
> Author of 5 novels

Don't let fear of rejection keep you from trying. Rejections only make that first sale all the sweeter.

> Gayle Kasper
> AKA Gayle Kaye
> *Here Comes the Bride* (Bantam)
> Author of 6 novels

Pay attention to your rejection letters but don't let them dissuade you from sending your work out again. Never give them more significance than they deserve. Many times a rejection letter represents only ONE person's opinion.

> Rosalyn Alsobrook
> *Beyond Forever* (Zebra)
> Author of 22 novels

When you think you've completed your last draft and are ready to send your manuscript in, set it aside for a few days instead. Then, after you've had time to allow your memory to dim each and every word, pick it up and read it again. The parts you read are the good parts. Don't touch them. The parts you skim are the parts that need work. Revise them one more time.

> Rita Clay Estrada
> AKA Tira Lacy and Rita Clay
> *Twelve Gifts of Christmas* (Harlequin)
> Author of 29 novels

After you've polished a piece of writing, let it sit for a few days. A week is even better. Don't look at it. Work on something else. When you read the first piece again, you'll be amazed at the rough places you'll find.

> Heather MacAllister
> AKA Heather Allison
> *Jilt Trip* (Harlequin)
> Author of 8 novels

Before you submit your work, polish your manuscript until it shines. This sounds so obvious, but I can't tell you how many new writers fail to do this. Check for word repetitions, vary your sentence structure, learn what is meant by sentence rhythm. Polish, polish, polish!

> Julie Caille
> *A Family for Ronnie* (Silhouette)
> Author of 6 novels

Nothing is sacred; everything can be revised. Write passionately; edit like the frozen tundra.

> Pam Hart
> *Lies and Shadows* (Meteor)
> Author of 1 novel

Write the book all the way through before perfecting what's been done. You keep the excitement and flow that way. Changes occur throughout, and you will probably have to repair anyway, so why do it twice, or three times, or a million.

> Patricia Potter
> *Wanted* (Bantam)
> Author of 21 novels

Don't stop to edit until you type "the end." Writing is like riding a wild horse. If you try to control the outcome, you'll only diminish the thrill, and rob your readers of your uninhibited creativity. The best plots are often a free rein away.

> Neesa Hart
> AKA Mandalyn Kaye
> *Forever After* (Pinnacle)
> Author of 6 novels

SECTION III

Markets

♡　♡　♡

Marketing Your Romance

ROBIN GEE

*Y*our heroine and hero have surpassed seemingly insurmountable obstacles to their love and are finally together; now they can begin to live happily ever after. As the writer of their story, however, it's only the beginning for you. A well-written manuscript with exciting characters and a well-developed plot is only your first step; the next is to market your book to editors in a way that will get it more than just a quick glance.

This isn't as difficult as it may seem. Overall, the market is good for romance fiction. Romances account for almost half of all mass market paperback sales. According to industry figures, 140 new and reprint romances are published *each month*. Recent figures indicate the largest romance publisher, Harlequin, sold more than 190 million books last year worldwide.

Nevertheless, publishers continue to be cautious, spending more time and advertising dollars on established authors rather than newer writers. More and more shelf space is being devoted to reissues of early books by bestselling authors, leaving less room for books by new authors. Competition remains keen and it takes a combination of a good story, talented writing and marketing savvy to make it.

Finding a publisher requires as much care and effort as researching and writing your novel. With romance, it's primarily important to know exactly what type of romance you are writing. Is it historical? Is it contemporary? Does it contain a lot of humor? Do your characters travel through time? There are publishers and imprints for each of these types and more, but sending to the wrong ones will mark you as an amateur and result in unnecessary rejection.

The cardinal rule is: Read. Reading what's on the shelves is the easiest way of determining which publisher will be interested in your manuscript. If, for example, you plan to submit your book to Harlequin's Temptation line, read the current Temptation releases and then go to a used bookstore and look for as many past releases as you can find. Beware that this is a love-it-or-leave-it genre; if the idea of reading a lot of romance novels puts you off, you shouldn't be trying to write them.

NOVEL MARKETS

Most romance novels are published by large, commercial publishers. Some, like Harlequin, are devoted entirely to romance, while others, like Kensington or Avon, have large romance imprints. There's a wide variety of romances being published, too. You'll find lines devoted to historicals, contemporaries, paranormal romance and time travel. Each line may also include several series such as Women of the Frontier, featuring stories set during the opening of the American West, or Love and Laughter, a series of humorous romances. Some series feature one author, while others feature several authors writing about a common theme.

As mentioned earlier, almost half of all mass-market paperbacks are romance novels. This is where romance publishing got its start. Mass-market paperbacks are the small, paperbound books usually priced between four and seven dollars. Writers on all career levels are published in this format, but most new writers start out here.

Paperback romances have changed drastically from the early days of romance publishing. With a few exceptions, category romances used to be sold by the line, each one with a different cover logo so readers could identify the different lines. Authors' names were mostly pen names and were not displayed as prominently as the name of the line. While publishers continue to publish books in each of several different and distinct lines, books are now sold less by line and more by author and series.

Although you'll still find the popular "clinch" cover, with the hero and heroine in a steamy embrace, many publishers are moving away from this. Some romances now have subtle floral patterns or other such designs on the cover. Others use a combination called a "step-back" cover. A step-back is really two covers; a pattern, title and author's name on an outer cover with a couple embracing on the inside. The outer cover is usually shorter than the width of the book and sometimes has a window cut into it, framing the couple's faces.

Bestselling authors and those who write romances with wide appeal also appear in hardcover. In fact, more romances than ever are being published in hardcover. Some are brought out in both hard and softcover formats; buying the rights to both formats from a writer is typically called a hard/soft deal.

Right now there are few markets in the small and independent press for romance, unless it's a book that is literary or is aimed at a specific audience. Christian romances, for example, do very well with Christian publishers. Young adult romances can appeal to both large and small book publishers specializing in titles for young adults and children. Book packagers produce books for other publishers and quite often work with series books. Romances, especially those aimed at teens, do well in this area and some packagers may also be open to romance series for adults.

There are a few audio book publishers interested in new romance. For the most part, however, well-known authors have a better chance than new authors at having their books published on tape.

SHORT STORY MARKETS

Magazines devoted exclusively to romantic fiction appear from time to time, but, unfortunately, they don't stay on the scene long. Two currently in business are *Romantic Interludes* and *I'll Take Romance!* (see **Resources** for more information). Mainstream women's magazines, however, remain open to stories with romance elements and some of these pay very well. Stories that mix genres—especially romantic suspense— are in demand by some of these publications. Christian magazines are also open to romance stories as are magazines aimed at seniors and at teens.

Most of the large, commercial romance publishers also publish anthologies, another market for short fiction. These tend to be open to established authors, but one or two slots are usually left open to new writers who have published at least one promising novel. Many are themed; holiday and travel-themed anthologies are very popular. The best way to find out about these is to watch your bookstore shelves for possible anthology series. If there's an anthology you think your story would fit, write the editor to find out if a new edition is being planned. Also, visit conventions and attend meetings of organizations such as the Romance Writers of America—networking can bring you leads on new anthology projects.

CHOOSING A MARKET FOR YOUR NOVEL

The first place to learn about book publishers and their various lines is your local bookstore or library. It's easier than ever today to find romance series or all the books of a favorite author. More and more publishers are reissuing series of bestselling authors and, with more shelf space in the big superstores, you're sure to find all the books you're after. There are a large number of independent used bookstores devoted to romance and, now, many of these have added new titles as well. An avid reader can stock up on past books by favorite authors and even trade old ones in for others.

A membership to Romance Writers of America can be most beneficial to the marketing efforts of both new and established romance authors. The group publishes the *Romance Writers Report*, a monthly publication chock full of market information and advice along with news about the organization. Magazines aimed at readers as well as authors, such as *Romantic Times*, can also keep you up-to-date with what's happening in the field. RWA also sponsors several conferences across the country and maintains a presence in the many online services. America Online, Prodigy, GEnie, Compuserve and others have areas and forums devoted to romance, and many established romance authors are accessible through them.

As an important part of your research of the market, study the listings in this book. The interviews with editors offer inside information specific to the needs and interests of romance writers. Pay close attention to the articles, especially the Anatomy of a Sale, pieces to see exactly what does and does not appeal to these editors.

Develop a short list of publishers you think might be interested in your romance, then write to request their guidelines. Publishers once issued long, involved writers' guidelines for each of their lines. Now the guidelines are shorter and more flexible, but you can still obtain these and descriptions of the various lines from all the major publishers. Guidelines highlight the differences between lines and series, making it easier to identify the right publisher for your book.

ABOUT AGENTS

You do not need an agent to send a short story to a magazine. Most agents will handle short stories only if they already handle your novel, and then they do it mostly as a courtesy. For book submissions, however, a good agent can give you an edge.

It is still possible to send unagented submissions to most romance publishers and many writers do. Because of the volume of submissions, other types of publishers have turned to agents as a way to screen out some manuscripts, treating agents almost as "first readers." In the romance field, however, most publishers still rely on their editors to do this initial screening. Many offer standard contracts to new authors and it's hard for a writer or agent to negotiate for a better deal.

While romance publishers say having an agent does not necessarily give you the edge, you may want to secure one anyway to look out for your interests or just for the peace of mind an agent can give you. Many writers who secure agents early on feel it is worth the money because they can let the agent be the "bad guy," handling contract negotiations, calling editors about late payments and acting as a liaison for any author-editor disputes, regardless of how minor. Since they are just establishing a relationship with the editor, they feel these services are worth the agent's commission. Others simply feel that it is their job to write the book, and an agent's job to sell it, acknowledging that a good agent knows much more about the market and has much better contacts.

Once you become an established name, however, an agent is a necessity. When discussing multi-book contracts and foreign rights, a good agent is a definite asset. And as your career grows, your agent will assist you in keeping it on track and can advise you of the best ways to handle any non-romance projects you might wish to pursue.

Since it can be as hard to find a good agent as it is to find a publisher, some writers market their first book themselves and then look for an agent once they have a published book or at least a contract in hand. If you decide to look for an agent, look first at the listings of agents in this book. These agents specialize in romance and know the different lines and their editors. The Romance Writers of America also publishes a list of romance agents and the *Guide to Literary Agents* (Writer's Digest Books) is another good source of agent listings. In addition to its detailed entries, the *Guide* includes articles on finding and working with an agent.

Word-of-mouth is another good way to find an agent. The RWA regularly invites agents to speak at its conferences and you can often make appointments to meet with one. Talking to other romance writers at conferences, at group meetings or on computer bulletin boards is a good way to find out about various agents.

Approach an agent as you would a publisher, with a query letter and sample chapters or a complete manuscript, depending on the agent's guidelines. It is generally acceptable to query more than one agent at a time, but avoid sending complete manuscripts to more than one agent for consideration.

Take your time when looking for an agent and don't be afraid to ask questions. After all, your agent will be your business partner. You want to go into business with someone you trust, someone you feel has your best interests at heart. Don't hesitate to ask for references and be wary of agents who charge large fees up front. Agents who do not charge up front fees make their money from their commission (usually 15 percent) when the book is sold. An agent who charges a lot of money just to read your manuscript has less incentive to sell your book and paying a reading fee is not a guarantee of representation.

Finally, read "How to Find and Work With an Agent" in the **Agents** section of this book. In that article, agent Denise Marcil gives you her perspective on why you need representation.

MANUSCRIPT MECHANICS

Professional presentation is important whether you are approaching an agent or a publisher. Granted, a poorly written manuscript will not make much of an impression, no matter how dazzling its presentation. Yet, a well-written manuscript will remain in the slush pile only to be returned if it is sloppy and hard to read.

Ensure that your manuscript will be read and your talent has a fighting chance by making your manuscript as easy for the editor to read as possible. Manuscripts should be double-spaced with wide margins and free of typos and errors. Pay attention to the details. Before typing or computer printing, make sure the print is dark. Use a fresh ribbon, ink cartridge or toner cartridge if necessary, and choose a paper that will hold up to being passed around from editor to editor—white bond rather than erasable paper or onion skin.

Photocopies are fine as long as they are clear. Most publishers do not want unsolicited computer disk submissions. If you've been requested to send a complete manuscript and would like to send it on disk, check with the publisher first. If you are sending a disk, be sure to include a hard copy as well. Do not send fax or modem (email) queries. Few publishers can handle a volume of submissions tying up their fax lines.

Include your name, address and phone number with your submission; put your name and a consecutive page number at the top of each page. With all this in mind, however, don't worry too much about where your name or title should be placed. The bottom line is that your manuscript must be as accessible and easy to read as possible.

QUERIES, COVER LETTERS AND MANUSCRIPT FORMATS

If you are approaching book publishers and are asked to query first, chances are you will need to include a sample of your writing and some form of story outline. In fiction, your query letter should be as brief as possible (see the Sample Book Query Letter on page 93). You are simply asking if they would be interested in seeing your manuscript. Keep the letter to one page, preferably only a few paragraphs. You may choose to start your letter with a hook—something special about your story, something to catch the editor's eye—but keep the hard sell to a minimum.

Be sure to identify what type of romance you have written. Show that you've done your research by mentioning which of the publisher's lines it would best fit. Information about yourself that lends credibility to your story should also be included, but avoid extraneous personal material. For example, if your heroine meets her hero in Spain and you lived in Spain for two years, by all means mention it. If she's an independent bookstore owner and you work in such a store, that would be worth mentioning, too. Beyond this, though, avoid giving details about your job, hobbies, family or pets if they have nothing to do with your story. Other information to include in your query would be an estimated word count and a few of your publishing credits, if you have any. Occasionally, you will be asked to send a bio. This is usually a one- or two-paragraph biographical statement, including a brief description of your achievements.

When sending sample chapters, send three *consecutive* chapters. Most publishers prefer the first three. Editors want to know how your work flows and how you move from one chapter to the next.

Include a cover sheet (see the Sample Cover Sheet on page 94) with either a partial or a complete manuscript. Put your name, address and phone number in the upper left-hand corner of the page and the word count in the right. Agented authors often leave the right-hand corner open for their agent's name and address, and some agents prefer their contact information to be the only material included on the cover sheet.

Center your title and byline about halfway down the page. Start your first chapter on the next page. If your chapter has a title, include it about one-third of the way down the page. Include your last name and page number in the upper right-hand corner of this and subsequent pages. Be sure to number the entire submission consecutively, all the way through to the end of the manuscript.

Along with a query and sample chapters, you may be asked to include a synopsis, outline or summary. Unfortunately, publishers tend to use these terms interchangeably, so when in doubt, check with the publisher first. A *synopsis* is a brief summation of your story, condensed into a page or a page-and-a-half, single spaced. An *outline* can run from five to twenty pages, double-spaced. An outline usually follows the chapters throughout the book, listing chapter headings and a few lines about what happens in each chapter. A *summary* is the most subjective of these terms. Before submitting a summary of your manuscript, it's best to ask the publisher how long and detailed it should be.

For magazines and many book publishers, you will be asked to send a complete manuscript. With a complete story or novel, you include a cover letter rather than a query (see the Sample Short Story Cover Letter on page 95 and the Sample Novel Cover Letter on page 96). Cover letters should be kept simple, and again, short. Don't tell too much about your story. After all, it's all there for the editor to read. Basically, you're saying: "Here I am. Here is my romance novel." As with a query letter, include what type of romance it is, what line you feel it best fits, the estimated length, a brief list of your previous publication experience (if you have any) and only the personal information that lends credibility to your story.

Whenever you correspond with an agent, editor or publisher, include a self-addressed, stamped envelope for their reply. Some writers send a disposable copy of the manuscript, but if you want it returned, you must include enough postage and a big enough box. Some writers cut costs by sending a self-addressed stamped postcard with places for the publisher to check off a reply. Also, when sending to a magazine or book publisher in another country, include International Reply Coupons instead of stamps. These may be purchased at the main branch of your post office.

For more information on submitting to either a book publisher or a magazine, several books by Writer's Digest Books can be helpful. For information on submitting your work, see *Novel & Short Story Writer's Market* or *Writer's Market*. For specifics on manuscript format see *The*

Writer's Digest Guide to Manuscript Formats by Dian Dincin Buchman and Seli Groves or *Manuscript Submission*, by Scott Edelstein, a part of the Elements of Fiction writing series.

MORE ABOUT SUBMISSION

Many romance writers choose to write their books under pseudonyms. In the past, some writers found themselves in messy contract disputes when the publisher owned the writer's pen name. The authors could not take the name (or their following) with them when they switched publishers. Today, thanks to organizations such as the RWA and to changes by publishers themselves, this is not as much of a problem. Many writers, however, select a pseudonym that is close to or another form of their own name. Whatever you decide, be sure you include your legal name on all correspondence with your publisher.

As do agents, most publishers will look at simultaneous queries, but they do not like simultaneous submissions. On the other hand, publishers understand that writers cannot wait a long time for their decision, so more are willing to look at them now than in the past. Keep in mind, however, that if more than one publisher expresses interest, you must decide. It's considered common courtesy to let other publishers know right away if your manuscript is sold.

Response time varies greatly with agents, magazines and book publishers. It's best to wait two to three weeks beyond the stated response time before sending a letter to check the status of your submission. A follow-up letter should be courteous and brief, and you should include a SASE for reply.

Keep careful records of your submissions. In addition to the name of the magazine or publisher and nature of the submission, be sure to include the date you mailed it and the dates of any subsequent correspondence. If your work is accepted, keep track of your rewrite and any other deadlines. If rejected, record any useful comments or notes of encouragement accompanying the rejection. The information will not only help you manage your submissions, but also help you make informed decisions when making future submissions.

While waiting for a response, one of the best ways to relieve the anxiety is to dive into your next book. Not only does it take your mind off the wait, but it also prepares you for the very good possibility that the editor will want to buy your *next* book, as well as your first.

Jennifer Williamson
8822 Rose Petal Ct.
Norwood OH 45212

January 6, 1996

Ms. Laverne Lamour
Historicals Editor
Romantic Book Publishers
113 W. 75th Ave.
New York NY 10101

Dear Ms. Lamour:

I met you briefly at the Lovers and Writers Convention in Cleveland last June and I'm following up on your suggestion to send you a few sample chapters of my manuscript.

I teach history at Parkdale Middle School and am a volunteer at the Cincinnati Historical Society, specializing in riverboat history. This background has helped me with my novel, a 75,000-word historical romance set along the Ohio River in the 1880s. *Lady Luck* would fit well into your Rivers of Romance line.

My heroine is Paulette Waterson, owner and captain of the Lucky Lady, a small riverboat. The boat was a gift from her father, a Civil War veteran, who raised her on the river. When Charlie Waterson died, he left his daughter just two things: Lucky Lady and the fierce Waterson pride. Paulette is barely making ends meet ferrying cargo and passengers from the little town of Anders Mill to and from Cincinnati when she meets Thomas Langdon, a charming, but notorious gambler and new owner of the Cincinnati Shipping Company. When Paulette refuses to sell Lucky Lady at any price, Thomas makes her a wager, one that will change their lives forever, no matter who wins.

Enclosed are the first three chapters of my novel and a brief synopsis. May I send you the complete manuscript?

I look forward to hearing from you.

Sincerely,

Jennifer Williamson

Encl.: Three sample chapters
        Synopsis
        SASE

Sample Book Query Letter

Jennifer Williamson   75,000 words
8822 Rose Petal Ct.
Norwood OH 45212

Lady Luck
by Jennifer Williamson

Sample Cover Sheet

Jennifer Williamson
8822 Rose Petal Ct.
Norwood OH 45212

January 15, 1996

Rebecca Rossdale
Young Woman Magazine
4234 Market St.
Chicago IL 60606

Dear Ms. Rossdale:

As a teacher and former assistant camp director I have witnessed many a summer romance between teens working at camp. One romance in particular touched me because the young people involved helped each other through a very difficult summer. It inspired me to write the enclosed 8,000-word short story, "Summer Love," a love story about two teens, both from troubled families, who find love and support while working at a camp in upstate New York.

I think the story will fit nicely into your Summer Reading issue. My publishing credits include stories in *Youth Today* and *Sparkle* magazines as well as publications for adults. I am also working on a historical romance.

I look forward to hearing from you.

Sincerely,

Jennifer Williamson

Encl.: Manuscript
          SASE

Sample Short Story Cover Letter

Jennifer Williamson
8822 Rose Petal Ct.
Norwood OH 45212

January 6, 1996

Ms. Laverne Lamour
Historicals Editor
Romantic Book Publishers
113 W. 75th Ave.
New York NY 10101

Dear Ms. Lamour:

I met you briefly at the Lovers and Writers Convention in Cleveland last June and I'm taking you up on your suggestion to send you my 75,000-word historical romance novel.

Lady Luck is set along the Ohio River in the 1880s and involves my heroine Paulette Waterson, owner and captain of the Lucky Lady, a small riverboat. The boat was a gift from her father, a Civil War veteran, who raised her on the river. When Charlie Waterson died, he left his daughter just two things: Lucky Lady and the fierce Waterson, pride. Paulette is barely making ends meet ferrying cargo and passengers from the little town of Anders Mill to and from Cincinnati when she meets Thomas Langdon, a charming, but notorious gambler and new owner of the Cincinnati Shipping Company. When Paulette refuses to sell Lucky Lady at any price, Thomas makes her a wager, one that will change their lives forever, no matter who wins.

I teach history at Parkdale Middle School and am a volunteer at the Cincinnati Historical Society, specializing in riverboat history. This background has helped me with my novel. I have also published short stories in several magazines including *Sparkle* and *Woman Today*. *Lady Luck* would fit well into your Rivers of Romance line.

I look forward to hearing from you.

Sincerely,

Jennifer Williamson

Encl.: Manuscript
        SASE

Sample Novel Cover Letter

Romance Novel Markets

*T*he publishers listed in this section either publish romance fiction exclusively, have a strong romance imprint or maintain a strong romance presence in their fiction lines. Since it is crucial for you to be well-informed about the publishers you submit to, we've gathered as much information as possible to shortcut your search for the perfect home for your novel.

Before each profile, there is a list of the types of romance that most interest the publisher. These will help you find the editors most receptive to the type of book you've written. Read the interview and a few of the publisher's recent books, however, to get a more in-depth feel for the types of material they look for.

You'll also find submission information included in each listing, including reporting times. Keep in mind that this information is averaged, and that such things as reporting times and contract terms vary and change. Keep careful records of submissions and correspondence, and allow three or four weeks beyond the stated reporting time before writing to check on the status of your query or manuscript.

Contract terms vary greatly within romance, so many publishers declined to provide us with average advance and royalty information. Generally speaking, however, a new category romance writer can expect an advance of about $4,000, and should ask for royalties of 8% on the first 150,000 copies sold and 10% on any copies sold thereafter. A new historical romance writer can get a slightly higher advance, usually around $7,000.

Finally, be aware that the romance market (and the publishing industry in general) is extremely dynamic. Editors change positions or move to other companies; new series begin and unpopular series end; likes and dislikes fluctuate; and addresses and phone numbers change. Therefore, it is vital to keep abreast of changes in the market. Join the Romance Writers of America and pay careful attention to their *Romance Writer's Report*. Also watch market reports in *Publishers Weekly*, *Romantic Times*, *Gila Queen's Guide to the Markets*, and *Writer's Digest* magazine. If you have a computer and a modem, explore the online resources listed later in this book. And if you become aware of a change that others might not know about, send a note to *RWR* and to us, as well.

AEGINA PRESS AND UNIVERSITY EDITIONS, INC.

Established: 1984

Romance Editor: Ira Herman, Managing Editor

CATEGORIES
Contemporary Romance, Fantasy, Ghost, Historical, Over 45, Romantic Mystery, Romantic Suspense

Wants: Strongly plotted fiction with non-stereotyped characters.

An average of 10-15 books per year are first novels. Recently published *Where the Whipoorwill Sings*, Barbara Chambers; *Captive Bold*, Judie Kleng; *A Little Different Love Story*, Helen E. Boyce and Linda L. Drury.

HOW TO CONTACT: Accepts unsolicited manuscripts. Send full manuscript. Simultaneous submissions accepted. Receives 50 manuscripts each month. 5% of accepted submissions are agented. On average reports on queries in 1 week. On average reports on manuscripts in 1 month. Send SASE for writer's guidelines.

TERMS: Each project is negotiated individually; most new titles are subsidy published. Buys First North American rights. Manuscript is published an average of 6-9 months after acceptance. Author receives bionote in book or on jacket. Author receives 5 copies of book; additional copies available at a 50% discount.

ADDRESS: 59 Oak Lane, Spring Valley, Huntington, WV 25704

PHONE: (304)429-7204

AVALON

Established: 1948

Marcia Markland, Vice President and Publisher

> **CATEGORIES**
> Contemporary Romance, Multicultural, Over 45, Romantic Mystery, Romantic Suspense

"We're the Family Channel of publishing," says Avalon's vice president and publisher Marcia Markland. "We publish sweet romances, and our audience ranges from teens to elderly people and everybody in between. We try to make what we publish suitable for anybody in the family."

Therefore, steamy sex-scene novelists should steer clear of Avalon. "There's absolutely no graphic sex in any of our books," Markland says. "We promise the libraries we will not send them books that have lots of sex and violence. So we're sort of wholesome."

Few people know the publishing industry better than Markland. While she has been at Avalon only since 1992, Markland has a long, diversified publishing career. "I've been working in publishing since 1972. I started at Prentice Hall, went from there to Penguin and then to St. Martin's where I stayed a long time throughout the 70s and 80s. I was the editor of the Mystery Guild at the Literary Guild. Then I went to England and came back and worked briefly at Bantam before coming here."

Although a relatively small house, Avalon has found a niche that demands a large and consistent number of books annually. "We publish 60 books a year, 12 of which are mystery, 12 westerns and 36 romances," Markland says. "We sell primarily to libraries that subscribe to our books. Every two months we publish ten books and send them to our libraries—six romances, two mysteries, and two westerns. It's a nice way for us to publish because we know we have a market and they know what they're getting."

Don't think that just because Avalon publishes unadulterated romances, their books are dull. A book's potential to enlighten, to broaden the reader's knowledge, is imperative at Avalon. They publish stories in which readers can actually learn something besides who's going to end up with whom. "Most of our romances are very contemporary," says Markland. "What's different about us is that we're really into career romances with characters who have interesting occupations—varying from a quilt store owner to a radio station manager to an archaeologist. This really helps our readers learn a lot about different vocations. It's fun to learn about what takes place at an archaeological dig. I guess that's what makes us unique: our characters have lives outside of their romances. You actually learn about things other than romance from our books. And we're very interested in publishing ethnic romances."

Does Avalon's refusal to publish sexy romances indicate they're old fashioned? Not really. Says Markland: "In many ways we're old fashioned, but we're also looking to the future. We try to emphasize the relationship, the getting to know the other person, not the physical part of the romance. We want well-written love stories. And love stories do not have to have lots of sex. Often our characters are more like platonic friends than lovers. Or they become friends before having a sexual relationship. So in that regard we're very contemporary and even future-oriented, especially with the rise of AIDS and other sexually transmitted diseases. We're learning you must get to know your partner well as a person before sleeping with him."

One noteworthy characteristic of Avalon's publishing philosophy is their receptivity to unagented authors. "Our contract is very simple, so you don't really need an agent. Not every good writer in this country has a literary agent. I'd guess about 90% of our writers do not have agents, and we're very open to new writers. We are a very good place to get started. Because we're mostly limited to libraries, however, you're not going to hit the bestseller list, but you'll have a hardcover published that will remain on the library shelves indefinitely. We were founded in 1948, and there are still books on library shelves from that first year."

While open to new authors and unsolicited submissions, Markland refuses to look at full-length manuscripts. "We do not want manuscripts unless we request them. We ask authors to submit three chapters and a two-page synopsis along with a SASE. If we think the manuscript is suitable for our company then we'll write to you and ask you to send us the entire manuscript. Very often, since we do publish only wholesome books, we have to reject many manuscripts that are well-written and publishable but just not suitable for our line."

Be sure to write for guidelines. "I receive a couple hundred query letters a week. Many of them have nothing to do with what we publish. And we have a length requirement. Our books cannot exceed 50,000 words. So it is a good idea to write for guidelines first and include a SASE."

Since libraries are Avalon's sole market, the publisher rarely does a lot of author promotion. "Now and again we'll pick a book we can do some special promotion with. But most of our authors belong to local writing associations and do regional promotions themselves, like library readings and book signings. We encourage all our authors to do that and we help them, particularly on a regional level. It's very good practice for authors to meet the public. We try to find writers who are going to have a long career in writing even after they leave Avalon."

Markland does have some advice for those trying to get published. "Try to have an original concept, especially regarding situation. I would recommend beginning writers read their work aloud, that helps them focus on what's they've written. And don't write what you're reading, because that's already been done. Do something new. We've been seeing way too many replicas of *The Bridges of Madison County*."

And if your manuscript is original, interesting and well-written but still hasn't found a publisher? "Don't get at all discouraged by rejection," says Markland. "The key to getting published today is to keep sending your manuscripts out. Send simultaneous submissions. Editors are curious to find something new. Your manuscript should be out somewhere getting a chance to be read, not stuck in some drawer at home. Besides, if you're a writer you must write. And your writing should be read."

HOW TO CONTACT: Accepts unsolicited manuscripts. Submit query letter and 3 sample chapters. Simultaneous submissions accepted. 10% of accepted submissions are agented. On average reports on queries in 1 month. On average reports on manuscripts in 3 months. Send SASE for writer's guidelines.

TERMS: Contracts negotiated on an individual basis. Buys all rights.

Manuscript is published an average of 6 months after acceptance. Author receives bionote in book or on jacket. Author receives 10 copies of book; additional copies available at a 50% discount.

ADDRESS: 401 Lafayette Street, New York, NY 10003

AVON BOOKS

Established: 1941

Romance Editors: **Ellen Edwards, Executive Romance Editor**; Carrie Feron, Executive Editor; Lyssa Keusch, Associate Editor; Christine Zika, Associate Editor; Ann McKay Thoroman, Assistant Editor; Micki Nuding, Assistant Editor

> CATEGORIES
> Contemporary Romance, Ghost, Historical, Multicultural, Over 45, Paranormal, Reincarnation, Time Travel, Vampire

"The fun part of being an editor is helping an author fulfill her vision for the book. It's so gratifying to see writers grow and fulfill their potential," says Ellen Edwards, executive editor of romance at Avon Books. "It's also been great to see how the whole romance genre has matured over the last 15 years—the quality of the writing is up, the number of writers is greater than ever, and the number of books being sold keeps growing. The genre has achieved a tremendous variety over the years."

Edwards has always gravitated toward women's fiction, even as a child. "My mother was a school librarian and was always bringing home Newbery winners for me to read, but I'd also read women's fiction, particularly 19th century novels—the Bronte sisters, Willa Cather, Jane Austen." Although a lover of women's fiction, Edwards didn't read many romances until she graduated from college. "I didn't read paperback romances until I got a job 15 years ago as an editorial assistant at Dell working on the Candlelight romances. I fell into the niche quite comfortably."

Since that first introduction to the genre, Edwards has remained committed to romance. After leaving Dell, she "did a 5-year stint at Berkley working on the Second Chance at Love line. We also published a line called To Have and To Hold, which was about married love, but that lasted only about 50 books." Edwards has been at Avon nine years, learning much about the genre over the years. "Since coming to Avon I've switched from working on category romances to historicals, which opened up a whole new avenue of reading and working with new authors. I'm working with a lot of top authors."

There are three core romance programs at Avon. Avon Romantic Treasures are historicals, published once a month, written by somewhat established authors. "This line is a step above the starting point," says Edwards. Then there are two Avon romances published every month, which are also historicals, and "this is the area where beginning authors come out." And there's the recently launched Contemporary romance program, which has more mainstream elements and ranges from the extremely sensual to the sweet love story. Edwards is looking for new voices for this program. "Many authors we're buying are category romance writers who are feeling the constraints of that genre and are looking for a longer format that will give them a bit more creative freedom."

Recently, Avon intensified its interest in the contemporary market. "We're taking steps to establish a stronger presence there, especially with people like Susan Elizabeth Phillips, Kathleen Eagle and Christina Skye. What we're after are specific stories with universal appeal. Kathy Eagle writes very realistic stories, but they're also very uplifting and emotional. Susan Elizabeth Phillips writes light, funny, sexy and sophisticated stories. And Christina Skye writes romantic suspense with paranormal elements; all her stories are set around Draycott Abbey and feature a guardian ghost. She always includes a past story that relates to the present one.

"In some of our historicals, we're looking for new angles on American history," says Edwards. Take, for example, Elizabeth Grayson's *A Place Called Home*, which traces one woman's venture along the wilderness trail in Kentucky. It tells about her settlement, the two men in her life, her children, and her encounters with Native Americans. "We're exploring

American expansion from a female perspective here. This is really new and compelling reading. Elisabeth Macdonald also publishes in this vein. So this is another subgenre of the women's market we're entering."

When discussing her company, Edwards tells of Avon's long tradition and the respect it's garnered in the industry. "Avon was the first romance publisher. In 1972, we published *The Flame and the Flower* by Kathleen Woodiwiss. It was the first paperback original historical romance. Ever since, we've been known as the premier publisher of historical romance. We've had a huge presence in the genre. We publish so many books of high quality, and our romance programs have so such stability and continuity, that people are honored to publish with us. Our reputation is very distinct, even worldwide. We do well in Europe, and we have a very strong following in Australia."

Since she's been an avid student of literature written by women, Edwards has noticed one big problem: women's fiction in general has not been taken seriously over the years. "Women read so-called 'men's' fiction all the time, so I don't see why men can't read and appreciate so-called 'women's' fiction," says Edwards. "Women writers, especially romance writers, have not been given the respect they deserve."

But that's beginning to change. "Romance writing is in the midst of an ongoing evolution. The women who write romances today are more sophisticated in the way they write, and in the way they present themselves to the press, resulting in more positive articles and programs about romance. The quality of the books has certainly improved, gaining more respect from those who take the chance to read them. Much of the bad rap comes from sheer ignorance, from those who have never read a romance."

Edwards knows what she's looking for, regardless of what other houses are publishing. "We want exceptional writers who have the potential to grow. We're in the business of building authors," she says. "We publish writers, not trends."

Even if you write well and have the growth potential Edwards wants, keep in mind what she doesn't want. "We're not looking for futuristic romances. And I'm very leery of romantic suspense; it's been tried often and keeps failing. The romance must be the focus, not the suspense. We're not interested in category romances or old-fashioned Gothic romances either. However, if you've figured out how to adapt the Gothic to the 90s, or have a great concept for a romance that includes top-notch suspense, I'd love to see it!

"We publish light, funny books and more serious, sexy ones. Some books have a strong fantasy element whereas others are more realistic. Yet all our books are fantasies and people know the difference between fantasy and reality. Our books are intended to be entertaining. We like the women in the stories to be empowered and there must always be a strong, happy ending. Our books reinforce the value of relationships."

Avon is also looking for multicultural romances. Says Edwards, "We publish Beverly Jenkins, who is our only African-American romance writer, and her book *Night Song* has gotten lots of attention. So we'd love to have more multicultural romances, particularly multicultural historicals. There are lots of ethnic historical stories that have yet to be told."

Edwards warns that if you send an unagented submission to Avon, your chances of getting published are slim. "We do read slush, but we give careful attention to our agented submissions. Most of what we buy is agented. Still, if you think what you write is good enough, request our guidelines. But study the market and be savvy about it. And when I say 'study the market,' I don't mean to imitate what's hot. Remember that a writer makes a trend; a trend doesn't make a writer. So challenge yourself and take risks; that's the only way you'll write something fabulous."

RECENTLY PUBLISHED: *It Had To Be You*, Susan Elizabeth Phillips (won RITA Award for Favorite Book of 1994); *Three Weddings and a Kiss*, Kathleen E. Woodiwiss and others; *Beyond Scandal*, Brenda Joyce.

HOW TO CONTACT: Accepts unsolicited manuscripts. Submit query letter and 3 sample chapters. Simultaneous submissions accepted. Receives 200 manuscripts each month. 99% of accepted submissions are agented. On average reports on queries in 4 weeks. On average reports on manuscripts in 6 months. Send SASE for writer's guidelines.

TERMS: Contracts negotiated on an individual basis. Manuscript is published an average of 9-18 months after acceptance. Author receives bionote in book or on jacket. Author receives copies of book; additional copies available at a 50% discount.

ADDRESS: 1350 Avenue of the Americas, New York, NY 10019

PHONE: (212)261-6800

FAX: (212)261-6895

AVON FLARE

Established: 1941

Romance Editor: Gwen Montgomery, Editorial Director

> CATEGORIES
> Young Adult

"Young adult romance focuses more on first love than adult romance, and they are more emotional," says Gwen Montgomery, editorial director of Avon Books for Young Readers. "There's very little, if any, sex. Young adult romances can be more bittersweet; they don't necessarily have to have happy endings, because, realistically, whoever you fall in love with at sixteen is not going to be the love of your life."

Romance titles for ages 12 and up are published under Avon Flare, Avon's young adult imprint. (Avon also publish books for middle readers, ages 8-12, under the Camelot imprint. "You could say we do 'romance' for middle grade readers—books about the discovery of boys for the first time—although you couldn't classify them as true romance," Montgomery says.) The young adult line includes historicals such as Nancy Covert Smith's Apple Valley trilogy, following 15-year-old De-Lanna from her childhood antics in 1820s Pennsylvania through her covered-wagon trip to Ohio as a new bride. Sales of the series were so encouraging that Avon released a follow-up fourth book.

The Avon Flare line also includes contemporary romance such as *The Wind Blows Backward*, by Mary Downing Hahn. This young adult novel is an emotional tale of first love, delving into the feelings and fears of heroine and hero Lauren and Spencer. Although the teens, deeply in love, do give in to their passion for each other, sex is not the focus of the story, just a small part of the coming-of-age tale. "All the characters in these stories are coming into their own," says Montgomery. "Readers might learn something about the maturation process; they might learn something about American history; but basically they're just good, solid, well-written recreational books."

Montgomery has been with Avon for 12 years, working on middle grade and early chapter books as well as young adult fiction. Avon had published young adult contemporary romance in the 80s, but stopped for several years as horror became the dominant force in the young adult fiction market. Today, the market for young adult romance seems to be getting better, so Avon is diving back in. "The market for so long has been heavily teen horror and suspense, I think, at the expense of everything else. Not every girl wants to read slasher books. Publishers are looking into other untapped areas," Montgomery says. "The young adult books are really stepping stones for kids that are past Judy Blume, but not quite ready for LaVyrle Spencer. That's the gap we're trying to fill."

Avon Flare is fairly full on historical titles although still accepting submissions for them. They are more open to submissions of contemporary fiction, as Montgomery feels there is still a dearth of contemporary young adult books in the marketplace. Their guidelines plainly state "while romance can be a plot element, we are not interested in formula romance." About 20 submissions a day arrive at Avon's offices and all of them are read. They buy about four or five manuscripts a year from the slush pile, but also work through agents, although they evaluate everything on its own whether it's represented by an agent or not. "The only advantage having an agent might get you is that you might have your project looked at a little quicker," Montgomery says.

Montgomery encourages beginning writers to be aware of what's on the market for young adults. "Visit libraries and bookstores, see what kids are checking out and buying, and keep abreast of what's new. A lot of stuff in the stores is a year or two old, which might be the tail end of a trend. Do your research. Don't send things out blindly. Know what different houses publish and publish well."

HOW TO CONTACT: Accepts unsolicited manuscripts. Submit query letter and 3 sample chapters. Simultaneous submissions accepted. Receives 200 manuscripts each month. 99% of accepted submissions are agented. On average reports on queries in 4 weeks. On average reports on manuscripts in 6 months. Send SASE for writer's guidelines.

TERMS: Contracts negotiated on an individual basis. Manuscript is published an average of 9-18 months after acceptance. Author receives bionote in book or on jacket.

ADDRESS: 1350 Avenue of the Americas, New York, NY 10019

PHONE: (212)261-6800

FAX: (212)261-6895

BALLANTINE/DEL REY/FAWCETT/IVY

Established: 1952

Romance Editor: Barbara Dicks, Acquisitions Editor

CATEGORIES
Publisher accepts all types of romance fiction.

Recently published *Hellion*, Bertrice Small (Ballantine); *Tall Dark Stranger*, Joan Smith (Fawcett Crest).

HOW TO CONTACT: Accepts unsolicited manuscripts. Submit query letter and 3 sample chapters. "All our romances have been bought through agents for the last five years."
TERMS: Contracts negotiated on an individual basis.
ADDRESS: 201 E. 50th Street, New York, NY 10022
PHONE: (212)751-2600

BANTAM BOOKS

Established: 1945 • Imprint: Fanfare

Romance Editor: Wendy McCurdy, Senior Editor

CATEGORIES
Publisher accepts all types of romance fiction.

"I started out as a romance reader when I was 12, reading books like *Gone With the Wind* and *Rebecca*. I just loved them," says Wendy McCurdy, senior editor at Bantam Books in New York. She's been hooked on romances ever since.

McCurdy took her love of romances with her when she entered the working world. "I already had an interest in publishing," she says, "so I naturally went toward romances. It just seemed to be something I had a feeling for." Starting at Bantam right out of college as an editorial assistant, McCurdy moved to Zebra Books, where she stayed for eight years before returning to Bantam as senior editor four years ago.

Bantam has three imprints for their romance titles. Their main line of romances falls under the Bantam Books imprint; Bantam Fanfare often features the work of new writers; and Bantam Loveswept publishes a series of category romances with four new titles each month. Within these imprints, they publish a wide spectrum of romances covering just about every subject imaginable. From tales of futuristic encounters on distant planets, to historical stories set in 1860s Victorian England, to contemporary tales of lust and longing in the 1990s, Bantam is "open to everything," says McCurdy.

"I would have to say that most of what gets bought comes from agents," McCurdy says. "We don't get much that's unagented." But she's open to finding manuscripts wherever she can, including unsolicited manuscripts. Some come from already signed authors. "One of my authors might say to me, 'Have you read this book by such and such? It's one of the best books I've ever read.' That will pique my interest. Once, one of my author's fans turned out to be a writer and gave her some material to look at. She was impressed enough with it to send it to me; it was wonderful and I ended up buying it." Some authors can be found in unexpected places. McCurdy relates the tale of the manuscript she discovered at her husband's high school reunion while she was working at Zebra Books: "I sat down next to one of my husband's old friends, and he heard that I was an editor. Over his wife's strenuous objections, he told me all about the manuscript she had written that was languishing in her closet. I had to ask her to send it to me, thinking it would be terrible—but it was good, and I ended up buying it. So, you never know."

When reading a manuscript, McCurdy tends to trust her instincts rather than look for a certain formula. "What I react to is the quality of the writing," she says. "Close on the heels of that is, does this person have a sense for the romance? Is there something special going on here? It really isn't something all that tangible." The characters in Bantam's romances don't fit into any one category, and McCurdy doesn't have any specific guidelines as to what kind of heroine she's looking for. "If the author is able to masterfully portray a heroine of any different kind and make it work," she says, "I'm going to react to that. It's possible I always end up reacting to a strong heroine, but it all depends on the author. Betina Krahn [author of Bantam books *The Last Bachelor* and *The Perfect Mistress*, among others] has some very sweet heroines but she gives them a lot of spunk and a sense of humor and they work really well." When it comes to the hero of a story, however, McCurdy has some definite ideas. "My favorite type of male character, which I think is everybody's favorite, is strong and intelligent, yet ultimately sensitive, understanding and passionate underneath it all."

One of the biggest mistakes a writer can make when writing romances, asserts McCurdy, is thinking that anyone can write one. "If you don't really love reading romances, then you probably shouldn't be writing them," she says. "I don't think you're ever going to have that true feeling for it. So much of writing a successful romance is in the feelings and instincts for it. You can't just follow a formula."

The lack of a formula may be the key to recent success of romance novels. "It's become not so much a genre category field anymore; it's really entered the mainstream," McCurdy says. "People who would never have picked up a romance ten years ago are now fans of a particular author. It's become more varied, with intelligent writers coming into the market and trying different things. The quality has gone way up." Along with the increased success, however, comes increased competitiveness to get a novel published. "The romance field is more competitive than it was ten years ago," McCurdy says. "But it's a much more mature field now, and you can get the kinds of things published today you couldn't have gotten published ten years ago."

McCurdy offers some basic advice for writers wanting a career in this competitive field. "Be true to your own instincts and don't try to mold yourself into someone else's mold," she says. "Just do what you feel you do best and be inspired by the best of what you're reading. Be your own harshest editor—and get a good agent. Having a good agent is very important; they can direct you to the right places and give you the kind of feedback you need."

In her quest for the next *Gone With the Wind*, McCurdy is eager to hear from new writers. "I'm very open to new material and I always get a big charge out of finding new talent," she says. "I definitely hope people will submit things to me."

An average of 5-6 books per year are first novels. Recently published *Vanity*, Jane Feather; *Star-Crossed*, Susan Krinard; *See How They Run*, Bethany Campbell.

HOW TO CONTACT: Does not accept unsolicited manuscripts. Submit query letter and first 2 sample chapters. 95% of accepted submissions are agented. On average reports on queries in 2 weeks. On average reports on manuscripts in 2-3 months.

TERMS: Average advance varies; pays royalties of 8% on first 150,000 sold, 10% thereafter. Buys all rights. Manuscript is published an average of 1-2 years after acceptance. Author receives bionote in book or on jacket. Author receives 25 copies of book.

ADDRESS: 1540 Broadway, New York, NY 10036

PHONE: (212)782-9696

BANTAM BOOKS

Established: 1945 • Imprint: Loveswept

Romance Editors: Beth de Guzman, Senior Editor; Wendy McCurdy, Senior Editor; **Shauna Summers, Editor**

> CATEGORIES
> Publisher accepts all types of romance fiction.

Whether you're a new writer asking Shauna Summers how to get your first book published or an established writer asking her how you can improve your sales, the Bantam editor has the same advice: Write a great book. "It's always difficult to find good single-title contemporaries," she says, "but beyond that, we're simply looking for great books."

Summers's definition of a great book is a well-written story told with the author's individual tone. "With the market being as competitive as it is, the writing must be really strong. Writers can't just be storytellers anymore; they need to stand out. Knowing their craft well, having strong writing and being true to their own unique voice—that is what's going to make any writer stand out."

Bantam has two main romance lines and publishes romance in their general line, as well. The general line, Summers says, is more for established authors, while Loveswept and Fanfare are more likely to buy from newer writers. Fanfare's guidelines are fairly liberal, accepting all time periods and lengths of books. Loveswept is a bit more defined, wanting contemporary category romances of 55,000 to 60,000 words.

Bantam's dedication to its authors is evident in the awards it has garnered. Bantam won the 1995 *Romantic Times* Award for Favorite Publisher, which says quite a bit as the award is voted on by authors. One of those authors, no doubt, was Glenna McReynolds, whose *Avenging Angel* won the 1994 RITA Award for Best Short Contemporary Romance. And winning the 1995 ARTemis Award for Best Historical Cover Artwork was Bantam's Alan Ayers, for his cover of Amanda Quick's *Mistress*. Bantam has won many other romance industry awards in previous years, as well.

A new writer wishing to publish with Bantam does not need an agent, Summers says. "I've acquired quite a few authors who aren't agented. It's certainly not necessary, and I generally tell writers who are trying to get published for the first time that they should concentrate on their writing and on making their books really strong, rather than worrying about getting an agent. I think it eliminates another step in a very difficult process." Summers does admit, though, that they buy slightly more books from agents than they do over the transom.

A writer should know the market, however. "Read the books from the house you want to be published by, and not just a few. Read and read and read. It gives you an idea of the diversity of the house, which is especially valuable when you're submitting to a large house like Bantam." But it all comes back to the writing. Says Summers, "Writing a great book is the number one thing you can do for your career."

RECENTLY PUBLISHED: *Avenging Angel*, Glenna McReynolds (won 1994 RITA for Best Short Contemporary Romance); *Fairest of Them All*, Teresa Medeiros; *Mystique*, Amanda Quick; *The Perfect Mistress*, Betina Krahn; *Brazen*, Susan Johnson; *Violet*, Jane Feather; *Dark Rider*, Iris Johansen.

HOW TO CONTACT: Does not accept unsolicited manuscripts. Query before submitting. Simultaneous submissions accepted. On average reports on queries in 8-12 weeks. On average reports on manuscripts in 8-12 weeks. Send SASE for writer's guidelines.

TERMS: Contracts negotiated on an individual basis. Author receives bio-note in book or on jacket.
ADDRESS: 1540 Broadway, New York, NY 10036
PHONE: (212)354-6500
FAX: (212)782-9523

BARBOUR & CO., INC.

Established: 1992 • Imprint: Heartsong Presents

Romance Editors: **Stephen Reginald, Vice President, Editorial**; Rebecca Germany, Editor

> CATEGORIES
> Contemporary Romance, Historical, Multicultural, Over 45

"There is a thread throughout each of our books," says Stephen Reginald, Heartsong Present's Vice President of Editorial, "an inspirational, Christian message of the importance of the spiritual dynamic that exists in a relationship between a man and a woman." All of Heartsong's books share the theme that a faith in God is the foundation for any romantic relationship.

Heartsong Presents romances are made available to readers through a monthly book club, which releases four books per month to its almost 25,000 members. Any books not sold at the end of each month are then sold in retail outlets. Since most Heartsong Presents readers are women who consider themselves born-again Christians, each story must confirm the values and beliefs of their faith. With such a specific agenda, Heartsong romances must follow fairly strict guidelines. The story, which can be historical or contemporary, should present a conservative, evangelical world view. Controversial subjects are discouraged, and the Christian characters must act according to Christian beliefs. The hero and heroine cannot be divorced, for example, nor should they engage in activities such as drinking, swearing or dancing. Characters should be moderately dressed, and detailed descriptions of romantic moments are to be avoided. A particular biblical message should be conveyed throughout the story if possible.

Reginald looks for all of these components in the manuscripts he receives, and he's open to anything within Heartsong's guidelines. "We're looking for certain elements," he says, "but we're also looking for something unique, and that's always hard to identify. It's important for the hero and heroine to get together at the end of the book—that's a must. But in between, there's a lot of creativity and flexibility. We look for unusual locations, settings, and job occupations." Many of Heartsong's books feature heroines in unusual occupations. VeraLee Wiggins's *Llama Lady* tells the story of a woman who runs a llama ranch; Eileen M. Berger's *Escort Homeward* is about a woman whose job it is to drive an escort truck behind vehicles that transport mobile homes. The stories of women in non-traditional jobs have been extremely popular with readers. "Whether she's traditional or an entrepreneur, I don't think there is one particular heroine that the audience seems to like," Reginald says. "In the historical genre, the heroine that seems to stand out is the one that's down on her luck. Readers love the woman who is abandoned then scratches her way back up . . . and finds romance at the end."

In order to create entertaining stories that readers can relate to, Reginald reminds writers that they must respect their audience. "The biggest mistake a writer can make is taking for granted that the readers of romances will read anything," he says. "There's a general misconception that romances are not well written, or that the audience is somehow more naive than the rest of the population. And I don't think that's true. Because most romance readers, at least from my understanding of the market, read all kinds of books. They like romance, obviously, but they do read other more literate works and they're probably better educated than most."

Reginald offers some advice for beginning romance writers. "The best thing you as a romance writer can do is read as much as you can about the market," he says. "Get the guidelines from the publisher you'd like to work with and follow those. And keep plugging away. It's a numbers game; the more stuff you have out there the better your possibilities. Try to keep a thick skin, because it's really tough."

Reginald loves to hear from new writers, and most of the manuscripts he signs come to him unsolicited. The key to writing Heartsong Presents romances lies in balancing a Christian message with an entertaining story that isn't preachy. "A lot of readers read our books for entertainment," Reginald says. "They're not necessarily expecting to be taught a big lesson, although there are lessons to be learned in a lot of the books. But mostly they want to be entertained. They want to be uplifted; they don't want to feel depressed after they've finished a book."

While manuscripts must advocate a Christian lifestyle, the true essence of the story should be romance. "Writers really need to keep the romance in the forefront. That's what our readers are looking for. Technical skill, setting, all of the other factors involved with good novel writing are important. But if the romance isn't there . . . the audience will forgive a multitude of sins, but the one thing they will not forgive is lack of romance!"

Publishes 52 mass market paperback books per year. An average of 12 books per year are first novels. Recently published *Angel's Cause*, Tracie J. Peterson; *Winding Highway*, Janelle Burnham; *Distant Love*, Ann Bell; *Iditarod Dream*, Janelle Jamison (a.k.a. Tracie J. Peterson) (voted Favorite Inspirational in *Affaire de Coeur*'s 1994 annual readers' poll).

HOW TO CONTACT: Accepts unsolicited manuscripts. Submit query letter and 2 sample chapters. Simultaneous submissions accepted. Receives 20 manuscripts each month. 5% of accepted submissions are agented. On average reports on queries in 6 weeks. On average reports on manuscripts in 6 months. Sometimes comments on rejected manuscripts. Send SASE for writer's guidelines.

TERMS: "We purchase manuscripts for a fee." Buys all rights. Manuscript is published an average of 6 months after acceptance. Author receives bionote in book or on jacket. Author receives 10 or more copies of book; additional copies available at a $1 per copy.

ADDRESS: P.O. Box 719, 1810 Barbour Drive, Uhrichsville, OH 44683

PHONE: (614)922-6045

FAX: (614)922-5948

BERKLEY PUBLISHING GROUP

Established: 1954 • Imprint: Berkley, Jove, Diamond

Romance Editors: Judith Stern, Senior Editor; Hillary Cige, Senior Editor; Gail Fortune, Editor; Denise Silvestro, Editor

> CATEGORIES
> Contemporary Romance, Ghost, Historical, Paranormal, Time Travel, Vampire

"Variety is key to our program," says Judith Stern, senior editor at Berkley Publishing Group. Publishing approximately 50 paperback titles each year along with several hardcovers, Berkley's romances cover a wide spectrum of subjects. Running the gamut from contemporary and historical themes to stories of the paranormal, vampires and time travel, Berkley prides itself on the diverse nature of the titles they present to romance readers.

Berkley does not accept unsolicited manuscripts, and prefers writers to contact Berkley's editors through an agent. Agents play an important role in an author's career, Stern says, because they can relieve an author from the negotiating process of signing a contract. They can also troubleshoot for their clients, advising them as to what to look out for when signing with a publisher and basically helping them guide their careers.

Whether they have an agent or not, Stern advises beginning romance writers to read the competition and polish their writing skills. The romance field is a competitive one, she says, and an author should be creative, but at the same time not become too outrageous in plot and characters. Romance readers like variety, but stories shouldn't stray too far from their original intention of telling a romantic tale. The best place to start is with Berkley's writer's guidelines, which are available to aspiring authors for a SASE. Following such guidelines is the easiest way to discover exactly what Berkley is looking for.

Publishes approximately 50 mass market paperback romances per year. Recently published *Born in Ice*, Nora Roberts; *Red Velvet*, Barbara Boswell; *Heartless*, Mary Balogh; *Forever in Texas*, Jodi Thomas.

HOW TO CONTACT: Does not accept unsolicited manuscripts. **Accepts agented submissions only.** Simultaneous submissions accepted. On average reports on queries in 6 weeks. On average reports on manuscripts in 3 months. Send SASE for writer's guidelines.

TERMS: Contracts negotiated on an individual basis. Buys all rights. Manuscript is published an average of 2 years after acceptance. Author receives 25 copies of book; additional copies available at a 40% discount.

ADDRESS: 200 Madison Avenue, New York, NY 10016

PHONE: (212)951-8800

BETHANY HOUSE

Established: 1956

Romance Editor: Barbara Lilland, Series Editor

> CATEGORIES
> Contemporary Romance, Historical

Not typically labeled a romance publisher, Bethany House publishes a broad range of religious fiction including romance. As a series editor for the evangelical publisher, Barbara Lilland is responsible for acquiring manuscripts for the house's adult romance category.

An avid reader of the romance genre since her teen years, Lilland looks for authors who know Bethany House and know the romance market. "The best thing an author can do to help sell her book is to know what the current trends are and how to put something together that fits the current trend but is also unique and compelling." Unfortunately, this is advice many authors do not follow, Lilland says. "We get a number of unsolicited proposals from writers who don't know what we publish and don't know what's out there in the marketplace. They either give us something that doesn't fit our list or is a duplicate of something we are already doing."

Authors submitting to Bethany House also must keep in mind—and adhere to—what Lilland and her fellow editors call the "Big Four." "We want to see a query letter that describes the book idea, outlines their qualifications and experience, lists the similar books in the religious market and tells why theirs would be better or unique, and then identifies the target audience. We want to see authors clearly define who their book is aimed at." Lilland says writers who follow these simple guidelines will make their manuscripts stand out from the piles of submissions that fill her desk.

To help their manuscripts even more, writers should supply Lilland with a list of publication credits. "Many of our authors got their start writing for periodicals. It's a good example of their writing talent and we like to see that." Because there are few periodicals that accept Christian romance fiction, Lilland is open to a publication history of nonfiction articles covering everything from the writing field to parenting. "We want to see writers who have been able to pull an article together and get it published."

As well as knowing the market and following guidelines, authors also must be able to write romance stories from the Christian perspective—a task that sometimes can cause problems. "It is very important that a book be written from a Christian perspective, and yet the theme and the message of Christianity be a subtle part of the story. Some writers will leave the [religious] aspect out completely and others will have the plan of salvation presented so clearly and so overwhelmingly that it has detracted from the story itself."

Bethany House looks for books with a balance between the Christian message and a story that is memorable and enjoyable. Further, they need to have some sort of insight, some sort of inspiration that will underscore God's perspective on the world." Lilland refers to this insight and inspiration as "take-away" value and says it is this value that makes Bethany House publications unique in the romance market. "It isn't *just* an entertaining story that we are looking for, but a novel that will inspire the readers and give them a deeper understanding of the characters' lives and their own world."

Writing Christian romances also differs from writing standard romances because the relationship aspect is emphasized and any sexual overtones are kept to a minimum. And Christian romance novels provide character growth outside the realm of the romantic relationship. "You see growth in the main characters' lives beyond the romantic aspect of the story," says Lilland. "So, at the end, you not only see this resolution of the romance, but you also see emotional and mental growth in the main characters. And, hopefully, the reader has grown with them."

Lilland's final advice for authors looking to publish in the Christian romance market is to submit a story that offers something different— "Something that will capture the eye of an editor but not a repeat of what they read last week. There are a number of good writers out there who have just missed that magic. The magic isn't elusive, however, and they can incorporate it into their story if they work hard."

An average of 12 books per year are first novels. Recently published *Empire Builders*, Linda Chaikin (won Silver Angel Award for Excellence in Media); *Trial of the Innocent*, Sara Mitchell; *A Door of Hope*, Neva Coyle.

HOW TO CONTACT: Does not accept unsolicited manuscripts. Submit synopsis and 3 sample chapters. Accepts faxed queries. Simultaneous submissions accepted. Submissions on computer disk also accepted. Format: 3.5" IBM. Receives 170 manuscripts each month. 20% of accepted submissions are agented. On average reports on queries in 6-9 weeks. Send SASE for writer's guidelines.

TERMS: Contracts negotiated on an individual basis. Buys all rights. Manuscript is published an average of 1 year after acceptance. Author receives bionote in book or on jacket. Author receives 15-25 copies of book.

ADDRESS: 11300 Hampshire Avenue South, Minneapolis, MN 55438
PHONE: (612)829-2500
FAX: (612)829-2768

BOOKCRAFT, INC.

Established: 1942

Romance Editor: Cory H. Maxwell, Editorial Manager

> **CATEGORIES**
> Contemporary Romance, Historical, Romantic Mystery, Romantic
> Suspense

Taboo: "Bookcraft publishes to a religious market—primarily to members of the Church of Jesus Christ of Latter-Day Saints (Mormons), so we avoid gratuitous violence and explicit sex in our books."

An average of 3-4 books per year are first novels. Recently published *A Face in the Shadows*, Susan Evans McCloud; *Jimmy Stillman, I Will Always Love You*, Eric Hendershot; *Shannon*, Gordon T. Allred.

HOW TO CONTACT: Accepts unsolicited manuscripts. Send full manuscript. Simultaneous submissions accepted. Receives 50 manuscripts each month. 5% of accepted submissions are agented. On average reports on queries in 2-3 weeks. On average reports on manuscripts in 1-2 months. Send SASE for writer's guidelines.

TERMS: 5% royalties minimum and 15% royalties maximum. Buys all rights. Manuscript is published an average of 5-7 months after acceptance. Author receives bionote in book or on jacket. Author receives 25 copies of book; additional copies available at a 40% discount.

ADDRESS: 1848 West 2300 South, Salt Lake City, UT 84108

PHONE: (801)972-6180

DUTTON SIGNET, A DIVISION OF PENGUIN USA

Established: 1935 • Imprint: Topaz

Romance Editors: Audrey LaFehr, Editorial Director; Hilary Ross, Executive Editor; Jennifer Sawyer, Senior Editor; Leah Bassoff, Associate Manuscript Editor

> **CATEGORIES**
> Contemporary Romance, Erotic, Ghost, Historical, Humorous,
> Multicultural, Over 45, Regency, Romantic Suspense, Time Travel,
> Vampire

One of the major publishers in the romance industry, Dutton Signet's

Topaz imprint currently receives more manuscripts than its editors can handle, according to Audrey LaFehr, editorial director. Subsequently, they are only accepting manuscripts submitted through agents. Dutton Signet also publishes romance in its Dutton, Signet and Onyx imprints, but these receive many manuscripts per month, so authors should not send unagented submissions to these imprints as well. An average of 3-6 books per year are first novels. Recently published *Again*, Kathleen Gilles Seidel (won RITA Award for Best Contemporary Single Title Romance of 1994); *Dancing In The Wind*, Mary Jo Putney (won RITA Award for Best Long Historical Romance of 1994); *Mrs. Drew Plays Her Hand*, Carla Kelly (won RITA Award for Best Regency Romance of 1994); *Lord of the Storm*, Justine Davis (won RITA Award for Best Paranormal/Fantasy/Time Travel Romance of 1994).

HOW TO CONTACT: Does not accept unsolicited manuscripts. **Accepts agented submissions only.** Simultaneous submissions accepted. On average reports on queries in 4 weeks. On average reports on manuscripts in 6 weeks. Sometimes comments on rejected manuscripts.

TERMS: Contracts negotiated on an individual basis. Buys all rights. Manuscript is published an average of 14-18 months after acceptance. Author receives bionote in book or on jacket. Author receives 10-20 copies of book; additional copies available at a 40% discount.

ADDRESS: 375 Hudson Street, New York, NY 10014

PHONE: (212)366-2000

FAX: (212)366-2888

E. M. PRESS, INC.

Established: 1991 • Imprint: R&M Books

Romance Editor: Ellen Beck, Editor

> CATEGORIES
> Historical, Romantic Mystery, Romantic Suspense

According to 1996 *Writer's Market*, 10% of books published are subsidy. Publishes a total of 8 books per year.

HOW TO CONTACT: Accepts unsolicited manuscripts. Submit query letter and 3 sample chapters. Simultaneous submissions accepted. Receives 100 manuscripts each month. On average reports on queries in 4 weeks. On average reports on manuscripts in 8 weeks. Send SASE for writer's guidelines.

TERMS: Average advance is $250, with 6% royalties minimum. Buys all rights. Manuscript is published an average of 18 months after acceptance. Author receives bionote in book or on jacket.

ADDRESS: P.O. Box 4057, Manassas, VA 22110

PHONE: (540)439-0304

FAX: (703)250-4009

DONALD I. FINE BOOKS/DUTTON, A DIVISION OF PENGUIN, USA

Romance Editors: Donald I. Fine, Editor-in-Chief; Jason Poston, Editor

> CATEGORIES
> Publisher accepts all types of romance fiction.

"We just publish what's good—and what will sell—from legal thrillers to cookbooks. (No children's books)."

Wants: Quality women's fiction, historical, fantasy.

Taboo: "We get huge numbers of submissions of mystery and suspense because we publish a good deal of it—which is exactly why we don't need more. Don't bother unless it's exceptional. Also, we do hard cover only; send manuscripts with paperback original potential elsewhere. (We do license paperback rights and, in certain cases, make hard/soft deals as well.)"

An average of 16 books per year are first novels.

HOW TO CONTACT: Does not accept unsolicited manuscripts. Send full manuscript. **Accepts agented submissions only.** Simultaneous submissions accepted. Receives 25 manuscripts each month. 99% of accepted submissions are agented.

TERMS: Advance and royalties. Buys all rights. Manuscript is published within 24 months after acceptance. Author receives 10 copies of book; additional copies available at a 40% discount.

ADDRESS: 375 Hudson Street, New York, NY 10014.

HARLEQUIN AMERICAN ROMANCE

Established: 1983

Romance Editor: Debra Matteucci, Senior Editor & Editorial Coordinator

---

CATEGORIES

Contemporary Romance, Historical, Humorous, Romantic Mystery, Romantic Suspense

---

Debra Matteucci wears not one, not two, but *three* hats at Harlequin, editing not only the American Romance line and the Intrigue line, but acting as editorial coordinator, as well. In her 13 years with the company, she's worked with many authors and has watched the industry grow and evolve.

"In 1992," she says, citing an example, "we made a major change in our American Romance line. We moved from realistic stories to contemporary fairytales and stories with fictional credibility." Matteucci defines "fictional credibility" as meaning anything the author can make believable to the reader. "In that vein, we've done some of our best books and some of our reader favorites. We have an ongoing series called 'More Than Men' that features heroes with super powers. Not superheroes, wearing capes and avenging crimes and all that, but otherwise normal guys that have a special power. One is immortal, another is a healer by touch. They each have a special power that makes them more than a man." Obviously, this is not your realistic, everyday kind of story, Matteucci says. "You're not going to find this kind of man walking down Fifth Avenue, and yet, our authors have made them credible. That is fictional credibility, and that is something that our readership has responded to enormously. We've done space travelers from the 21st century coming back to America now in the 1990s. We've done heroines and heroes who are genies. We've really pushed the envelope as far as that fictional credibility area goes."

As for contemporary fairytales, Matteucci says those are also popular American Romance stories. "The Cinderella story is always something that sells. Something like *How to Marry a Millionaire*, where an ordinary person becomes a millionairess in the end. Or the waitress who goes from slinging hash in a sleazy diner to becoming royalty of some European country. Those are also the kinds of stories we'd like to see more of in our American Romance line."

American Romances are 70,000 to 75,000 words long, and should also have a lighter tone, she says. "Humor is key for us, and we have found a number of authors who can do that very well. Many times the comedy of errors works well." Matteucci says that, although some of the plots may seem too standard, they are nevertheless still very popular. "Weddings of convenience, kidnapped brides and those types of classic situations are ever popular, so we'll be looking for much more of that."

Harlequin Intrigue, the other line Matteucci edits, "is a completely different animal; a much more dramatic series. Intrigue is a line in which we can do almost every kind of subgenre of mystery and suspense. Of course, the main ingredient is still romance. We need to have a fully developed romance that progresses in much the same way that it would in a regular series romance book." Woman-in-jeopardy, psychological suspense, legal thrillers, medical thrillers and the standard whodunit are all viable plots for an Intrigue book. The mystery the characters are involved with should directly affect them. "It's not an international espionage ring; the fate of the world does not rest on the outcome. It's *her* life in danger. The heroine is at the center of the mystery and plays a role in solving it." The latter is probably the most important aspect, Matteucci says. "She's not just sitting there in peril while the hero goes out and brings the bad guys to justice. She's right in the thick of it. In that way it's quite a bit different than the old Gothics."

Intrigues should be 70,000 to 75,000 words long, and should never let the reader off of the edge of her seat. As Harlequin's guidelines sum up, "shared dangers lead right to shared passions. Their lives are on the line—and so are their hearts!"

Whether writing for Intrigue, American Romance or any other line, writers should know what is selling, Matteucci says. Be aware of what the trends are within the industry and then within a given series. "Weddings and babies and blendings of families and marriages of convenience—the classic types of plots are very popular right now, and I think you're going to see that popularity across all of the series. But how American Romance handles it versus how Intrigue handles it is completely different. You need to identify the key selling trends within the industry and then see how they apply to the given series and how they're handled within those series." Matteucci recommends becoming active in the RWA, establishing a rapport with booksellers and going to conferences as ways of keeping your ear to the ground. "Conferences are ways for us to disseminate information on the kinds of books we're looking for and what's doing well for us. From a writer's standpoint, attending conferences and networking with other authors and editors are invaluable."

After you make that first sale, Matteucci says to cooperate with your editor. "Many times we will come back to an author and say, 'This book needs a new title.' The title of a book is one of the few major selling tools we have, along with the cover copy, the art and the author's name. Cooperating with your editor is saying, 'Okay, I really like that title, but I can see that you have a point. It isn't capturing the hook of the book, it isn't shouting out one of those key selling themes.' And then working with us to come up with a new title. Believe it or not, a lot of times that's not the case. The author is wedded to the title she has and doesn't want to see it changed. It really makes it difficult, and it seems like a small thing, but it really does help us to help the author sell better."

Most important, Matteucci feels, is that you write the best book you can possibly write. "Many times, authors are saving some of their best plot ideas and best writing for their breakout book, the book that will take them out of romance and move them into the mainstream. I say, no way. Every time you sit down to write, whether it's for category or for mainstream, you should be writing the best book you can possibly write. The authors who are very successful in category and have had long, successful category careers are the ones who approach each and every book with that kind of attitude. I can't say enough about writing the best book you can possibly write for that moment."

Publishes 48 mass market paperback books per year. An average of 0-4 books per year are first novels. Recently published *Falling Angel*, Anne Stuart (won RITA in 1994); *Eight Second Wedding*, Anne McAllister; *Cinderman*, Anne Stuart.

HOW TO CONTACT: Accepts unsolicited manuscripts. Query before submitting. Receives 20-25 manuscripts each month. 50% of accepted submissions are agented. On average reports on queries in 3 weeks. Sometimes comments on rejected manuscripts. Send SASE for writer's guidelines.

TERMS: Contracts negotiated on an individual basis. Manuscript is published an average of 9 months minimum after acceptance. Author receives bionote in book or on jacket.

ADDRESS: 300 East 42 Street, New York, NY 10017

PHONE: (212)682-6080

FAX: (212)682-4539

HARLEQUIN HISTORICALS

Established: 1983

Romance Editor: Tracy Farrell, Senior Editor

> CATEGORIES
> Historical, Humorous, Romantic Suspense

Tracy Farrell, senior editor for Harlequin Historicals, says she enjoys working in the historicals area because it allows herself, the writers and the readers flexibility. "Historical fiction is not so specific an area. It can cover a lot of ground, a wide range of settings and time periods, and I find readers of historical romances are willing to explore many different things. For example, they are very open and interested in different elements in stories such as suspense or mystery."

Harlequin publishes four books per month in the historical line and these come in a wide range of time periods and settings. "We generally ask for books set pre-1900, more than 95,000 words, but even that is a little flexible," Farrell says.

American westerns and medieval Europe (especially Scotland) are the two most popular areas. While Harlequin no longer has a separate, regular Regency line and most of their Regencies are published in another division, a few stories set in the Regency time period are also published as Harlequin Historicals.

Farrell is always interested in good American westerns. The term "westerns" in romance covers a range of material. Frontier or prairie romances tend to be about survival, people against the elements, she says. Some westerns are set in towns or on ranches and involve people living in the generation after the first settlers. These people have more of a stake in how things are run than the earlier generation.

Overall, the trend at Harlequin, as well as other romance publishers, has been toward books that are broader in scope and more complex no matter what the time period. Farrell, who has been with the company for 11 years, does not agree, however, that the central characters of Harlequin's various lines have changed much. "From the beginning, Harlequin characters were not the traditional younger woman and powerful man. We've always tried to portray the hero and the heroine as equals, both in control of the story and their lives. I think the rest [of the publishers] have just caught up with us in terms of characters and style."

"Some readers have said that our historical heroines seem too modern, but if you look back in history, you'll find women very much in control. Just read the biographies of these women. Sure, in the Regency period, and certainly in medieval times, women were constrained, but they could also be very powerful. It's not necessary to be 'modern' to be powerful and in control."

Strong characters are a must for Harlequin romances, says Farrell. Writers should also keep in mind in westerns, as well as other historicals, they need not always be Europeans. Farrell would like to see more manuscripts featuring Native American characters. "We did a book in 1991 [*Cloud Dancer*, by Peggy Bechko] set before the Mayflower landed in which the hero and heroine were from two different Native American cultures. With the overlying threat of the conquistadors, it was an exciting read. I'd love to see more pre-European history. I grew up in New England, but I rarely ever see books featuring Native Americans from New England. There are many more time periods and cultures in American history for people to explore."

Farrell says she'd really like to see more variety in settings and time periods across the board. "A lot of writers seem afraid to try more 'exotic' time periods. Perhaps, they seem like a harder sell and people are not willing to take a risk. They have to do a lot more research and this may hold them back."

The ability to do good research is vital in historical fiction, she says. "If you don't know what you're talking about it's going to be obvious to the reader. It's very important if you plan to bring the reader into another time, you must know the possibilities of that time. You have to know what could and could not have happened. It's a real gift to be able to incorporate that research into a story and not let it look like research."

Echoing the advice given by so many writers and editors, Farrell says you must read and love romantic fiction to be able to write it. "You really have to know what's been done before. You also have to love the genre and that can really show up to me. Some people have a special sensitivity to the genre that's a little hard to explain. They just know what makes a good historical romance.

"The saddest thing for me as an editor is that I see work from many writers who do have a real sense of the genre, but who don't have the skills or natural talent to pull it together. I've also seen work from writers who have it down technically, but whose hearts are not really there. I need to find a good mix."

Farrell and her colleagues try to meet writers whenever they can. Collectively, they manage to attend most major romance conferences— about 15 each year. She says she's amazed with the amount of work these writers do and their determination to succeed. "We solicit complete manuscripts and it's incredible to me how many people do complete these huge projects. We see 700 to 1,000 projects a year—partials, queries and manuscripts."

About half of those submissions come to her through agents, but at

Harlequin it's not necessary to have an agent submit your work. "We try to take care of all manuscripts on a first in, first read basis. Agents are really most helpful during the contract negotiation time, even though we always offer a standard contract. They can talk money for you and many other mass-market houses require you have an agent."

Interested writers can send to Harlequin for submission guidelines, but Farrell says these are no longer very important. "Our current guidelines are only a little over a paragraph long. I would rather we didn't have any. I don't want to constrain anyone. I don't want anyone to hold back."

Her own personal guidelines are simple: Writers interested in historical romance should read well within the genre and not be afraid to try something new and different. Even a story that has been told before can become new, she says, if you make it your own.

Publishes 48 mass market paperback books per year. An average of 6 books per year are first novels.

HOW TO CONTACT: Accepts unsolicited manuscripts. Query before submitting. Receives 20-25 manuscripts each month. 50% of accepted submissions are agented. On average reports on queries in 3 weeks. Rarely comments on rejected manuscripts. Send SASE for writer's guidelines.

TERMS: Contracts negotiated on an individual basis. Manuscript is published a minimum of 11 months after acceptance. Author receives bionote in book or on jacket. Author receives negotiated copies of book.

ADDRESS: 300 East 42 Street, New York, NY 10017

PHONE: (212)682-6080

FAX: (212)682-4539

HARLEQUIN INTRIGUE

Established: 1983

Romance Editor: Debra Matteucci, Senior Editor & Editorial Coordinator

> CATEGORIES
> Contemporary Romance, Romantic Mystery, Romantic Suspense

Editor's note: For more information on the Harlequin Intrigue line, see the interview with Debra Matteucci under the Harlequin American Romance listing.

Publishes 48 mass market paperback books per year. An average of 0-4 books per year are first novels.

HOW TO CONTACT: Accepts unsolicited manuscripts. Query before submitting. Receives 20-25 manuscripts each month. 50% of accepted submissions are agented. On average reports on queries in 3 weeks. Sometimes comments on rejected manuscripts. Send SASE for writer's guidelines.

TERMS: Contracts negotiated on an individual basis. Manuscript is published an average of 9 months minimum after acceptance. Author receives bionote in book or on jacket.

ADDRESS: 300 East 42 Street, New York, NY 10017

PHONE: (212)682-6080

FAX: (212)682-4539

HARLEQUIN LOVE & LAUGHTER

Established: 1996

Romance Editor: Malle Vallik, Editor

> CATEGORIES
> Contemporary Romance, Historical, Humorous, Multicultural

While Harlequin's Love & Laughter line may be very new to the romance industry (the first books will be published in the fall of 1996), editor Malle Vallik is not. "I've always read romance in one form or another throughout my life," she says. "Even the mysteries I've read had a little bit of romance."

Vallik has worked in publishing since 1982, doing everything from driving a truck and putting the books on the rack to publicity to her current editorial job. She's been with Harlequin for the past six years, starting as an associate editor for the Temptation line. "I said to myself, I like this business and if I'm going to stay in it, I might as well work for a company that is very successful, that people really respond to and that publishes the books I enjoy so much."

Harlequin's success is evident in its growth and its addition of new lines, such as Love & Laughter. For Love & Laughter, Vallik wants 50,000-word, fast-paced, contemporary romantic comedies. "I want to stress that they are contemporary. These are characters who would know what *Seinfeld* is, or *Mad About You*, and have the same concerns that we do in the 90s. They're not timeless love stories; they're very specific to our age."

Although "romantic comedy" should give you a good idea of what Vallik is looking for, she is surprised by the number of unusable manuscripts she receives. "I'm finding people are forgetting the two basic things. One, there has to be a fairly strong comic premise in the book, as in the movie *While You Were Sleeping*. The heroine has daydreamed over this man for quite some time and is in love with him. She saves his life but he goes into a coma, and the family is convinced she is his fiancee. This is a strong romantic-comic premise that you can develop from. The characters go through changes; she learns what he's really like, what his brother is like. There are suspicions that develop. And then the guy actually wakes up and the story goes on from there. This has a very strong comic premise."

A comic premise is not the only way to approach a Love & Laughter story, however. "The other thing you can have with a comic premise or with a story that's slightly more adventurous or serious is to have a comic perspective in your voice as the writer and in the voice of the characters," Vallik says. "It's the way the character looks at the world and finds the humor in the disaster." Vallik again cites an example from the movies. "Like Meg Ryan's character in *Sleepless in Seattle*, which is much more of a drama, although it's also a bit of a romantic comedy. It's her way of looking at things, the way she looks at love, the slapstick that she does that brings the comedy into the story."

Vallik is surprised at some of the submissions she gets, because they are straight dramas with a few jokes thrown in here and there. "That's not what I'm looking for," she says. "I would love to see more screwball comedies, full of misunderstanding and based on an appealing and original idea." Originality is the key. "Don't let the rules hold you back. Write the story as you would like to tell it. The things that really strike an editor's eye are the things that are kind of different and fun."

One writer who writes what Vallik is looking for is Temptation author Jennifer Crusie. "She is great, and she's actually one of the launch authors for the Love & Laughter program. Jennie has a very contemporary voice and a comic perspective." A fine example of her voice is Crusie's *Getting Rid of Bradley*, which won the RITA Award for Best Short Contemporary Romance of 1994. (See Crusie's "Happily Ever Laughter" in the **Craft & Technique** section for more on writing romantic comedy.)

"For every writer that gets published in category, it is because they have a strong voice and they don't sound like anyone else," Vallik says. "The thing that we see over and over again are stories that sound exactly like every other one that we've published, and of course that's not what we want. We want something new and different and appealing. A lot of people don't seem to go very high concept in Love & Laughter, and to me that seems like a pretty obvious technique. Asking 'what if' again and again, putting all the combinations together and seeing what happens. People should not worry about what anyone else is writing and just think of the best idea they can."

Vallik says that when submitting to Love & Laughter, new writers should send the full manuscript, while established writers can send a proposal and the first three chapters. Established writers should also include a list of recent titles, and both new and established should summarize the unique selling point or hook that their book has. "If you can say what the strong hook of your book is in a paragraph, and it's something interesting and appealing, that's fairly impressive."

A strong hook also helps sell a book to the readership, Vallik says. A strong image for the cover, a title and the back cover copy are all things that can be drawn from a strong hook, and if the author considers that in advance, it helps sell the book to the editor. Vallik points to Tiffany White as an author who considers all the angles when submitting a book.

"She is one of our Silhouette Yours Truly launch authors," Vallik says. "The whole concept of Yours Truly is that some kind of written communication starts the story. So she had a bachelor auction, which is kind of a neat hook, and she called it *Male for Sale*, which is good. It was a fun story, because the way the auction worked the heroine wasn't sure which guy she was bidding on. She thought she was picking a very conservative looking fellow, and she got the motorcycle rider. Kind of the fun opposites attract, which I can talk about on the back cover." The strength of the title and concept of the bachelor auction also made the front cover more effective. "Tiffany considers the whole angle when she first has an idea; what title will work nicely, how can my editor get the story across in a hundred words. She considers what the book will look like on the shelf. And of course, that's backed up by an entertaining story and great characters."

Writers do not need an agent to sell to Love & Laughter. "Our negotiations are pretty much the same across the board. The only benefit to having an agent would be if that agent was one I've dealt with before, and that agent phones me to say, 'I've got something for you that's appropriate for Love & Laughter.' I'm going to read that one first. But we read everything." Vallik adds that it takes them a little longer to get to unagented writers, and that 55 to 65 percent of books bought by Harlequin are through agents.

Many writers make the mistake of reading a lot of one type of romance, and then trying to copy that type, Vallik says. "Writers are often told by their critique groups, 'No, no, this will never work. You'll have to change all of this if you want to sell this to Harlequin.' What we actually like is that it is different, that it's fundamentally your story told your way." Vallik says that although the odds seem to be against unpublished writers, it's important to remember that there are new openings all the time. "We're always beginning new projects and some of our established authors are moving into other programs, so there is opportunity and space. We have never turned away a good book because we didn't have the space; we'll always find the space." Also, since Love & Laughter is new, it's wide open. "Your chance of being bought as a new author is much higher in it than in Temptation, which is looking but not looking that hard.

"The other thing about Harlequin in general," Vallik says, "is how much we work with unpublished people in developing their talent. That's one of the fun parts of the job, reading a manuscript that you think has potential and going through the revision process once, twice or more times. There are many people published by Harlequin now that went through several manuscripts with us before they hit it, but after that they were fine." Vallik says she remembers the names of promising writers and looks forward to hearing from them again. "The best moment of all is when you can make that phone call and offer the deal. That's one of the things that keeps us editors going, and we do that a lot at Harlequin."

Publishes 24 mass market paperback books per year.

HOW TO CONTACT: Does not accept unsolicited manuscripts. On average reports on queries in 3-4 weeks. On average reports on manuscripts in 8-12 weeks. Send SASE for writer's guidelines.

TERMS: Contracts negotiated on an individual basis. Buys all rights. Manuscript is published an average of 1-3 years after acceptance. Author receives bionote in book or on jacket. Author receives 25 copies of book.

ADDRESS: 225 Duncan Mill Road, Don Mills, Ontario, Canada M3B 3K9,

PHONE: (416)445-5860

HARLEQUIN MILLS & BOON, LTD.

Established: 1908 • Imprint: Harlequin Romance, Harlequin Presents (North America); Mills & Boon, Love on Call, Legacy of Love (United Kingdom)

Romance Editors: E. Johnson, Senior Editor, Medical & Historicals; T. Shapcott, Senior Editor, Harlequin Presents; Linda Fildew, Senior Editor, Harlequin Romance; S. Hodgson, Senior Editor, Mills & Boon

> CATEGORIES
> Contemporary Romance, Historical, Medical Romances, Regency

The depth and variety of romances offered, developed from strong author participation and reader feedback make Harlequin Mills & Boon unique, according to the editors. "We continue to evolve in those terms."

Wants: Medical romances, i.e. romances involving medical professionals as hero/heroine, and incorporating some medical information in reference to patients.

Taboo: Novels with psychiatry/social workers as characters are received with caution. Contracted authors normally discuss plots/settings before writing.

Advice to writers: "Check current output, then use your own voice.

Make sure any research is accurate but don't write a textbook. Don't forget emotion is as important as any professional technique in writing romances."

Publishes 260 or more mass market paperback books per year. An average of 3-4 books per year are first novels.

HOW TO CONTACT: Accepts unsolicited manuscripts. Submit query letter and first 3 chapters. Sometimes comments on rejected manuscripts. Send SASE for writer's guidelines.

TERMS: Contracts negotiated on an individual basis. Buys all rights. Author receives bionote in book or on jacket. Author receives 6 copies of book; additional copies available at a 50% discount.

ADDRESS: Eton House, 18-24 Paradise Road, Richmond, Surrey, TW9-1SR, United Kingdom

PHONE: 0181-948-0444

FAX: 0181-940-5899

HARLEQUIN SUPERROMANCE

Established: 1949

Romance Editor: Paula Eykelhof, Senior Editor

> CATEGORIES
> Contemporary Romance

"Characterization is the key to writing Superromance," says Paula Eykelhof, senior editor of Harlequin's Superromance line. "We're looking for characters who stand out as believable people—characters that the reader not only understands, but cares deeply about. That's the hallmark of our books."

With a length of about 80,000 words, Superromance novels allow writers the room to develop characters with dimension—detailed personal histories; family, community and workplace relationships; and, of course, intense and tempestuous romantic involvements. It is the characters—their actions and reactions, their motivations and emotions—which move the story, Eykelhof says.

"The plot has to stem believably from these people, so their motivations must be explained and explored, not so much through exposition, but through all the other novelistic means at the writer's disposal—action, dialogue and plot," Eykelhof says. "The characters are the reader's way into the story, and through her commitment to the characters, she becomes engaged with the story."

The Superromance line was begun in 1980 to offer series romance readers longer, more in-depth stories than were offered in Harlequin's other, more traditional, lines. Harlequin publishes 48 Superromances each year, in a wide range of story types and tones—from highly dramatic to humorous, from suspenseful to adventurous.

The level of sensuality in each book also varies, Eykelhof says: "The books can have very little overt sensuality—although there always has to be sensual tension—or they can be quite erotic. It depends on the author's comfort in writing about sex, her ability to do so in a fresh, moving and believable way, and its appropriateness to the story."

Because Superromance allows authors such latitude, there is a danger in creating a story in which the romance is secondary, Eykelhof cautions. Writers need to be aware that while subplots, interesting secondary characters and complex plot lines are important, the primary story is a love story. "This is still series romance fiction," she says, "and the relationship between the hero and the heroine has to be central to the book.

"Newcomers to series romance writing should also take care to keep their writing fresh, avoiding formulaic approaches to plotting, imitative phrasing and time-worn fictional devices. But good style can salvage even the most exhausted techniques," Eykelhof says.

"If you do use a standard element, by which I mean cliched plot developments, stereotypical character traits and so on, you need to do something unique and convincing with it. Love at first sight, for example, is very difficult to pull off, but it can be done," Eykelhof says. "A plot device like the overheard conversation is one we've all seen far too many times and it's too easy a way of writing yourself out of a plot difficulty. Yet even that you could probably get away with, if you can find a convincing way of doing it."

Time-tested story lines can also be revisited again and again if the writer has a fresh take on the idea. "The secret baby, the marriage of convenience, the rancher-hero story, all are still tremendously popular," she says. "And we find they work really well for us if they're written with a contemporary sensibility, and the characters are so real and believable that the reader buys into the story. The author's version of one of these standard plots has to be very particular to her characters and their circumstances."

A fresh, individual writing style is one quality Eykelhof looks for among the manuscripts Superromance receives, "something that says this story could never be told by anyone else other than the author, and has never been told before in quite the same way," she says. "It's an involving style that draws the reader into the story's world, yet it can't be self-conscious to the degree that it interferes with the reader's involvement in the story. What we're looking for is the perfect blend of story and style."

Like many other series romance publishers, Superromance accepts both agented and unagented material. "The majority of submissions we receive each month are unagented. Whether or not you have an agent is a purely personal decision, and it has no impact on our decision to buy or not to buy. Every manuscript gets read and assessed whether or not the writer has an agent."

For initial contact, writers should send a query letter, a brief synopsis of the plot and characters, and pertinent information about the author. Eykelhof also likes to receive two or three completed chapters. "The reason for that is it gives me a much better sense of the writer's ability, her understanding of the genre and our series, and the appropriateness of her writing for romance fiction."

Aside from sending a clean, professional submission package, what can authors do to make their work stand out? "Above all, strive for quality. If you send us a well-written, well-crafted story with a compelling plot that stems from believable, sympathetic characters, we'll notice it. Take the time to do it right."

Writers struggling with their first romance novel can learn a lot about structure, pace and characterization from published authors. But remember to "write from the heart, and write with sincerity," Eykelhof says. "That's where that real sense of individuality comes from."

Publishes 48 mass market paperback books per year. An average of 3-4 books per year are first novels.

HOW TO CONTACT: Does not accept unsolicited manuscripts. Submit query letter and 1 sample chapter. Receives 100 plus manuscripts each month. 50% of accepted submissions are agented. On average reports on queries in 2-3 weeks. On average reports on manuscripts in 10-12 weeks. Sometimes comments on rejected manuscripts. Send SASE for writer's guidelines.

TERMS: Contracts negotiated on an individual basis. Buys all rights. Manuscript is published an average of 1 year after acceptance. Author receives bionote in book or on jacket. Author receives 25 or more copies of book.

ADDRESS: 225 Duncan Mill Road, Don Mills, Ontario, Canada, M3B-3K9

PHONE: (416)445-5860

FAX: (416)445-8655

HARLEQUIN TEMPTATION

Established: 1949

Romance Editor: Birgit Davis-Todd, Senior Editor

> CATEGORIES
> Contemporary Romance, Fantasy, Humorous

"We are the most contemporary, the most sensuous of all the Harlequin and Silhouette lines," says Birgit Davis-Todd, Senior Editor at Harlequin Temptation. "Silhouette Desire comes close to Temptation, but it has a little more traditional feel to it. We are the steamiest of them all."

Romances have been a part of Davis-Todd's life since childhood. "I grew up reading historicals. What I liked about them was the fanciful feel they have, the larger than life characters. Even then, I was fascinated with Harlequin as a company; it was a household name, like Coca Cola. Who doesn't enjoy a love story? My eyes still water when I read a good romance."

With a degree in English from the University of Toronto and a diploma in Book Editing and Design, Davis-Todd joined Harlequin as an assistant editor two years after graduation. "I've been at Harlequin 12 years. I started with Temptation in 1983 when they were about to launch this sexy new series, which at the time was quite controversial. Interestingly, what was considered extremely sexy then is the norm in romances today. We've come quite a long way gaining acceptance from readers."

In fact, Temptation has become one of Harlequin's strongest lines, especially in terms of international sales. "We're published widely overseas, from England and France to Japan and Australia," says Davis-Todd. "Foreign readers particularly like Temptation because it has a young, sexy, 90s feel. There's a real fascination abroad with North American culture and that includes romance as well as North American television shows and movies."

Temptation publishes sensuous, contemporary category romances (of approximately 60,000 words), which makes it quite distinct in the marketplace. "We have very sensual love scenes in our books, based on a 90s attitude. Relationships today between a man and woman are very sexually oriented. The characters in our books should reflect this. They should be people our readers can relate to. We're not into classic, timeless, sweet and safe romances. There's a real titillation factor in our line."

Does emphasizing the physicality of a relationship undermine the love relationship, which is typically at the heart of all romances? "The love story is essential to any romance," says Davis-Todd. "That's what romance readers want, expect and get. They're looking for the emotion that goes into a love story, but our Temptation readers want it in the context of sexiness. They are quite willing to admit that they like a spicy book, or that they like to be turned on. If readers want a tamer, less sensuous love story, they have plenty of other lines to choose from. But in the 90s, sex is an indispensable part of every romance, every love story. We're not soft porn; we're romantic and erotic. Porn is geared strictly toward men and relies solely on sex, not romance. Even if we have eroticism in a Temptation, the romance comes first."

Another defining Temptation characteristic is the line's strong female characters. "Our heroines have careers, hobbies and sex drives. They've established themselves in life, know what they want, have great jobs— are always on the go. Yes, they have flaws and vulnerabilities. They're looking for Mr. Right, but they are all women our readers can relate to. Most of the heroines are quite feisty, independent and fun; they know their own minds, know what they want, and how to get it."

Many readers find themselves both falling in love and laughing while they read Temptation books. "There's a lot of humor in the line, and that sets us apart. Humor and sexiness work very well together for us," says Davis-Todd. "The awkwardnesses of new relationships, the funny things that can happen, the unexpected surprises all work hand-in-hand to make a great book. We're known as a sensual line but also as a humorous line. Almost 50% of our books are funny as well as sexy. One author, Jennifer Crusie, has really made a name for herself by incorporating her own wry brand of humor into romance." (See Crusie's piece "Happily Ever Laughter: Writing Romantic Comedy for Women" in the **Craft & Technique** section of this book).

Davis-Todd is receptive to a range of ideas and stories in the Temptation line. "There's not much we don't want to see in a manuscript, because generally we're pretty open-minded and innovative. Sometimes an author can take an idea, a topic or a character and make it work, even if it at first seems unlikely."

But there are a few categories and themes Temptation is not looking for. "The paranormal trend, I think, is waning, so I'm not very interested in that. And I want more authors who can push the erotic boundaries, but I don't want stories that are too terribly real. Temptation is still a fantasy-oriented line, after all. And avoid heroes or heroines who are artists (musicians, painters, actors, etc.). We've found most of our readers aren't interested in the artsy types. There's a built-in perception, right or wrong, that artsy people are dull and unromantic. Our readers like masculine types such as cowboys and cops. Although it's just perception, we have to publish what our readers want."

One pet peeve of Davis-Todd's comes from writers who simply submit manuscripts without directing them to a specific editor or line. "New writers must target the line that is right for them," she says. "Read the line and know it and the market. And read recent releases—lines can change dramatically over time. Never forget that, above all, a romance is a love story between a man and a woman. Be knowledgeable about what we want before you send something to us."

Davis-Todd stresses that romance writers not only need to master the writing aspects of the genre, but they need to know the ins-and-outs of the industry, as well. "The romance genre is a world unto itself, and you don't realize this until you start working in it. You, and everyone involved, become so immersed. What I find fascinating is that for the most part the books are written by women, published by women and bought by women. It's a big business, too. Romance is a $600 million industry and represents 49% of mass-market paperbacks sold. People are giving romance much more respect today. It's becoming legitimized, as it should. Writers need to know all these things."

In addition, Davis-Todd encourages authors not to forget there's a world of books outside of romance. "Keep up on current novels, especially bestsellers, to try to understand why these books sell so well. What is it about a Grisham novel that appeals to millions of readers? What can you learn from other authors? What successful writing techniques do writers like Danielle Steel use, and why do people like her sell so many books? At Harlequin, we keep track of these things and try to find writers who can tap into similar techniques.

"Temptation has a large regular author base," says Davis-Todd. "But we are always looking for new writers. About half of our authors have agents. An agent will help you get in the door, but at Harlequin, we read everything that is submitted so an agent is not essential. Keep in mind we receive several hundred manuscripts and queries a month, and we buy only a small percentage. From first-time authors, we prefer to see a query letter, the first chapter and a 2-3 page synopsis. In the query letter tell us about yourself and outline your writing credentials."

A final word of advice from the editor of the steamiest of all romance lines: "Writers have to think in terms of building a career. You can't just write one book and rest on your laurels. You've got to keep coming up with more good stories. That's the only way you can make it in this business. You must make your writing a career, not a hobby."

Publishes 48 mass market paperback books per year. An average of 3-4 books per year are first novels. Recently published *Getting Rid of Bradley* (Temptation #480, Feb '94), Jennifer Crusie (won RITA Award for Best Short Contemporary in 1994); *A Human Touch* (Temptation #356, July '91), Glenda Sanders (won RITA Award for Best Short Contemporary in 1991).

HOW TO CONTACT: Does not accept unsolicited manuscripts. Submit query letter and 1 sample chapter. Receives over 100 manuscripts each month. 50% of accepted submissions are agented. On average reports on queries in 2-3 weeks. On average reports on manuscripts in 10-12 weeks. Sometimes comments on rejected manuscripts. Send SASE for writer's guidelines.

TERMS: Contracts negotiated on an individual basis. Buys all rights. Manuscript is published an average of 1 year after acceptance. Author receives bionote in book or on jacket. Author receives 25 or more copies of book.

ADDRESS: 225 Duncan Mill Road, Don Mills, Ontario, Canada, M3B-3K9

PHONE: (416)445-5860

FAX: (416)445-8655

HARPERPAPERBACKS

Established: 1819 • Imprint: Monogram

Romance Editor: Carolyn Marino, Editorial Director

> CATEGORIES
> Contemporary Romance, Fantasy, Ghost, Historical, Paranormal, Time Travel

If you want to send your manuscript to a broad-minded, diversified, and flexible publishing house, HarperPaperbacks just might be what you're looking for. "We consider each book individually, without any category or genre quotas to meet," says Carolyn Marino, editorial director. "We are flexible at Harper because our one guideline is to acquire the strongest books possible, and to do that we need to have an open mind about what works. Since we're somewhat youthful, being in the business only five years, we're pretty willing to experiment."

Marino has experimented quite a bit as well: she has a bachelor's degree from the University of North Carolina (history), a master's degree from George Washington University (history), and has done further post-graduate work at Columbia. She's also been a reporter for the *Washington Post* and an editor for children's books—all before entering "mainstream" publishing. "I've been at Harper since January of 1990. Before that I was an editor at St. Martin's Press."

So how did Marino become a romance editor? "The training for an editor is to read a lot, and people who study history certainly do read a lot and they write a lot, too. Being a reporter gave me quite a bit of experience in writing and editing, as well."

Harper has one imprint that is devoted strictly to romances and women's fiction: Harper Monogram. This line enforces few parameters regarding what subgenres of romance it will publish. "We publish all kinds of romances," says Marino. "We probably publish more historical romances than any other subgenre, but we certainly do contemporary romances, romantic suspense, time-travel, humorous—we'll try anything, really. If someone has written something that is very unlike anything we've ever published and it really is fascinating, then we're happy to consider it.

"We have no series romances. We might do a few sequels or trilogies or books in which the same character keeps popping up, but that's about it. I think our consistency rests in that we consistently publish quality books."

Editors at Harper work hard to ensure that their books are of the highest caliber. "I have a lot of respect for other romance publishers. They're doing a really good job," Marino says. "But that makes my job that much harder. Because it's such a crowded marketplace, we have to do our best to make our books stand out, which is why we don't try to anticipate trends or limit our subject matter. We acquire the best books we can, the strongest manuscripts that come our way. We don't just push numbers. We're quality-driven."

Unlike other romance publishers that have strict word-length requirements, HarperPaperbacks leaves it up to authors to determine the size of their books. "A writer should tell the story in however many words it takes. We have no length requirements or stipulations." For Marino, it's not length that matters, but content and writing quality. "We look for strong writing, well-developed characters, a sense of place, good plotting, and an individual voice that really makes the writing standout. What really appeals to me is a unique voice, one that doesn't sound like all the others."

You can get Harper's editorial staff to hear your unique voice, even if you don't have an agent. "We do take unagented submissions, and they are read—although agented submissions may get read before the unagented material. But we read all of it, eventually. It's just that getting a response takes a bit longer when something comes in over the transom." Harper Monogram editors usually respond in six to eight weeks.

Regarding submission, Marino has some specific criteria. "If writers want to submit to Harper, we ask that they send us a SASE, write a cover letter with a synopsis and two or three chapters of the manuscript. And please double-space the manuscript! We also suggest that writers research the publishing house they're submitting to; get to know the kinds of books being published."

One final word of advice: "Writers wanting to publish must have confidence in their writing, even if it keeps getting rejected. Don't give up."

Publishes 48 mass market paperback books per year.

HOW TO CONTACT: Does not accept unsolicited manuscripts. Submit query letter and 3 sample chapters. On average reports on queries in 6 weeks. On average reports on manuscripts in 6 weeks. Send SASE for writer's guidelines.

TERMS: Contracts negotiated on an individual basis. Manuscript is published an average of 1 year or more after acceptance. Author receives bionote in book or on jacket.

ADDRESS: 10 East 53rd Street, New York, NY 10022

PHONE: (212)207-7724

FAX: (212)207-7759

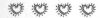

HARVEST HOUSE PUBLISHERS

Established: 1974

Manager: Pat Smith

> CATEGORIES
> Historical, Romantic Suspense with a Christian emphasis

An average of 1 book every 2 years is a first novel.

HOW TO CONTACT: Accepts unsolicited manuscripts. Submit query letter and 3 sample chapters. Simultaneous submissions accepted. Receives 300 manuscripts each month. 1% of accepted submissions are agented. On average reports on queries in 2 weeks. On average reports on manuscripts in 2-4 weeks. Send SASE for writer's guidelines.

TERMS: Manuscript is published an average of 1 year after acceptance. Author receives bionote in book or on jacket. Author receives 10 copies of book.

ADDRESS: 1075 Arrowsmith, Eugene, OR 97402

PHONE: (503)343-0123

FAX: (503)342-6410

♡ ♡ ♡ ♡

KENSINGTON PUBLISHING

Imprint: Arabesque, Denise Little Presents, Pinnacle, Zebra

Executive Editors: Sarah Gallick (hardcover); Tracy Bernstein (trade paperbacks); **Ann LaFarge** (mass market). Senior Editors: Denise Little, John Scognamiglio, Monica Harris, Kate Duffy.

> CATEGORIES
> Contemporary Romance, Futuristic, Historical, Multicultural, Paranormal, Regency, Reincarnation, Time Travel, Vampire

Spirited, savvy and outspoken, Ann LaFarge, executive editor of Zebra Books, could be the protagonist of one of the books she edits. In fact, she once graced the cover of a Zebra novel. Pick up a copy of *A Bid For Love* by Carol Finch and check out the back cover. The attractive heroine perched atop the fence is none other than Ann LaFarge. Her publisher chose LaFarge for the cover because she exemplifies the spirit of the To Love Again heroines—independent women who, at 40-something and beyond, find new careers, new lives and new loves.

Sadly, the To Love Again program has been put on a long vacation, says LaFarge. "Not enough loyal readers," but she hopes the program can be picked up again soon. Publishers have to publish what sells. "The market is changing so fast it reminds me of that sign over McDonald's telling you, every second, how many burgers have been sold." Time was when readers walked into a bookstore and said "Give me all the Zebras." No more. The world of genre publishing is changing.

Barriers between subgenres are falling, taboos are being lifted, and formulas are going out the window. Despite the protest of a few stalwart devotees, certain subgenres—such as the Gothic—have fizzled out. Some readers demand formulaic writing and even the couple in a clinch on the cover, but more and more buyers are reading eclectically, says LaFarge. The competition is fierce. Subgenres crop up, fall by the wayside, and rise again. This makes it difficult for a new writer to get started—it's hard to find your way around the world without a map, but the challenge is a valid one.

The changes are evident at Kensington Publishing Corporation, the large umbrella under which Zebra, Kensington Books and Pinnacle fall. Each month Editor-in-Chief Paul Dinas, LaFarge and her ten colleagues set out to fill their lists. The type of manuscripts they seek depends on what readers are buying. Month to month, the list changes and certain sub-genres are acquired more agressively than others. At any one time, editors could be in search of a historical romance, a time travel novel, a supernatural romance, or a contemporary relationship-based story.

Founded in 1975 by Walter Zacharius, an astute businessman known for his keen instinct of the market, Kensington has remained family-owned for more than 20 years. Though a major house, its atmosphere has a family feel rather than a corporate culture. The company's loose structure does not restrict editors to certain manuscripts. All are free to acquire any type of book Kensington publishes. Since Kensington has several active romance programs, all editors acquire romances. Quite naturally, each follows his or her own preferences.

Kate Duffy and John Scognamiglio, for example, prefer editing Regencies. Denise Little has a weakness for paranormal and anything with vampires, ghosts, ghoulies or things that go bump in the night. Time travel and other alternative fantasy subgenres can be addressed to either Tracy Bernstein or Denise Little. LaFarge longs for more relationship-based fiction that focuses on what happens in everyday life—in families, in the workplace, in friendships. The company's newest imprint, Kensington Mass Market, features books of every genre chosen to appeal to the widest range of readers.

Zebra's Heartfire imprint has been discontinued, and the Lovegram program is so heavily inventoried "we're buying very, very selectively," but some imprints are very open to new writers. Monica Harris, the editor for Arabesque, a relatively new program under Pinnacle, is looking for African-American writers to write historical or contemporary romances about African-American couples. The imprint will eventually include other ethnic sensitivities as well.

Kensington accepts novels set in all time periods—the Regency period, the Old West, the 1890s, the 1990s, or the future. Lengths range from 70,000 to 110,000 words.

Your submission should include a cover letter, a two- to three-page synopsis, the first three chapters of your novel or the entire manuscript, if it is finished, and a SASE. A synopsis is a summary of your story from beginning to end. "Think of the way an eight year old describes a movie he's just seen." The writing should be simple and straightforward. Its purpose is not to show your writing style but to help editors process your submission. They'll judge your writing skills on the merits of your manuscript.

Submissions addressed simply to "Zebra," "Kensington," or "Pinnacle" without an editor's name, will be sent back unread, says LaFarge. Address your manuscript to an editor you think will like it. If it's not right for her, she'll pass it on to a colleague. Keep up with editorial changes by reading *Publishers Weekly* and *Romantic Times*, and call Kensington to verify the editor is still on staff *before* you mail your submission.

Simultaneous submissions are fine as long as you are upfront about it, says LaFarge. State in your cover letter that the manuscript has been sent to other publishers, and that you will withdraw it if you accept another offer.

LaFarge has one criterion for judging a manuscript: "I look for a story I can't stop reading. It must be so good I'm not tempted to put it down and turn on the television. I must care what's happening inside the head of the character, and (this goes without saying) the writing must be smooth and unpretentious and adverb-free."

LaFarge is adamant about adverbs, which she says can sabotage your prose: " 'Help Help! she exclaimed fearfully' is the worst mistake you can make. Don't use more tags than you absolutely need, then use only 'he said,' or 'John said,' or maybe 'Mary asked.' Eliminate five out of every six adverbs. Then go back and throw out the rest."

Don't use dialogue to advance the plot as in "Remember how that madman killed mother and then we all had to lie on the floor tied up for three days until the police came?" Coincidence- inspired conflict introduced just to keep the plot going or to heat up the relationship is "old-hat, formulaic, and cheap, and causes me to reach for a copy of my form rejection letter." Certain plots have worn thin: twins; revenge ("Brianna vowed to find the man who'd killed her beloved brother . . . "); rags to riches; serial killer stalkings.

Details and nuance add power to your writing. "I like to know what a room looks like, where the dog sleeps, what the characters had for dinner, how it tasted, how the new car smells, what kind of curtains are at the window. Read *Cousins* by Rona Jaffe (check out the funeral scene in the beginning), *So Big* by Edna Ferber, *Beach Music* by Pat Conroy, *Fault Lines* by Anne Rivers Siddons for examples of great telling details.

LaFarge doesn't believe in "tip-sheet fiction," where characters must kiss by page 75. "The Bronte sisters didn't have tip sheets, and look what a good job they did!" Tip-sheets often advise romance writers to create only strong, independent, self-reliant heroines. "Nonsense," says La-Farge, "I like deeply flawed people, both men and women. Maybe we need to to stop thinking of our main characters as 'heroes and heroines' and start thinking of them as people"—like the characters Margaret Mitchell brought to life in *Gone with the Wind*. "When I was in high school, my best friend and I used to argue about who was sexier, Rhett or Ashley." When characters are that real, when writing is so good editors can't put it down, your fiction will be in demand.

LaFarge advises writers to "read, read, read." Read every kind of fiction: literary fiction, bestsellers, the top romance writers, the new romance writers. "If I were a nutritionist, I'd recommend a balanced diet; as an editor I recommend a balanced diet of reading." Learn by listening to yourself respond: what attracts you? What bores you? What angers you? Then, find your own voice.

"We are struggling, as hard as writers are, to find the book that will crack the market wide open and make us rich and famous. All we need to set that in motion is The Perfect Manuscript. Send it to me!—and don't forget the synopsis."

LaFarge understands writers because she's a writer, too. After acquiring and editing manuscripts all day, she leaves her Manhattan office and heads for home where, surrounded by two Jack Russell terriers and a cat named Riffraff, she becomes Phoebe Gallant, or another of her three pseudonyms, and gets to work on her latest novel. "I'm struggling with my next proposal just like everyone else, and I could paper my walls with rejection slips. It's a tough world out there!" says LaFarge, who is the author of five published books, both fiction and nonfiction.

Above her desk, LaFarge keeps a quote from William Faulkner describing his work: "A life's work in the agony and sweat of the human spirit, not for glory and least of all for profit, but to create out of the materials of the human spirit something which did not exist before."

"Try it," says LaFarge. "And God bless."

RECENTLY PUBLISHED: *Natchez*, Pamela Jekel; *The Ring*, Sylvia Halliday; *Homecoming*, Barbara Bickmore.

HOW TO CONTACT: Does not accept unsolicited manuscripts. Send full manuscript. Submit query letter and 3 sample chapters. Simultaneous submissions accepted. Send SASE for writer's guidelines.

TERMS: Contracts negotiated on an individual basis. Buys first worldwide rights. Buys all rights. Author receives 25 copies of book.

ADDRESS: 850 Third Avenue, New York, NY 10022

PHONE: (212)407-1500

FAX: (212)935-0699

LEISURE BOOKS/LOVE SPELL, A DIVISION OF DORCHESTER PUBLISHING CO., INC.

Established: 1970 • Imprint: Leisure Books, Love Spell

Romance Editor: Joanna Cagan, Editor

CATEGORIES
Futuristic, Ghost, Historical, Paranormal, Reincarnation, Time Travel, Vampire

"It makes more sense to write from what you know and enjoy writing about, rather than respond to the 'market,' or what you perceive as a trend," says Joanna Cagan, editor for Leisure Books and Love Spell. "It's easy for editors to spot writing that comes from the heart versus writing done in an attempt to answer a perceived trend."

While this may be good advice for any writer, it is especially important for a writer submitting to Leisure and Love Spell. Both imprints are widely varied in the types of romance they seek, and authors of less traditional books stand a great chance of finding a home in those imprints.

"The tone varies greatly for Leisure," Cagan says. "While a well-written book is always the first criterion, the humorous ones often catch our eye. Good, emotional ones that make you cry will get us sometimes, as will darker romances."

Love Spell is even more non-standard. "In Love Spell, we publish the time travels, the futuristics and the paranormals. We're looking for a more quirky tone. If you come up with a well-written romance, no matter how strange, we'd love to have a look at it."

The crucial aspect writers should keep in mind, however, is still the writing. Don't think a quirky tone or odd story will make up for poor quality. "Pay attention to the basics, like point-of-view, plot continuity and character development," says Cagan.

Likewise, writers should not concern themselves with how they will promote the book until they've actually written it. "The most important thing you can do to help the sales of your book is to put most of your energy into the writing of that book. Series change and vary in terms of what kind of promotion works or doesn't work, but we always start with the basic approach that we need a strong product in order to sell it successfully. Some writers spend too much time worrying about grand self-promotions, and their writing gets lost in the shuffle."

Writers shouldn't look too far ahead, either. Says Cagan, "Sometimes writers—especially new writers—have planned out a sequel or a whole series of books based on the first romance they've written. I encourage new authors to take it book by book. When you submit an unsolicited manuscript, for example, I'm not concerned about whether you will follow up with romances for the secondary characters. I want to see that first book done well, then we'll move on to the second one. But having a sequel in the works does not increase your chances of having the first one accepted or published."

New authors also might feel they need an agent to get published, but that is untrue as well. "The importance of an agent really depends on the author," Cagan says. "For a company like Leisure/Love Spell, we're willing to look at your submission whether it's agented or not. If you're someone who is not so comfortable negotiating or discussing the business side of things, you might prefer to have an agent do that for you. It varies from author to author, and we're certainly willing to look at and accept submissions from authors who are unagented. We have some authors we've worked with to build their careers, without them ever having an agent."

A good agent can be an ally in the sometimes intimidating world of publishing, and can also help new authors to think of their writing in career planning terms. In addition, most houses, including Leisure/Love Spell, look at agented manuscripts before the over-the-transom submissions. "Agented manuscripts do get looked at first, but they vary in quality, just as the unagented submissions. In some ways, a good agent can be a screening step for the publisher. If we have a positive relationship with an agent, their sending us a manuscript makes it likely we'll look at it earlier, because someone who knows the industry has deemed it a quality product."

Cagan says the best way to sell a book to any publisher is to know the market. "Be familiar with the kinds of books we publish." While you don't want to write to what you think they're looking for, you should know if the book you've already written is a good fit before you send it off. "Rejection is a huge part of this business, as is trying again and again," says Cagan. "It takes a lot of patience."

Publishes 132 mass market paperback books per year. An average of 12 books per year are first novels. Recently published *Love's Legacy*, an anthology of 11 authors to benefit literacy (Leisure Books).

HOW TO CONTACT: Accepts unsolicited manuscripts. Submit query letter and 3 sample chapters. Receives 75 manuscripts each month. 50% of accepted submissions are agented. On average reports on queries in 4-5 months.

TERMS: Contracts negotiated on an individual basis. Manuscript is published an average of 10 months to 3 years after acceptance. Author receives 25 copies of book; additional copies available at a 40% discount.

ADDRESS: 276 Fifth Avenue, Suite 1008, New York, NY 10001

PHONE: (212)725-8811

PHOTO: S. MACERO

POCKET BOOKS

Romance Editor: Caroline Tolley, Senior Editor

> CATEGORIES
> Contemporary Romance, Historical, Time Travel

Growing up reading books by Victoria Holt, Phyllis Whitney, Daphne Du Maurier and Barbara Cartland, Pocket Books senior editor Caroline Tolley has a long, personal history with romances. "My junior high English teacher turned me on to these writers. And I'm still a big romance reader, even aside from my job. I think they're great."

Her love and devotion to romance led Tolley into publishing when she graduated from Skidmore College, back in the mid-80s. "My first publishing job was at the Doubleday Book Club as assistant to the editor-in-chief. Then I was approached by Pocket to join their romance division. I've been here almost six years, and the whole time I've been working on romances. To try to be an expert in something you must love what you're doing; you must be committed to it. I am."

Although she loves the genre, Tolley is insistent about what types of manuscripts she will not consider. "In my *personal* opinion, there are certain time periods and locales that just aren't as desirable as others, namely the historical romance mainstays. I will not purchase anything before 1066, for example, because I feel its archaism will put off too many readers. What are also hard sells, in my opinion, are romances set in France, Russia and Italy. England, Scotland and Ireland would be better choices. I don't purchase what I call 'exotic' romances: those set in the Far East, Australia, Hawaii, Mexico, Brazil, and Spain, as well as some island locations. Settings on the Eastern seaboard of America can be difficult as well as some Eastern to mid-America locations and Canada.

Colonial America, the Elizabethan Period and the French Revolution are all time periods I would advise staying away from if you are trying to make a first sale. I just don't believe there is a big enough romance audience for books in these settings. Again, these are my opinions alone. I do not wish to speak for the industry as a whole."

What, then, should you send her? "100% of what I acquire are 100,000-word traditional paperback historical romance novels that take place between 1066 and 1895. I like romances set in the Scottish Highlands, the Antebellum South, or the American West. Pocket does publish some contemporary novels, but I do not acquire them at this time. We usually publish a total of three to four romances per month."

While Tolley gravitates toward books with traditional historical settings, she's far from traditional in her approach to love scenes. "Romance readers like to see the culmination and the consummation of love. I believe there is a market for the very sweet romance, but there's also one for the more sensual. There are audiences for the gamut of passion-related love stories. I draw the line at really graphic sex, but with every book I buy there has to be at least one consummated love scene, and the readers expect this. If they bought a romance and there were no love scene, I think they'd be very disappointed."

Tolley's philosophy is that the best way to know what readers want is to know what editors want. "Part of an editor's job is to know her market. Your first responsibility is to keep abreast of the business," says Tolley. "Those wanting to publish with Pocket must be aware of what I want and what I buy. The only way you can do that is to be knowledgeable about the industry today. Read the new romances that are selling, not the big stars, to get a feel for what is currently working. Educate yourself as much as possible. Be professional and courteous, and always be open to critiques. Be patient with the editor, too. We work with lots of authors, so we can't devote all of our time to just one author."

Tolley warns that unpublished writers should try not to take too many risks when trying to break into the market. "Write a commercial product that the market can absorb. And if you're having trouble, stay in a commercial vein. Be aware that trends come and go in romance. For a first sale, pay attention to the mainstays, the locations and time periods that are the favorites; Regency England, for example, will never go away. Don't write anything too wacky or off the beaten path. While there will be some editors and readers who are exceptions to these rules, personally

I don't believe they are the majority. So much of this business is word of mouth. Don't spread yourself too thin. Try to focus on one genre at a time, and be versatile in that genre so you can encompass as much of the romance audience as you can; try a Medieval, a Regency and Western, etc. until you find your niche. Then hone your craft. You need to establish an audience and develop it."

Before you establish that audience, however, your manuscript must be published. If you plan on publishing with Pocket, you might want to get an agent. "I will look at unsolicited material if it fits my very specific guidelines such as those I mentioned previously. But in all the time I've worked here, I have not acquired a book without an agent," says Tolley. "I think that, especially on a first sale, I rely greatly on the agent to channel things in my direction, to know what I'm looking for. Agents are also a big part of the screening process. A beginning writer should definitely get an agent."

So what can you expect if Pocket decides to buy your manuscript? Above all, you'll get lots of respect in the industry. "We simply publish a higher quality of women's fiction. That's one of the many things we're known for, that's what our authors aspire to. Publishing the highest quality book possible is our governing principle. And that's what we're going to continue to publish."

Recently published *Angel of Midnight*, Jo-Ann Power; *The Last Duke*, Andrea Kane; *Weeping Angel*, Stef Ann Holm.

HOW TO CONTACT: Does not accept unsolicited manuscripts. **Accepts agented submissions only.** On average reports on queries in 5 months. On average reports on manuscripts in 5 months. Sometimes comments on rejected manuscripts. Send SASE for writer's guidelines.

TERMS: Contracts negotiated individually.

ADDRESS: 1230 Sixth Avenue, 13th Floor, New York, NY 10020

PHONE: (212)698-7000

FAX: (212)632-8084

PREP PUBLISHING

Established: 1994

Romance Editor: Anne McKinney

> CATEGORIES
> Contemporary Romance, Historical, Romantic Mystery

"We enjoy romance that tries to integrate religious and ethical values in a way that does not preach. Christian romance interests us."

Advice to writers: Rewrite and edit carefully before submitting manuscript.

An average of 2-6 books per year are first novels.

HOW TO CONTACT: Accepts unsolicited manuscripts. Send full manuscript. Simultaneous submissions accepted. Receives 50 manuscripts each month. 1% of accepted submissions are agented. On average reports on queries in 3 months. On average reports on manuscripts in 3 months. Send SASE for writer's guidelines.

Terms: Advance with 6% royalties minimum and 15% royalties maximum. Buys all rights. Manuscript is published an average of 18 months after acceptance. Author receives bionote in book or on jacket.

ADDRESS: 1110½ Hay Street, Fayetteville, NC 28305
PHONE: (910)483-6611
FAX: (910)483-2439

READ'N RUN BOOKS

Established: 1982

Romance Editor: Michael P. Jones, publisher

> CATEGORIES
> Contemporary Romance, Fantasy, Futuristic, Ghost, Historical, Multicultural, New Age, Paranormal, Reincarnation, Romantic Mystery, Romantic Suspense, Time Travel, Vampire

"We are brand new in the romance field. We have no books—other than some great romantic poetry books—to show, so we are wide open, very selective, but interested in finding good writers to work with."

Wants: "More Western history! Think about the Oregon Trail, the American Indians, and the fur trade. These are rich literary areas that few people have tapped into."

Taboo: Cheap sex and violence.

Advice to writers: "Don't copy other writers. Develop your own style and have faith in your creativity. Ideas flow like an endless waterfall, learn how to tap into this."

HOW TO CONTACT: Accepts unsolicited manuscripts. Send full manuscript. Simultaneous submissions accepted. Receives 20 manuscripts each month. 10% of accepted submissions are agented. On average reports on queries in 2-4 weeks. On average reports on manuscripts in 8 weeks. Send SASE for writer's guidelines.

TERMS: Paid in published copies. Manuscript is published an average of 11 months after acceptance. Author receives bionote in book or on jacket.

ADDRESS: P.O. Box 294, Rhododendron, OR 97049

PHONE: (503)622-4798

ST. MARTIN'S PRESS

Romance Editors: Jennifer Weis, Executive Editor; Jennifer Enderlin, Senior Editor

> CATEGORIES
> Contemporary Romance, Fantasy, Historical, Paranormal, Romantic Mystery, Romantic Suspense, Time Travel

One of the nation's largest commercial publishers, St. Martin's Press, upholds a reputation for publishing top-of-the-line books, fiction and nonfiction alike. Their romance line is no exception. As Executive Editor Jennifer Weis says, "We're very hungry and we're very aggressive. Also, we don't publish large quantities of romance, so we're highly selective. Because we don't have that many authors, we really believe in and are very committed to those we do acquire. We're very author-driven, not category-driven."

Weis knows how to distinguish the wonderful from the mediocre, too. She's been reading romances most of her life, and she has a strong background in romance publishing. Her love for the genre started at a young age, while she was doing a little unsupervised snooping in her mother's room. "When I was eleven, I opened my mother's drawer when she was gone one day and found a bunch of romances. I started reading them and couldn't quit. I had to sneak them, of course, because she never would have let me read them. So for me, reading romances was this wonderful clandestine activity."

With both a B.A. and M.A. in English from Yale, Weis has now made reading and acquiring romances her career—she's been in romance publishing since she graduated. "I first started with Bantam, and then I did a stint at Atlantic Monthly Press. From there, I went to Dell and worked on their Candlelight Romance line. Eventually, I came to St. Martin's and have been here the past six years."

Although many romance publishers have strict genre specifications and limitations, St. Martin's accepts, publishes and welcomes variety. "We publish a wide range of material. We do historicals, time-travels, paranormal, fantasy, contemporary, women's suspense, and whatever else we think worthy of putting into print."

Weis's openness to bring variety into St. Martin's line does not mean that she doesn't have her preferences. "We publish no category romance and no series novels. I'm also not too interested in ancient-period romances or international suspense. I prefer domestic love stories. At the same time, I know great manuscripts will come along that will totally defy my stipulations."

If you don't have an agent, you should probably get one if you hope to see your name on the cover of a St. Martin's romance. "To me, agents are very, very important," says Weis. "Having an agent puts you at the top of our list. We have one pile for agented material and another for unagented. The agented pile always get priority. And agents have clout that regular submitters don't. For example, if we don't respond to an agent's submission, that agent will hound us until she gets a response. And that manuscript will get attended to, much sooner than any of those in the unsolicited pile. In fact, nearly 100 percent of our acquisitions are agented."

Nonetheless, Weis and her associates do accept—and try to read—unsolicited submissions. But she wants her submission guidelines followed. "What I want in a submission is a brief outline or synopsis and three sample chapters with a query. I want the synopsis to be very brief, preferably only one page. I don't want writers to spend lots of time telling me what they're going to do. I like to actually read the story. Many times I skip the outline and synopsis and go straight to the material. Often an outline can be wonderful but the actual story is awful. If you prefer to send the full manuscript that's fine, but don't expect we'll read it in its entirety—unless it's a real keeper.

While a knowledge of romance, a strong writing style, and a love for the genre are prerequisites for writing a good romance, Weis wants authors not to forget what, in her opinion, is the essence of a potent love story. "Romance is all about conflict. It's about conflict between a hero and a heroine, about building a believable conflict that can be resolved in a romantic way. This conflict must be engaging, intriguing, and suspenseful.

"You can have an author who's better at doing humor, an author who's better at developing characters, an author who's better at writing sex scenes, but what it all boils down to is the story's conflict. A truly happy ending—and we know that's a necessity—must be preceded by a strong, page-turning conflict. A burning conflict always makes the ending so much sweeter."

HOW TO CONTACT: Accepts unsolicited manuscripts. Send full manuscript. Responds in 3 months.

TERMS: Contracts negotiated on an individual basis. Books are published, on average, 9 months after acceptance.

ADDRESS: 175 Fifth Avenue, New York, NY 10010

PHONE: (212) 674-5151

FAX: (212) 677-7456

SILHOUETTE BOOKS

Established: 1979

Romance Editor: Isabel Swift, Editorial Director

CATEGORIES
Contemporary Romance, Fantasy, Futuristic, Ghost, Historical, Humorous, Multicultural, New Age, Over 45, Paranormal, Regency, Reincarnation, Romantic Horror, Romantic Mystery, Romantic Suspense

---

"I've been in the romance publishing business for over sixteen years, and I'm still totally swept away by a good love story," says Isabel Swift, editorial director of Silhouette Books. "I've always had a fascination with people and the dynamics between them. When I read Jane Austen's *Pride and Prejudice* in grade school, I became hooked—and have been since. At heart I'm still just a delighted romance reader."

After college, Swift started her career in publishing as an editorial assistant at Pocket Books in 1979. Shortly thereafter, Silhouette Books was launched as part of Simon & Schuster, and in 1981, she joined Silhouette. When Harlequin acquired Silhouette in 1984, Swift moved with them. She hasn't left.

Silhouette Books is a brand-name category romance publisher that, with Harlequin, publishes around the world. "Most of our books are strongly branded and are published in particular series, with a specific series look,'" says Swift. "I'm responsible for six series—Silhouette Romance, Silhouette Desire, Silhouette Special Edition, Silhouette Intimate Moments, Silhouette Yours Truly and Harlequin Historicals. Each series publishes a set number of books monthly."

Series romances are not all Silhouette publishes, however. "We also put out a number of non-series titles. We publish short story collections, single titles, and have several reissue programs—from a romance digest magazine, to three-in-one theme-led anthologies, to repackaged category stories that have hit the *New York Times* bestseller list."

In addition to the Harlequin and Silhouette imprints, Harlequin Enterprises launched a new imprint called Mira in 1994, which publishes mainstream women's fiction single titles. And Harlequin/Silhouette does what they call "continuities," which are limited numbers of books that are interconnected in some way, yet are published individually. "For example," says Swift, "we're launching *Fortune's Children*, twelve independent, yet linked, stories about a family dynasty. The stories explore the bonds of love and lies that are created and revealed when the wealthy and powerful matriarch is presumed dead after her plane goes down, and foul play is suspected."

Despite such non-series endeavors, Silhouette is still primarily a series publisher. Ideally, Silhouette likes to forge a long-lasting relationship with its authors. Says Swift: "Once we buy one book, we're interested in publishing a second. We look to acquire an author, not just a story. Our belief is that with that first contract we've committed to building a relationship that with an author that will develop and grow. That's very exciting—and usually very different from mainstream publishing. This sense of mutual commitment can make it a delight for both writer and editor to work at Silhouette. Romance readers enjoy the ongoing relationship between publisher and author, too, because when they discover an author they like, they want more. Within series publishing, that favorite author is easier to find and follow."

Swift points out one major advantage to writing category romance: there's rarely a disagreement between the author and the editor about who the audience is—or what the audience wants. Both author and editor usually know and love the genre, so they have a gut understanding and appreciation for what the reader is looking for. "Most of our authors start out as romance readers, which is an enormous asset. The author's goal is to give other readers the pleasure she has received as a reader. There's a shared understanding and bond between reader and writer."

A great benefit of submitting to Silhouette is the publisher's receptivity to a wide spectrum of stories within the romance category. Silhouette will publish an incredible variety of subject matter, as long as the developing romance remains the story's focus. "Because we have the category framework and a strong brand to communicate to the reader, we have more flexibility to do different things within that framework than many mainstream houses. They often can't figure out a way to package an unusual story that will enable them to effectively reach a readership.

"The issue for us is meeting reader expectations. If we fail, that is a big problem—but as long as we satisfy those expectations, anything goes! Readers can find everything from a traditional Cinderella fantasy, to a paranormal, to time-travel, to characters dealing with real-life issues such as spouse abuse, a disability, or the melding of two families, to heart-warming stories of lovers reunited and families found. We look for stories that mean something to our readers, stories that give something to them, stories that will touch their hearts."

It's imperative that authors submitting to Silhouette have a good grasp of the relationship between reader and publisher and the obligations and expectations author and publisher need to meet. "There is definitely an unwritten contract between publisher and reader. When a reader buys a book from a particular Silhouette series, she brings certain expectations. We can surprise her—but we must never disappoint her."

Swift sees Silhouette's mission as two-fold. "Silhouette has two potentially disparate commitments: to address women's fantasies, but also to speak to their realities. Some stories represent one of those directions more than the other, but at times you can learn about yourself and your own reality through fantasy. An example might be a twin story that explores the different paths and opportunities offered the 'same' person, and the implications of her choices. Or a rags-to-riches fantasy that compellingly demonstrates the value of the simpler things in life."

Good news for new writers is Silhouette's policy regarding agents—you don't need one. "We accept both agented and unagented submissions. It's not necessary to have an agent to sell to us—just a great story! In fact, only about half of our authors have agents. Unlike many other kinds of publishing, an agent is not required to get your foot in the door."

Swift has some advice she tells all beginning romance writers. "When you submit, present yourself and your work professionally. Be committed to the genre and know the market. Your story must be a love story, an exploration of the challenges and the incredible joys we all experience in establishing and sustaining a fulfilling relationship with another person. But be warned—as one author noted, 'Just because romances are easy to read does not mean they are easy to write!' You will need a believable and intriguing premise, appealing characters, an effective conflict, a compelling attraction, a clean writing style and lively pacing. The author should just grab the reader's hand on page one and say, 'Come on, let me tell you this fabulous story.' There are also writer's organizations, such as the Romance Writers of America, headquartered in Houston, that can be of enormous help to an aspiring author."

Swift encourages those submitting to Silhouette to remember the following: "Read many books in the line to which you plan on submitting. When I say 'many' I mean twenty or more, not one or two. If you feel sad about the thought of reading twenty romances, just stop right there—because even though you're a talented, accomplished writer, if you have no genuine love for the genre, you'll lose to the competition. There are lots of romance writers out there who are devoted to their readers, the story and the genre. That's hard to beat, because Silhouettes are stories about emotion—and if they're not written from the heart, it shows.

"Romances in general are very much landscapes of the heart, not the intellect. A Silhouette should be an inspiring, positive reading experience. When a reader closes one of our books, she should feel satisfied, happy, strengthened and empowered. Who could ask for anything more?"

Publishes 400 mass market paperback books per year. An average of 10-25 books per year are first novels.

HOW TO CONTACT: Does not accept unsolicited manuscripts. Query before submitting. Receives 300 queries each month. 50% of accepted submissions are agented. On average reports on queries in 4-6 weeks. On average reports on manuscripts in 8-12 weeks. Send SASE for writer's guidelines.

TERMS: Contracts negotiated on an individual basis. Buys all rights. Manuscript is published an average of 1-2 years after acceptance. Author receives bionote in book or on jacket.

ADDRESS: 300 East 42nd Street, New York, NY 10017

PHONE: (212)682-6080

FAX: (212)682-4539

SILHOUETTE DESIRE

Established: 1979

Romance Editor: Lucia Macro, Senior Editor

CATEGORIES
Contemporary Romance, Romantic Mystery, Romantic Suspense

Every woman who wants to fall in love—who dreams of an exciting, beautiful, honest, loyal, extremely sexy man to fulfill her wildest sensual longings—need look no further than the pages of a Silhouette Desire romance, says Senior Editor Lucia Macro.

One of Silhouette's four lines of contemporary romance, Desire boasts the imprint's sexiest titles. "The emphasis is certainly on the romance and the love story, but it's a sensuous love story," Macro says.

Desire books are short and a therefore fast-paced. "At 55,000-60,000 words, there's not a lot of room to meander in your plotting." In tone, Desire romances "have to be sensuous and they have to be interesting. But they can be serious; they can be funny. Some authors are very skillful, and they manage to do both in the same book."

Macro has been with Silhouette for more than ten years, and Senior Editor of Desire since 1989. "I was a romance reader because my mother was a romance reader," she says. "As for being a romance editor, I just fell into it. I saw a job for an editorial assistant in the romance department at Berkeley, and I thought it would be fun. That's how I started."

Macro still enjoys bringing romance into the lives of Desire readers, which she says are the "ultimate decision-makers." "Editors have to offer contracts and buy books based on what they feel in their experience is going to go over with readers. A good editor really focuses on what readers are buying right now."

Macro and her staff have had success with a number of miniseries within the Desire line, which usually start out as three-book series (usually, but not exclusively, by the same author) then expand. Macro notes Joan Hohl's Big Bad Wolfe series, about the four Wolfe brothers; and Hawk's Way, a well-received series by Joan Johnston about the Whitelaws of Texas, as examples.

Unique in the Desire line is the Man of the Month, started in 1989, which, according to Macro, has been "extraordinarily successful, then and today." One of the six Desire romances published each month is chosen as the Man of the Month book (for example, Mr. May—Jake Taggert, *Mysterious Mountain Man*. These romances put more emphasis on the hero, and are more from his point of view. "There's more getting into his head."

There are definite criteria for a hero in any Desire title: "The hero has to be strong; he has to be very masculine. And he's definitely not the guy on the street—he's very sexy, and very true to his word. He's a larger-than-life man." The woman who interacts with this sensuous hero "must be a good person. She's a little more apt to show her vulnerabilities than the hero," says Macro. "The trick is that the reader relates to the heroine and falls in love with the hero."

Macro stresses that if you want to write for Desire, "make sure the book is sexy. Ideally, the whole book would be sensuous, and the reader would really feel what the characters are feeling. It's not just a couple of sex scenes plunked down because you think that's where they belong.

"If you feel uncomfortable writing love scenes, there are other lines which are equally romantic, but not quite so sensuous. I think there's sometimes a hesitancy on the part of the writers, and they think they're going too far—and really, they can't." The only thing that's taboo in a Desire romance is writing that's "more clinical than sensuous, and I think that's a question of writing style. If you read enough romances, you can pick up on the language."

Reading romances by other authors, in fact, is something Macro recommends. She advises "reading as many Desires as you can get your hands on" before submitting a manuscript to the line, which is open to both new and established writers.

"Desire is a very well-established line. It's been around for almost 14 years, so there are a number of writers that have been with us practically since the beginning," says Macro. "But people do go on to other things, so we're always looking for new writers. Publishing someone new is actually one of our great excitements." In general (for Silhouette as an imprint) new authors don't have agents when they are signed; most of their established writers do, but Macro and company accept submissions either way.

Her advice to new writers is simple. "Write the best book you can. The competition out there is very fierce, and the better you are at writing, the better chance you have." Just as important, Macro says, is knowing the marketplace, "because although trends do change, my contention is that they change very slowly. What I'm looking for now and what I'll publish in the next 12-18 months is generally not going to be radically different from what is published right now." Just remember that the reader is the ultimate critic—you've got to please her. "These books are escapism. They are uplifting. They tell you love is the answer—and everybody wants to fall in love."

Publishes 60 mass market paperback books per year. An average of 6 books per year are first novels.

HOW TO CONTACT: Does not accept unsolicited manuscripts. Query before submitting. 50% of accepted submissions are agented. On average reports on queries in 4-6 weeks. On average reports on manuscripts in 8-12 weeks. Send SASE for writer's guidelines.

TERMS: Contracts negotiated on an individual basis. Buys all rights. Manuscript is published an average of 1-2 years after acceptance. Author receives bionote in book or on jacket.

ADDRESS: 300 East 42nd Street, New York, NY 10017

PHONE: (212)682-6080

FAX: (212)682-4539

SILHOUETTE INTIMATE MOMENTS

Established: 1979

Romance Editor: Leslie Wainger, Senior Editor

CATEGORIES

Contemporary Romance, Multicultural, Over 45, Paranormal, Romantic Horror, Romantic Mystery, Romantic Suspense

---

"I always tell people it's my job to make thousands of women happy," says Leslie Wainger, senior editor for Silhouette's Intimate Moments, "and I don't see how that can be a bad thing. I like what we do."

Launched in 1992, the Intimate Moments line was created to combine the most classic elements of category romance—a relationship and a happy ending—with more mainstream plot lines, Wainger says. "We set out to marry those two in the line."

As a result, readers of Silhouette's Intimate Moments novels are not surprised to find suspense elements or even time travel underlying the romance plots. While the heroines must be believable, they're often caught up in extraordinary circumstances, swept away by heroes who work as government agents, international spies, and the like.

"We've gone from the basic Silhouette Romance line, which is our most traditional, to Intimate Moments, where you can have suspense or paranormal circumstances, and the characters do make love whether they're married or not," Wainger says of the line. "I think the change is evolutionary. Because so many of the writers are readers, they write the fantasy they would like to read."

Wainger has been around to witness much of that evolution. A 16-year veteran of Silhouette, she began as an editorial assistant and made her way up the ladder. Wainger signed on as senior editor when Intimate Moments was launched in 1992, and has seen the line grow by 50 percent in number of titles, from the original 48 to 72 per year.

While Intimate Moments authors have the latitude both in length (80,000-85,000 words) and in subject matter to experiment with depth and complexity, Wainger cautions that they must not lose sight of the love story.

"All of the books, whether they involve suspense or something paranormal, are still built around that strong romance," Wainger says. "If you use suspense, what I don't want is to have the characters figure out that they love each other two thirds of the way through the book, then spend the last part of the book being in love and solving the mystery. They can solve the mystery first and the romance later, or they can solve the two simultaneously, but that romantic tension has got to be maintained to the end of the book."

For new writers who've learned how to build, maintain and happily resolve that tension, there is an eager market of editors waiting, Wainger says. Openings are continually created by authors who move from category romance to mainstream fiction, and publishers launch new lines regularly to satisfy an increasing romance reader base, she says. And the readers are as receptive as the editors.

"It's a really welcoming readership," Wainger says. "They come to the books because they like a certain kind of book. And they're willing to give someone new a chance. Category is also one of the best places to gain exposure, because you're getting the same distribution as somebody who has written 27 books."

New writers do not need an agent's representation to get their novel in the door. In fact, writers "stand as good a chance without one," Wainger says. "Category romance is sort of the last bastion where you can get published without an agent. In the end, what I'm buying is the book, and I really don't care how it got to me. It's what I think of the manuscript when I read it that counts."

Silhouette does not accept unsolicited or partial manuscripts, so in the absence of an agent, a query letter is the first point of contact. A two-page plot and character synopsis should accompany the letter, in addition to SASE for reply. Writers should request specific guidelines before submitting. Beyond an intriguing storyline and characters, Wainger looks for professionalism in the query, "because this is a profession. It's not a hobby."

While Wainger hesitates to name the qualities she looks for in a writer ("editors tend to work on their gut instincts a lot," she says), there are a few problem areas new writers should try to sidestep.

"One of the things I see a lot is that the manuscript starts before the story really starts," she says. "They spend a lot of time on background, and really you want to start the book with a bang."

When romance readers buy books, Wainger says, they start by reading the back cover copy, then move to the front sales copy, and then open the book and start to read. "So you want to write a book that grabs them quickly, and is so compelling that they realize they either have to plunk down their money to buy the book, or they're going to have to stand there for three hours in the store and have the manager yell at them. So the beginning is really, really important."

The second error Wainger finds new writers often make is "the dreaded sagging middle," where the beginning and ending are well-crafted, but the author hasn't managed to sustain the tension between the characters with some substantial conflict that can be resolved progressively.

"So you have people who spend a lot of time going on dates, or talking to their best friends, or just sort of sitting on the front porch thinking about the other character," Wainger says. "There's nothing going on to pull you through the story."

One way Wainger suggests beginning writers work through plot, pacing and characterization issues is simply to read. "Read the newest books you can find, because the genre's changing all the time. And analyze what you read, because you can learn as much from books you don't like as from books that you like."

Publishes 60 mass market paperback books per year. An average of 6 books per year are first novels. Recently published *A Soldier's Heart*, Kathleen Korbel (won 1994 RITA Award for Best Long Contemporary); *The Fall of Shane McKade*, Nora Roberts.

HOW TO CONTACT: Does not accept unsolicited manuscripts. Query before submitting. 50% of accepted submissions are agented. On average reports on queries in 4-6 weeks. On average reports on manuscripts in 8-12 weeks. Send SASE for writer's guidelines.

TERMS: Contracts negotiated on an individual basis. Buys all rights. Manuscript is published an average of 1½-2 years after acceptance. Author receives bionote in book.

ADDRESS: 300 East 42nd Street, New York, NY 10017

PHONE: (212)682-6080

FAX: (212)682-4539

SILHOUETTE ROMANCE

Established: 1979

Romance Editor: Melissa Senate, Senior Editor

CATEGORIES
Contemporary Romance

"Whether a classic love story, a romantic comedy or an emotional heart-tugger, a Silhoutte Romance novel is always enjoyble and always about love," says Melissa Senate, senior editor for Silhouette Romance. "Romance is our traditional line, which means the characters never consumate their relationships before marriage. But the stories should be full of sensual tension, compelling conflict and vibrant emotion."

For the Romance line, classic plots are top sellers. Stories that focus on families, single parents, marriages of convenience and secret babies are reader favorites. But the popularity of the traditional does not rule out unconventional plot lines, Senate says. "The range is wide."

Sihouette Romance was launched in 1980, and publishes six books every month, ranging in length from 53,000 to 58,000 words. Senate, a seven-year veteran of romance publishing ("every one spent happily at Silhouette"), estimates some 50 submissions come in per month from writers new to Silhouette for the Romance line alone.

As with the other Silhouette lines, Romance editors will not consider unsolicited full or partial manuscripts. Authors should submit a query letter, two-page plot and character synopsis, and SASE. Both agented and unagented submissions are given the same consideration, Senate says.

Although Romance publishes only a fraction of the submissions it receives, writers should be aware there are ways they can make their material stand out the in the crowd. Says Senate: "The best way to learn what we're looking for is to read, read, read the line you want to write for. Study the structure, the character, conflict and emotional development, and most importantly the type of story we are publishing. Also, study back cover blurbs, which editors typically write themselves, to see what hooks we're highlighting as selling points to our readership.

"It's the cover letter and query that show an editor the author's talent and professionalism. Use that cover letter to show your understanding of the line's needs and wants. By studying the way we sell our books through back cover blurbs, writers can capitalize on the hook in their own story, and use it to grab an editor's attention in the cover letter."

Ultimately the quality of the story is its strongest selling point, and Senate recommends beginning writers remember that believable emotional conflict between the hero and heroine lies at the heart of successful romance novels. "What an author wants—always wants—to do is create a hero and heroine who fill essential emotional needs in each other, so they connect. They are two people who need each other, but there's a conflict standing in the way of romantic fulfillment—until it's resolved for a happy ending."

One sure way to throw that core emotional tension off track is to base it on an 'intellectualized' conflict, or introduce the other woman/other man plot device, Senate cautions. "We do get a lot of 'fighting city hall' books, where somebody wants to bulldoze something. The hero's the mayor and the heroine is a town administrator, and the whole conflict stems from an issue, rather than any kind of emotion between them. So if you took that one issue away, what would they be fighting about? The conflict doesn't arise out of their relationship—or their hearts."

The other woman/other man device fails for much the same reason, Senate says: "The writer is not relying on the characters as the real source of conflict and tension, she's relying on external sources. It's not something that arises out of the characters' relationship, and the conflict wouldn't hold together if you removed that third character."

Silhouette Romance remains open to new story types as the series romance genre evolves, Senate says: "Romance publishing seems to be changing as times change, to reflect readers' wants and needs. As for making predictions for the future? I can only predict that the one thing that will never change is a happy ending."

An average of 6 books per year are first novels. Recently published *Oh, Baby!*, Lauryn Chandler (won 1994 RITA Award for Best Traditional Romance).

HOW TO CONTACT: Does not accept unsolicited manuscripts. Query before submitting. 50% of accepted submissions are agented. On average reports on queries in 4-6 weeks. On average reports on manuscripts in 8-12 weeks. Send SASE for writer's guidelines.

TERMS: Contracts negotiated on an individual basis. Buys all rights. Manuscript is published an average of 1-2 years after acceptance. Author receives bionote in book or on jacket.

ADDRESS: 300 East 42nd Street, New York, NY 10017

PHONE: (212)682-6080

FAX: (212)682-4539

SILHOUETTE SPECIAL EDITION

Established: 1979

Romance Editor: Tara Gavin, Senior Editor

> CATEGORIES
> Contemporary Romance

The Special Edition line at Silhouette is, according to senior editor Tara Gavin, "sophisticated, substantial and packed with emotion." The contemporary romance line, which publishes six titles per month, recently celebrated the release of its 1,000th book with the publication of *The Pride of Jared MacKade*, written by *New York Time*'s bestselling writer Nora Roberts (the book is also Roberts' 80th book for Silhouette).

Silhouette Special Edition books "explore issues that heighten the drama of living and loving," Gavin says, "and the goal is to create a compelling romantic tale. Our readers look to Silhouette Special Edition to provide stories they can identify with, but have a depth and dimension that take them away from the mundane world of everyday cares and worries and into the realm of happily ever after."

Silhouette is open to new writers and is eager to publish the work of first-time authors. "We're proud of the fact that many of our now-established authors made their debut with us," Gavin says. "We're dedicated to continuing our record of finding the stars of tomorrow, today. Any month in the year readers will find new names in each of the lines." Once a year, Silhouette presents readers with Premiere, a cross-line promotion that showcases the work of a debuting author in each of their different lines.

The Special Edition line provides readers with longer stories (75,000-80,000 words) than a typical series romance. This allows writers to explore their characters more fully and perhaps even introduce subtle subplots. These subplots can be used to add more impact to the story, Gavin says, but they must always further or parallel the love story that's developing throughout the book.

First and foremost in the mind of a writer should be Silhouette Special Edition's goal, which is to please the reader and give her exactly what she wants to read. "Our goal is to meet our readers' expectations when they purchase our books—not only meet them, but in fact exceed them," Gavin says. "The readers are the ones plunking down their hard-earned money, and we want to be able to assure them that when they purchase a Silhouette novel they will receive an exciting, compelling, involving romantic book. We look for manuscripts that will help us fulfill that promise."

Gavin prefers to receive queries from interested writers, which should be accompanied by a short synopsis of the book. They do not accept unsolicited manuscripts, however, nor will they accept multiple submissions. "We will request further material if we feel the work is indeed suitable for our lines," Gavin says.

Readers must be able to identify with the characters in Special Edition books. They are contemporary romances, and plots can range from the innovative to the traditional. The romantic tension can be subtle or impassioned. There are few things Gavin finds unacceptable in Special Edition titles, but she does point out a couple of scenarios that readers have an aversion to. "Readers seem to have a bit of bias against heroes and heroines in the arts," she observes, "and a beginning writer may want to stay away from stories with those elements. I also feel that land development stories have seen their day. Topics that seem to be in vogue right now are more family-oriented stories, or twists on classic plots that traditionally have been satisfying to readers. What is always in vogue is a good, strong, compelling love story that leaves readers feeling hopeful and delighted by a wonderful happy ending."

Gavin is adamant about writers knowing the market they're submitting to, and knowing it well. "The best piece of advice I can give to any writer is to study the market," she says. "It is very helpful to me as an editor to work with an author who is aware of what is going on in the marketplace. See what is out there in bookstores, study books by bestselling writers—past as well as the present titles. Read as many books as possible, especially in the lines you feel best suit your particular style.

The romance market is an ever-evolving, dynamic market and a constant challenge. Reading just one or two books may not prepare an author very well for meeting that challenge."

Silhouette believes in career development for their writers as witnessed by the success of many of their authors, including the earlier mentioned Nora Roberts, who published her 80th book with Silhouette, and Diana Palmer, who recently presented her 60th book to Silhouette readers. Gavin looks for writers who can deliver books on a regular basis in order to build a following. "Maintaining a steady publishing schedule helps bring an author's work to the attention of the readership," she says. Once readers find an author they love, they'll come back again . . . and again . . . and again. Getting strong, good books out in a timely fashion is one of the best things a writer can do to gain an audience's loyalty.

With a roster of both new and established writers and a legion of loyal fans, Gavin predicts a happily ever after scenario for not only the characters in Special Edition books but for the romance market as well. "The growth within the romance industry in the last 15 years has been amazing," she says enthusiastically. "We're looking forward to a great future with new books by exciting, talented writers who will create the next 1,000 books in all our lines."

An average of 6 books per year are first novels.

HOW TO CONTACT: Does not accept unsolicited manuscripts. Query before submitting. 50% of accepted submissions are agented. On average reports on queries in 4-6 weeks. On average reports on manuscripts in 8-12 weeks. Send SASE for writer's guidelines.

TERMS: Contracts negotiated on an individual basis. Buys all rights. Manuscript is published an average of 1-2 years after acceptance. Author receives bionote in book or on jacket.

ADDRESS: 300 East 42nd Street, New York, NY 10017

PHONE: (212)682-6080

FAX: (212)682-4539

SILHOUETTE YOURS TRULY

Established: 1979

Romance Editors: Melissa Senate, Senior Editor; Malle Vallik, Editor

---

CATEGORIES
Contemporary Romance, Humorous

"The whole concept of Yours Truly is that some kind of written communication starts the story." Tone can be light and humorous or emotional and heartrending. Length of a Yours Truly submission should be 55,000 to 60,000 words.

Taboo: Paranormal stories. An average of 6 books per year are first novels. Recently published *Male for Sale*, Tiffany White.

HOW TO CONTACT: Query before submitting. 50% of accepted submissions are agented. On average reports on queries in 4-6 weeks. On average reports on manuscripts in 8-12 weeks. Send SASE for writer's guidelines.

TERMS: Contracts negotiated on an individual basis. Buys all rights. Manuscript is published an average of 1-2 years after acceptance. Author receives bionote in book or on jacket.

ADDRESS: 300 East 42nd Street, New York, NY 10017

PHONE: (212)682-6080

FAX: (212)682-4539

WARNER BOOKS

Romance Editors: None at press time. Address correspondence to Jessica Papin, Editorial Assistant

---

CATEGORIES
Contemporary Romance, Historical

Warner books looks for books they feel will appeal to the mainstream romance reader.

Advice to writers: "Read Warner books to see what makes us unique and what we mean by a non-series romance."

Publishes 15 mass market paperback books per year. Recently published *Wives of Bowie Stone*, Maggie Osborne (won Award of Excellence from Colorado Romance Writers and nominated for 1994 RITA for Best

Book of the Year); *The Veil*, Helen Mittermeyer; *Shield's Lady*, Jayne
Ann Krentz.

HOW TO CONTACT: Does not accept unsolicited manuscripts. **Accepts
agented submissions only.** 100% of accepted submissions are agented.

TERMS: Contracts negotiated on an individual basis. Manuscript is published an average of 12-18 months after acceptance. Author receives
bionote in book or on jacket. Author receives 20 copies of book;
additional copies available at a 40% discount.

ADDRESS: 1271 Avenue of the Americas, New York, NY 10020

PHONE: (212)522-5054

FAX: (212)522-7990

SECTION IV

Agents

♥ ♥ ♥

Finding and Working With a Romance Agent

DENISE MARCIL

*O*ne of the most important decisions you'll make in your career as a professional writer is choosing your literary agent. The agent is the author's business partner who handles the business, planning, career moves, strategies and problems. Having an agent allows you to do your job, which is to write. Few writers are good business people, and they usually don't even want to handle these situations. Virtually all published romance writers will agree that the right agent is essential to your success.

Romance represents almost 50 percent of all paperback publishing. It's here to stay, but it's constantly changing. Some years, it's flush and new authors are sought. Other years, it's tight, and all authors scramble for fewer publishing slots, advances, promotion and publicity dollars.

WHO NEEDS AN AGENT AND WHY?

New writers ask, "Do I need an agent?" I think any author of commercial fiction or nonfiction needs an agent. Most authors find it difficult to break into the market without one. Certainly, an author would want an agent to negotiate a contract with a publisher, even if the author has approached a publisher alone and received an offer. Why? Because the agent *may* be able to increase the advance and royalties, and the agent almost certainly will be able to improve other terms in the contract which may prove critical down the road.

Another reason to have an agent is that there is a *psychological* edge to an objective second opinion from a person who enjoys a good reputation with editors. For example, it's much different if *I* call an editor who has bought books from me and say, "I went to a conference in Florida this weekend and discovered a terrific novelist. I read the manuscript on the plane on the way home, and it's the *best* I've read in six months." If you were to send the same manuscript to the same editor cold, you wouldn't receive the same attention, and it might not even get read.

Another benefit of an agent is that we know the market. This is one of the most important advantages we provide. Agents know which houses and which specific editors are buying books, who's starting new lines, or who really needs a book to fill in a slot on an upcoming schedule. Agents know what publishers are buying and what they are paying. Knowing the range of advances and the royalty scale that each house gives, an agent is best prepared to negotiate on your behalf. The boilerplate contract that the publisher sends to an author is written to benefit the publisher. However, most writers don't realize that it's negotiable. Agents know where contract soft points are and can see that they are changed to benefit you.

Essentially, agents have greater bargaining power because they represent lots of authors. Editors want to deal with us because we generally have the best and most publishable material. Editors and agents develop relationships over the years, and an editor wants to be the first person who comes to the agent's mind when he or she begins to submit a manuscript. It's a competitive business.

Agents build relationships with editors over lunches, drinks, and endless phone calls, and by the process of submitting proposals to them and negotiating their acceptance. Agents discover which editors share their tastes in fiction. I know not only which editors buy romance but more importantly, their preferences in matters such as sensual stories or humorous ones, and American settings to European ones. Some editors like traditional romances; others are piqued by the unique and offbeat. As I read a manuscript, I think of *specific* editors who I think might like it. I have a list of editors I know and like and who know and like me, and it is them I first consider. I also consider who would be the *right* match for specific authors. Sometimes book ideas occur to these editors and they, sharing my likes and trusting my instincts, call me to match an author I represent to their idea.

WHAT AGENTS DO

Agents negotiate better contract terms for authors. They not only improve existing terms but can add unusual rights for authors, such as copy and jacket design approval, or at least consultation. Other special rights that can be negotiated include bestseller bonuses or advertising and promotion guarantees. Recently, one of my romance authors asked me to request *triple* the standard number of free author copies that the contract provided. She also wanted 75 free copies of the jacket. Because I knew that this author is an effective self-promoter and that those books and jackets would be used to sell more books, I was able to convince the publisher to agree. Few authors know their editors to say nothing of publishers that well, or what aspects of a contract are negotiable. That is our specialty; yours is writing. It's in your interest to leave the business aspects of selling your book to your agent. You would be doing yourself a disservice otherwise.

Agents can also handle some *subsidiary rights* that would otherwise be retained by the publisher. These are ancillary rights associated with the sale of a book, such as British and translation rights, audio and video and electronic rights, and magazine serial rights, to name just a few. All publishing houses have subsidiary rights departments that work like in-house agents selling these same rights, but an author's agent is usually a more effective and concerned advocate and negotiator. Also, when an agent retains subsidiary rights and sells those rights herself, the author retains *all* the income from that sale less only the agent's commission. If the publisher handles the rights, it keeps up to 50 percent of the income.

Assume your agent has marketed your book, sold it and negotiated a great deal for you. Now you are set, right? No way! Your agent must maintain contact with the publisher to make sure your book receives the attention the publisher should give it. This is not an easy task. In fact, this is how I spend most of my day. I push; I nudge; I call; I cajole; I fax editors, marketing and publicity directors, sales managers and *even* CEOs if necessary.

OTHER SERVICES

What else can an agent do for you? Say you've sold your book, it's published, sells well, and the money from royalties just rolls in, right? Wrong. Most publisher's royalty statements are shamefully lacking in information that reveals anything about a sale of a book. An agent should obtain prompt, accurate, and readable royalty statements from a publisher and show the author how to interpret the statement. An agent should request a printed reconciliation of all statements. This is a detailed accounting of a book's sales history that should, but does not appear on a royalty statement. It includes the number of copies printed and shipped, net sales, copies held in reserve against returns and current inventory. Without this extra effort on an agent's part, an author would not have a true picture of how his or her book sold.

Another detail agents handle is requesting reversion of rights on your books. When your book is no longer selling; it's not available from the warehouse and it's no longer in print, you have a right to request that the publisher either put the book back in print by printing more copies which the bookstores can order, *or* you can request that the publisher revert the rights to you and terminate the contract. Why would you want to do that? Well, at some point in time when you are a famous and successful romance author, you could resell that same book to another publisher for more money. So, your book has a second life.

WHEN TO BEGIN THE SEARCH

When do you contact an agent? First of all, if you're a new romance author, after you've completed your manuscript. The reality is it's virtually impossible for a first-time romance author to sell a book without having available a complete manuscript. Therefore, wait until your manuscript is as good as you can make it. Then start your search. If you have an offer from a publisher, even a category publisher, you'll still want an agent to negotiate the contract. The results may affect how well you do later. Consider pseudonym clauses. Few new writers know that this means that the publisher owns the pseudonym. If you'd become famous under the pseudonym and wanted to change publishers, you'd be out of luck.

FINDING AN AGENT

Do your homework. There's no use in querying agents who sell literary fiction or computer books. Research the agents. (More on this later; I'll give you sources.) The most important advice: Follow the submission instructions under the agent's listing. If it states "query only," don't send an outline. If chapters are requested, always submit consecutive chapters.

It's accepted and assumed that writers will query several agents simultaneously. State that you have done so in your query. What if you are fortunate enough to have several requests for your manuscript? Convey this in your cover letter when you send the requested manuscript. There's nothing more stimulating to an agent than reading, "I had an overwhelming response to my query, and several agents requested the manuscript."

That usually encourages a quicker reading to get a jump on the competition.

What about phoning, faxing, meeting? Remember, good agents are busy; time is our most valuable commodity. If you're a successfully published author, most agents will be happy to take your call. For newer authors or less established ones, the letter is your best bet.

READING FEES

Why would an author choose to pay a fee to an agent to read a manuscript, especially when many agents read for free?

The volume of unsolicited queries and manuscripts that agents receive is staggering. Eighty authors are about as many as I can handle. Yet, every year, more than 3,000 other writers ask for my time, expertise, advice and a promise of representation.

It is important for writers to understand the issue of compensation. Literary agencies work on small margins. Most agencies employ two to seven people including the owner. Our offices are hectic, with the phone constantly ringing while crises of one kind or another are dealt with. The agent has no time whatsoever during office hours to read manuscripts or even query letters. Rather, we read at home—nights and weekends. I even read during vacations. Am I expected to do this for free for writers I don't know, while my own clients pay me? Agents, like other business people, are in business to earn money. We may, indeed, love our work, but we need to make a living from it.

Many new writers are frustrated by rejections from nonfee agents with the comment, "Sorry, but it's not right for me." Nonfee agents can read a few pages and stop at any point, obviating the need for a considered response. This is what most of them do. Then many new writers wonder why they can't find an agent willing to read their work to say nothing of selling it.

The argument against reading fees is that they can lead to abuse, and sometimes they do. There are companies that charge hundreds of dollars with the promise of a critique and the implication of representation when none is really intended. These people are not agents, and this kind of abuse is why the AAR does not allow its members to charge fees. My reading fees, incidentally are one-quarter of what I estimate my costs to be; my income from reading fees is minimal. I read unsolicited manuscripts in hope of finding new, promising writers, not to earn money, but I want some return for my effort.

Writers concerned with the question should ask fee-charging agents what they can expect for the fee, and whether the agent will read their submission with the intention of deciding whether to represent them.

Editor's Note:

Whether you are considering the services of a fee-charging agent or a non-fee charging agent, it is always a good idea to evaluate their recent sales. An agent who regularly sells your type of manuscript will be more valuable to you than an agent who has little or no experience in your area.

Also, ask for references and check with editors the agent has worked with in the past. Ask for a *brief* idea of the quality of an agent's submissions to that editor. (If you cannot reach an editor, her assistant may be able to provide you with this information.) You can also check for complaints against an agent by contacting RWA's Professional Relations Committee. See the **Resources** section for more information.

Your agent can be either a great help or a great hinderance to your career, so research your prospects thoroughly before making a final decision and/or paying any fees.

THE RIGHT AGENT FOR YOU

This is like match-making. Agents look for certain attributes in the authors they want to represent. In my case, I look for passion in the writer's style, a distinct voice and a strong commitment to writing. I think the best writing comes from the heart. That always draws me to a writer's work. Other agents have different preferences. How do you find the right agent for you? There's a list of agents who specialize in romance later in this section. Here are seven other resources that will help.

1. You can begin by talking with other writers to find out about their agents. Some of my best clients have come through other clients' referrals.

2. Book editors: by writing to them, especially if you've had some contact or rapport, or certainly if they've made an offer on your book. An editor would rather negotiate with an agent than an author. Don't be afraid to botch the deal by bringing in an agent. It will make the editor's job easier, and she or he will appreciate this. So, ask the editor for three names of agents who *represent the type of book you write*. It's usually company policy for editors to do so.

3. Magazine editors: If you've written fiction or nonfiction for maga-

zines, they are fabulous for referrals.

4. *Literary Market Place*: This is the reference "bible" of the publishing industry. Agents are listed with some submission information.

5. *Guide to Literary Agents*: This book is published by Writer's Digest Books and is updated annually. Use this in conjunction with LMP. Many agents use these publications to advertise themselves and what they are seeking. Listings include recent sales by the agency which show the type of book an agent seeks.

6. Writer's conferences: At a conference you can meet agents, listen to them, and decide if the person represents your type of book, and if you like the agent's style and personality.

7. *Publishers Weekly*: This is the most popular trade magazine for publishing. Read it to keep up with trends. It does an annual survey feature on the romance business, and reports deals made by agents in the romance field, as well as other fields. Watch for agents handling the type of romance you write.

The following are some questions adapted from a list the Association of Authors' Representatives has available for writers. You may want to ask an agent before making a final decision:

1. Are you a member of the Association of Authors' Representatives?
2. How long have you been in business as an agent?
3. How many people does your agency employ?
4. Of the total number of employees, how many are agents, as opposed to clerical workers?
5. Do you have specialists at your agency who handle movie and television rights? Foreign rights? Do you have sub-agents or corresponding agents overseas and in Hollywood?
6. Who in your agency will actually be handling my work? Will the other staff members be familiar with my work and the status of my business at your agency? Will you oversee or at least keep me apprised of the work that your agency is doing on my behalf?
7. Do you issue an agent-author contract? May I review a specimen? And may I review the language of the agency clause that appears in contracts you negotiate for your clients?
8. What is your approach to providing editorial input and career guidance for your clients, or what would it be for me specifically?
9. How do you keep your clients informed of your activities on their

behalf? Do you regularly send them copies of publishers' rejection letters? Do you provide them with submission lists and rejection letters on request? Do you regularly, or upon request, send out updated activity reports?

10. What are your commissions for: (1) basic sales to U.S. publishers; (2) sales of movie and television rights; (3) audio and multimedia rights; (4) British and foreign translation rights?

WORKING WITH YOUR AGENT

Let's say you have an agent. How does the relationship proceed? First, you must convey your needs, questions, and anxieties (these usually surface later) to your agent. Mind reading is not one of our job skills. Do you need reports on submission, feedback from editors, your agent's response to the rejections? If so, then speak up.

Should you call, and how often? This depends on you. If you feel the need for information, feedback or an update, call; don't sit and stew.

Good communication will serve you well, especially when it comes to career planning. Your agent should guide your career, but you must articulate your aspirations. These may change. One of my top romance authors decided she also wanted to write mysteries. Decisions and planning were essential to building a mystery audience while maintaining her romance writing and her romance readers. Considerations included finding a new house and editor for the mysteries, maintaining a rapport and continuing to sign new contracts with her romance publishers, informing both publishers of each other's publishing schedules, and planning her delivery schedule.

What if you decide to change agents? Always give your agent the opportunity to respond to your needs. If you are dissatisfied, tell your agent why and what you expect, such as prompter responses to calls, better contracts, more visibility and higher sales. The worst thing you can do is to end the relationship without giving your agent the chance to respond to what you believe to be the agent's deficiencies. If you aren't satisfied with the response, then tell your agent of your decision. A letter is a coward's way out. This is a relationship and it demands the respect of personal contact. The agent also may be grateful to you for pointing out legitimate difficulties she or he wasn't aware of.

Once you've left, behave professionally. Most likely, the agent will continue to receive royalty statements and money, and control subsidiary rights on previously negotiated contracts. Badmouthing your ex-agent won't help you. Good behavior will. Word gets around; in the romance writing business, there are few secrets.

Looking at the big picture, a good agent guides an author's career. Most agents are not interested in one-shot book deals. Nor should *you* be. We help you realize your ideas and convey to you market trends and how they can help you. Good luck in finding the right agent for you!

Ten Tips For Your Next Book Deal

STEVE GILLEN

*I*f you've been published, then you've seen it before—a WHEREAS and a THEREFORE followed by eight pages of pre-printed, pedantic prose offered up by the editor as his "standard publishing contract." Other than a few tiny spaces for your name, the title of your work, and the manuscript delivery date, the bulk of it looks as though it was long ago locked down in Century Schoolbook type.

But the truth is that there is more to review than the spelling of your name, choice of title, and projected completion date, and more to negotiate than you might realize. Here are ten tips to get you started.

1. You have more leverage than you think. Editors are under ever increasing pressure to sign new titles, meet publication dates, and deliver sales results. For many of them, these factors have a direct bearing on their year-end compensation (a circumstance that can work to an author's significant bargaining advantage as year's end approaches). While there are many aspiring first-time authors out there, only a relative handful will be published. If you have attracted a contract offer, then you have already made the cut—a reasonable list of tactfully stated concerns and requested amendments will only reinforce the impression that you are a competent and thorough professional.

2. Only sell them what they intend to use. Beware of "work-for-hire" provisions, grants of "all right, title, and interest," and broadly stated grants of electronic rights. If your publisher intends to publish a hardcover edition for distribution in North America, then the grant of rights should convey North American hardcover rights only. Alternate editions can be addressed by amendment to your book contract if and when the publisher expresses an interest in publishing them.

3. Don't leave the back door standing open. It's one thing to be signed to a publishing contract, but unfortunately (and perhaps unfairly) quite another to actually be published. Editors come and go and markets change. An open-ended manuscript acceptability standard can leave you holding an unpublished manuscript. Most form contracts will require that you deliver a completed manuscript that is acceptable to the publisher in form and content. This arguably allows the publisher to reject your completed work for any reason (provided it is not acting in bad faith). You should strive for an acceptability clause that requires only that the finished manuscript conform in coverage and quality to the sample chapters provided with your prospectus or, alternatively, a clause that requires the manuscript to be professionally competent and fit for publication. You should also ask for language that obliges the publisher to provide you with detailed editorial comments and at least one opportunity to revise.

4. Don't promise what you can't deliver. Publishers usually require their authors to make certain representations and warranties about the work submitted—that it isn't libelous, that it doesn't infringe third party copyrights, and so on. Be careful that these representations apply only to work as supplied by you and not to the work of other contributors or editors. Also, we all know that every editor likes to put his mark on a work by changing the title. Be sure that you do not warrant that the title does not infringe trademark or other rights (unless, of course, it is indeed your title).

Most contracts will also require you to indemnify the publisher for any damage or cost incurred as a result of your breach of the foregoing warranties. It is reasonable for you to ask that such indemnification be limited to defects as determined by a court of competent jurisdiction and also to ask that your obligation to indemnify the publisher be capped at the total royalties and other payments you actually receive from the publisher's exploitation of your work.

5. Don't let the editor put words in your mouth. Contracts typically give the publisher the right to select an editor to edit the work. However, you can win the battle for editorial control (or at least negotiate a peace with honor) by asking that the editor's authority be limited to copyediting and changes reasonably necessary to conform the manuscript to house style and further that substantive changes not be made without your approval.

6. The copyright is yours . . . to have and to hold. U.S. Copyright law vests the copyright in the human creator at the moment the work is fixed in a tangible medium of expression—put pen to paper and the copyright is yours. Ask that the publisher register it in your name. The publisher's legitimate interests are adequately protected by an appropriate assignment of rights, and you are protected by holding all of the residual and derivative rights (not to mention having the psychic income that comes from being the record holder of a copyright—as writers, we have to take our income where we find it).

7. Don't take yourself out of the market. Watch out for the "no compete" provisions. Publishers often ask that you not publish or assist in publishing any other work that might compete. These restrictions are usually very broadly drafted and open-ended in scope. As such, they may be unenforceable as an unreasonable restraint of trade. Better, however, to try to narrow them before you sign.

8. A word about royalties. Royalties are the proverbial two birds in the bush. Far better to negotiate for non-refundable advances. In any event, know whether your royalties will be based on list price, invoice price, or net receipts. And if they are based on the latter, ask the publisher for its discount schedule and for some historical averages so that you can compare apples to apples in the event you are the happy holder of two or more contract offers.

9. Don't become an indentured servant. Some publishers still routinely include options clauses in their publishing contracts. This gives the publisher dibs on your next manuscript. Tell them that if they do a great job with the current one, you will certainly be back with the next.

10. Don't become trade bait. Publishers are merging, consolidating, and selling lists. The best thing you have going for you is the support and confidence of the editor who felt strongly enough about your manuscript to try to sign you—now, his interests parallel yours and his reputation is on the line. You lose this advantage if your book is sold to another house, so it is in your best interests to try to negotiate for the right to approve any assignment of your book contract. A great reluctance on the part of the publisher to agree should send you a signal about its own feelings of security.

Odds are, you will not prevail on all of these issues. But odds are equally as good that you will not lose on all of them either.

In any event, you will not get what you don't request. So ask away . . . at the end of the day you will have a better deal and a more informed relationship with your publisher.

♡ ♡ ♡

Please Release Me . . .
or
The Neglected Author's Lament

STEVE GILLEN

*I*t is an all too familiar scene: An author wined, dined, and dazzled with stories of a publisher's successes signs on the dotted line, giddy with the conviction that a cherished manuscript will finally roll off the high speed presses by the thousands of copies to long awaited critical acclaim and, not incidentally, financial reward. There is a flurry of editorial planning activity and then months pass, with an occasional overnight bundle from the publisher and an urgent request for the author to expedite revisions lest a critical market window be missed. Finally, the manuscript is completed and the long wait begins.

"Soon . . ." the publisher promises.

"Just a few last minute improvements . . ." the publisher asks.

And then, at some point, the process starts to sour. A change in editors, a merger, an acquisition, a list sale, disappointing results with other similar titles—the explanations are many and varied, but the results are predictable. A hopeful author's high expectations are gradually eroded by a parade of disappointing delays or slips as the publisher fails to follow through on unwritten targets. Or perhaps the book has already been published in one or more editions, but plans for the revision are dragging as the publisher's confidence flags and market share erodes.

Ultimately, an exasperated author looks back to the publishing contract, searching for the publisher's obligations and the disappointed author's recourse. Alas, there seems to be little comfort there.

But it *is* there, between the lines, where courts, concerned about a publisher's ability to use its leverage to unreasonable advantage, have found an implied obligation to deal in good faith and where they might be convinced to find an unreasonable restraint of trade. While most book deals are free from these problems, it is beneficial for authors to know what to do if they find themselves in such a situation.

TYPICAL TERMS

Let's take a look at the relevant terms in a typical book deal and see if we can find that elusive recourse.

By entering a publishing agreement, the author effectively agrees to entrust the publisher with the exclusive right to fully exploit the commercial potential of the work and agrees to take him/herself out of the market for any other similar book deal.

> **Grant of Rights.** The Author hereby grants and assigns this Work to the Publisher with the exclusive right to publish and sell the Work under its own name and under other imprints or trade names and with the exclusive right to exploit or otherwise dispose of all subsidiary rights in all countries and in all languages.
>
> **Competing Publications.** The Author agrees that during the term of this Agreement the Author will not, without the written consent of the Publisher, publish or furnish to any other publisher any work that is of a similar character on the same subject matter or that is likely to interfere with or injure the sale of the Work.

Inasmuch as most book deals are signed on the strength of an expectation and without a complete and final manuscript, the publisher generally reserves to itself broad discretion to determine publishability of that final manuscript. And this is more or less reasonable—after all, the publisher's good name and a significant financial investment are at stake.

> **Delivery.** The Author will deliver to the Publisher a complete and legible typewritten manuscript (and word-processed text-file) of the Work on or before [date], all to be satisfactory in form and content to the Publisher in its sole and absolute discretion.

The publisher does, however, typically agree to promptly put the manuscript into type and to timely publish the resulting work once its acceptance standard has been met, although editorial control, the details of printing and binding, pricing, and marketing are typically reserved to the publisher—all areas where it brings a special expertise and valuable resources to the relationship.

Publishing Details. When the manuscript is complete and accepted by the Publisher and is in proper form for use as copy by a printer, the Publisher will proceed to publish the same in such style and manner of paper, printing, and binding, and at such prices and under such titles as it considers most appropriate. From time to time during the life of this Agreement, the Publisher will print and publish the Work and the revisions thereof as long as there is, in its opinion, a reasonable demand for the same. The Publisher will keep the market supplied and make the Work and revisions thereof known by advertising and by giving copies to instructors for their examination and consideration. The Publisher reserves the right to publish or cause to be published other works even though such other works may compete with the Work.

In contemplation of success, the publisher generally further agrees to give the author what amounts to a first option to prepare a revision on substantially the same terms, though the publisher also typically reserves the right to determine when and if the work will be revised for subsequent editions.

Revisions. The Author will revise the Work when and if called upon by the Publisher to do so. The provisions of this Agreement (except where expressly stated otherwise) shall apply to each revision of the Work by the Author as though that revision were the Work being published for the first time under this Agreement. Should the Author decline or neglect or be unable by reason of death or otherwise to revise the Work, the Publisher may have the revision prepared and charge the cost of so doing (whether fee or royalty) against the Author's royalties.

The *letter* of the contract leaves all of these critical decisions to the publisher:

- Whether to publish
- Under what title
- In what manner and style
- At what price
- With what promotion and marketing
- Whether and when to revise

However, the courts have said that the spirit of the contract requires those decisions to be made in good faith, taking into consideration industry custom and practice.

THE OBLIGATION TO DEAL IN GOOD FAITH

In every contract whereby rights under a copyright are transferred or licensed, there is an implied covenant that neither party shall do anything which will have the effect of destroying or injuring the right of the other party to receive the fruits of the contract, which means that in every contract there exists an implied covenant of good faith and fair dealing. Moreover, at least where the grantor (author) is to receive royalties measured by the grantee's (publisher's) exploitation of the work, certain additional covenants on the part of the grantee are implied. In such circumstances, there is an implied covenant that the grantee will use reasonable efforts to make the work as productive as the circumstances warrant. Even where the publishing agreement reserves to the publisher the sole right to determine the number of copies to be printed and the advertising budget, the publisher is nonetheless obliged to undertake a first printing and to provide an advertising budget adequate to give the book a reasonable chance of market success. To read the contract without such an implied covenant would be to destroy the fruits of the agreement for the author, a construction resisted by the courts.

By logical extension, this supports the proposition that the publisher has an implied obligation to preserve the value of an author's work by either committing to a timely revision or releasing those revision rights to the author (provided that this can be done in a way that does not impair the publisher's ability to exploit those rights it lawfully retains). Such an argument played a significant role recently in producing a $3.2 million settlement for seven teacher/authors of a K-8 mathematics textbook published by Merrill Publishing in the 1980s. The genesis of the dispute was the acquisition of Merrill by Macmillan and Macmillan's subsequent decision to abandon the scheduled revision of the math series and at the same time to insist on holding the authors to their no compete commitments—patently unfair and ultimately unsustainable.

RESTRAINT OF TRADE

Where the issue is a publisher's reluctance to move forward with the timely revision of an existing work, there may also be a state law claim that the no-compete provision of the publishing agreement is unreasonably broad (and thus unenforceable) insofar as it might operate to preclude an author from preparing or assisting in the preparation of a potentially competing work that would not be published until the useful life of the existing edition has expired. The state law claim is premised on a common law restraint of trade theory most commonly encountered in employment cases or in connection with the sale of a business. The reasonableness of these types of no-compete provisions has generally been determined on an ad hoc basis and it is therefore difficult to predict a specific outcome with any degree of certainty. Nonetheless, the specter of a state law restraint of trade challenge to the publisher's no-compete provision might provide additional leverage in striking a reasonable compromise.

More imposing (as a result of the availability of treble damages) is the possibility, albeit remote, of a Sherman Act challenge. Such a claim would require evidence of an adverse market impact, which might be difficult to establish in the context of a one-author/one-publisher dispute. However, in a truly egregious case where it can be established that the publisher routinely seeks to enforce these clauses against all its authors even as their books are not revised and permitted to go out-of-stock and out-of-print, a Sherman Act challenge is within the realm of possibility. While there is a dearth of case law applying the Sherman Act to no-compete provisions, this approach has seen limited support in cases where one party obtains a large number of restrictive covenants not to compete from employees or franchisees.

PRESCRIPTION

The typical publishing enterprise is much like a marriage—recognized and respected by law, but with little remedy beyond dissolution should the parties lose interest in maintaining the relationship. The author contributes scholarship, creativity, and intellectual labor. The publisher advises, reviews, invests, and markets. If both parties live up to their respective obligations, and if the resulting work finds a receptive audience, then a contribution will have been made to art, science, or education from which both stand to profit and the union will prosper. If, however, either party disappoints the other, then the odds are good that neither will realize its expectations. While the letter of a publishing contract lays out the publisher's obligations in general terms (leaving a good deal to the publisher's discretion) and shows the publisher's corporate face, the spirit of that agreement is best revealed in the human face of an editorial champion who believed enough in the author and the work to see them signed.

If (or more likely, when) that editorial champion moves on to another assignment, another list, or another publisher, the author may find it necessary to help the publisher recall the true spirit of the deal. A letter from counsel experienced in publishing matters can go a long way in that regard. But if a new champion fails to step forward from the editorial rank and file, then a shotgun marriage to a reluctant stand in is probably not the path to happiness. In such event, your refrain should be "please, release me . . ."

All of this is not to say that only authors suffer disappointment from their publishing deals. It is perhaps more often the case that publishers are left standing at the altar by once enthusiastic authors who have since moved on to other loves and distractions. And it is an editor's truism that many must be signed to publish few. Nonetheless, when the ardor has cooled it is generally the publisher who holds the marital property and an author must pound the pulpit to get attention.

♡ ♡ ♡ ♡

THE AHEARN AGENCY, INC.

Established: 1992 • 25 clients

Romance Agent: Pamela G. Ahearn

> SPECIALIZES IN
> Contemporary Romance, Historical, Paranormal, Regency, Romantic
> Horror, Romantic Mystery, Romantic Suspense

Agency is seeking both new and established writers. Offers written contract, binding for 1 year. Author must give 30 days notice to terminate contract.

Recent sales: *Someone Like You* by Susan Sawyer to Avon; *The Rose of Rowdene* by Kate Moore to Avon; *Home Again* by Linda Shectzer to Berkley. Only charges reading fee to new authors who've never been represented before, ranging from $125-$400 depending upon book's length. Author receives 3-5 pages critique. Fee is non-refundable. 10% of business is derived from reading fees. Payment of criticism fee does not guarantee representation of writer. Usually meets new clients at conventions and conferences. Query first before submitting manuscript.

Seeks: "Strong characters, quality writing, good conflict, original ideas."

Attends the following conferences/conventions: RWA National and various regional conferences. Will be attending mystery conferences as well in 1996.

Advice: "Keep trying and don't give up!"

ADDRESS: 2021 Pine Street, New Orleans, LA 70118
PHONE: (504)861-8395
FAX: (504)866-6434

JAMES ALLEN, LITERARY AGENT

Established: 1974 • Signatory of WGA • 40 clients

Romance Agent: James Allen

> SPECIALIZES IN
> Contemporary Romance, Fantasy, Historical, Humorous, Romantic Horror, Romantic Suspense

Agency prefers to work with established writers, mostly through referrals. Offers written contract. Author must give 30 days notice to terminate contract.

Recent sales: *Wish List* by Jeane Renick to HarperMonogram; *Undercover Vows* by Judi Lind to Harlequin Intrigue; *Down to a Sunless Sea* by David Poyer to St. Martin's Press.

"I reserve the right to pass along costs of (1) photocopying full-length novel, (2) postage for airmail distribution of copies for translation-rights marketing, and (3) buying copies at author's discount for sub-rights marketing, as needed. In practice, only (3) is applied, and that, usually, is deducted from income rather than billed."

Usually obtains clients upon recommendations from others. Send outline or proposal initially.

Seeks: "The kind of romance I'm looking for is made saleable by the same criteria that makes any good writing saleable: a good story well told, with believable, three-dimensional characters."

Attends the following conferences/conventions: California Writers' Club conference in Asilomar on the Monterey Peninsula, and Writing On The Sea, a cruise-ship conference to the Bahamas.

Advice: "As an agent, I do not just sell books, I seek to build writing careers. Therefore, though of course category romance has its place, in new clients I seek authors of books that can stand, as books, on their own, without the framework of a line's requirements."

ADDRESS: P.O. Box 278, Milford, PA 18337
PHONE: (717)296-6205
FAX: (717)296-7266

MARCIA AMSTERDAM AGENCY

Established: 1970 • Signatory of WGA • 30 clients

Romance Agent: Marcia Amsterdam

> SPECIALIZES IN
> Contemporary Romance, Futuristic, Historical, Romantic Horror,
> Romantic Suspense, Time Travel

Agency is seeking both new and established writers. Offers written contract, binding for 1 year. Author must give 60 days notice to terminate contract. Usually obtains clients upon recommendations from others, at conventions and conferences, or through query letters.

ADDRESS: 41 W. 82 St., New York, NY 10024-5613
PHONE: (212)873-4945

JOSH BEHAR LITERARY AGENCY

Established: 1992 • 12 clients

Romance Agent: Josh Behar

> SPECIALIZES IN
> Contemporary Romance, Romantic Horror, Romantic Suspense, Time
> Travel

Agency prefers to work with established writers, mostly through referrals. Offers criticism service. There is no charge for criticism service. Critiques are written by Josh Behar. Usually obtains new clients through query letters and by reading unsolicited manuscripts. Send query and 1 sample chapter. Agency represents all genres.

Attends the following conferences/conventions: Mystery writers conferences, science fiction writers conferences.

ADDRESS: Empire State Building, 350 Fifth Avenue, Suite 3304, New York, NY 10118
PHONE: (212)826-4386

THE BARBARA BOVA LITERARY AGENCY

Established: 1974 • 35 clients

Romance Agent: Barbara Bova

> SPECIALIZES IN
> Contemporary Romance, Historical, Multicultural, Over 45, Romantic
> Horror, Romantic Suspense, Time Travel

Agency prefers to work with established writers, mostly through referrals. *This agency is not currently seeking new clients.* Usually obtains clients upon recommendations from others. Query first before submitting manuscript.

Attends the following conferences/conventions: ABA, science fiction conventions, Romance Conference in Naples.

ADDRESS: 3951 Gulfshore Blvd., Naples, FL 33940
PHONE: (813)649-7237
FAX: (941)649-0757

BRANDT & BRANDT LITERARY AGENTS, INC.

Established: 1919 • Member: AAR • Signatory of WGA • 200 clients

Romance Agent: Charles Schlessiger

> SPECIALIZES IN
> Contemporary Romance, Humorous, Romantic Suspense

Agency is seeking both new and established writers. Offers written contract. If there will be charges, they are discussed with author first. Usually obtains new clients in a variety of ways including recommendations from others, at conferences and conventions, and solicitation. Send outline and 3 sample chapters.

Attends the following conferences/conventions: Romance Writers of America conferences.

ADDRESS: 1501 Broadway, New York, NY 10036
PHONE: (212)840-5760
FAX: (212)840-5776

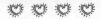

PEMA BROWNE LTD

Established: 1966 • Member: AAR • Signatory of WGA • 25 clients

Romance Agent: Perry Browne

> SPECIALIZES IN
>
> Contemporary Romance, Futuristic, Historical, Humorous, Multicultural, Paranormal, Regency, Time Travel

Agency is seeking both new and established writers. Offers written contract. Author must give 30 days notice to terminate contract.

Recent sales: *Taste of the Ton* by Dorothea Donley to Kensington; *Sleeping Tigers* by Sandra Dark to Silhouette; *Wings of Smoke* by Sandra Dark to Silhouette. Usually obtains clients upon recommendations from others, through query letters and by referrals from editors.

Seeks: "Uniqueness in style and storytelling."

Advice: "Consulting a freelance editor from LMP would be helpful for making a manuscript professional."

ADDRESS: Pine Rd HCR Box 104B, Neversink, NY 12765
PHONE: (914)985-2936
FAX: (914)985-7635

MARIA CARVAINIS AGENCY, INC.

Established: 1977 • Member: AAR • Signatory of WGA • 30 clients

Romance Agent: Maria Carvainis

> SPECIALIZES IN
>
> Agency handles all types of romance.

Agency is seeking both new and established writers. Offers written contract, binding for 2 years. Author must give 30 days notice to terminate contract.

Recent sales: 3 contemporary novels by Sandra Brown to Warner; 3 historicals by Mary Balogh to Berkley; 3 category romances by Kristine

Rolofson to Harlequin. Charges author for foreign postage and bulk photocopying. Usually obtains clients upon recommendations from others. Query first before submitting manuscript.

Seeks: "Strong and original story concepts with engaging characters."

Attends the following conferences/conventions: ABA, Novelists Inc., RWA conferences, London Book Fair.

ADDRESS: 235 West End Avenue, New York, NY 10023
PHONE: (212)580-1559
FAX: (212)877-3486

CISKE & DIETZ LITERARY AGENCY

Established: 1993 • 20 clients

Romance Agent: Francine Ciske

> SPECIALIZES IN
> Contemporary Romance, Futuristic, Historical, Inspirational, Regency, Romantic Suspense, Time Travel

Agency is seeking both new and established writers. Author must give written notice to terminate contract. "We ask that clients provide all copies of manuscripts for submission." Agent usually initiates contact with client. Send query and 1 sample chapter.

Seeks: "The best advice I can give regarding making a manuscript saleable is for the writer to read the type of books they want to write. Also attend RWA workshops and conferences, and join a good critique group."

Attends the following conferences/conventions: RWA conferences.

Advice: "It is important to mention the line you are targeting. We are not looking for fiction manuscripts with romantic elements woven in. We are looking for category and single title contemporary romance up to 125,000 words."

ADDRESS: P.O. Box 555, Neenah, WI 54957
PHONE: (414)722-5944

RUTH COHEN, INC. LITERARY AGENT

Established: 1982 • Member: AAR • 65-75 clients

Romance Agent: Ruth Cohen

> SPECIALIZES IN
> Contemporary Romance, Historical, Romantic Mystery

Agency prefers to work with established writers, mostly through referrals. Offers written contract, binding for 1 year. Author must give 30 days notice to terminate contract. Charges author for photocopying and mailings to foreign countries. Usually obtains clients upon recommendations from others. Usually meets new clients at conventions and conferences. Send query and 2 sample chapters.

Seeks: "A manuscript about characters who are appealing and well-defined and writing that is carefully edited and deftly and vividly presented."

ADDRESS: P.O. Box 7626, Menlo Park, CA 94025
PHONE: (415)854-2054

FRANCES COLLIN, LITERARY AGENT

Established: 1948 • Member: AAR • 100 clients

> SPECIALIZES IN
> Fantasy, Historical, Multicultural, Reincarnation, Romantic Horror, Romantic Mystery, Romantic Suspense, Time Travel, Vampire

Agent prefers to work with established writers, mostly through referrals. Offers written contract. Author must give 30 days notice to terminate contract. Charges author for photocopying, postage on special mailings. Usually obtains new clients through recommendations. Send outline and 1-2 sample chapters.

Seeks: "Good writing, strong characters, well developed plot."

ADDRESS: P.O. Box 33, Wayne, PA 19087-0033
PHONE: (610)254-0555

RICHARD CURTIS ASSOCIATES, INC.

Established: 1970 • Member: AAR • Signatory of WGA • 125 clients

Romance Agent: Richard Curtis

> SPECIALIZES IN
> Agency handles all types of romance.

Agency prefers to work with established writers, mostly through referrals. Author must give immediate notice to terminate contract.

Recent sales: *Notorious* and 2 untitled novels by Janet Dailey to HarperCollins; *Tigress in the Night* by Jennifer Blake to Fawcett; 3 untitled novels by Linda Ladd to Penguin Topaz.

Charges author for some extraordinary expenses such as express mail. Usually obtains clients upon recommendations from others. Query first before submitting manuscript.

Seeks: "Factual detail making writing rich."

Attends the following conferences/conventions: RWA annual conference

ADDRESS: 171 East 74th Street, New York, NY 10021
PHONE: (212)772-7363

ANITA DIAMANT AGENCY

Established: 1922 • Member: AAR • Signatory of WGA • 125 clients

Romance Agents: Robin Rue, Ashley Kraas

> SPECIALIZES IN
> Contemporary Romance, Historical, New Age, Regency, Romantic Horror, Romantic Suspense, Young Adult

Agency is seeking both new and established writers. Offers written contract, binding for 90 days. Author must give 30 days notice to terminate contract.

Recent sales: *All That Glitters* by V.C. Andrews to Pocket Books; *Jacqueline Kennedy Onassis* by Lester David to Carol; *Dream Man* by Linda Howard to Pocket. Query first before submitting manuscript.

ADDRESS: 310 Madison Ave., New York, NY 10017
PHONE: (212)687-1122

DIAMOND LITERARY AGENCY, INC.

Established: 1982

Romance Agent: Pat Dalton

> SPECIALIZES IN
> Contemporary Romance, Futuristic, Ghost, Historical, Humorous, Multicultural, Over 45, Paranormal, Regency, Romantic Horror, Romantic Mystery, Romantic Suspense, Time Travel, Vampire

Agency prefers to work with established writers, mostly through referrals. Offers written contract. "We charge a $15 reading fee if author is not yet published." The fee is refundable if published. Charges author $180 annual retainer if earnings under $5,000 in past year or $10,000 in past two years. Refunded out of commissions. 1% of business is derived from reading fees. Payment of criticism fee does not guarantee representation of writer. Usually obtains clients upon recommendations from others. Usually meets new clients at conventions and conferences.

Attends the following conferences/conventions: Novelist Inc., Rocky Mountain Fiction Writers, RWA conferences.

ADDRESS: 1932 Irving Avenue, San Francisco, CA 94122
PHONE: (303)759-0291

DOYEN LITERARY SERVICES, INC.

• 50 plus clients

Romance Agent: B.J. Doyen, President

> **SPECIALIZES IN**
> Historical, Humorous, Romantic Suspense

Agency prefers to work with established writers, mostly through referrals. Offers written contract, binding for 1 year. Usually obtains new clients through query letters.

ADDRESS: 1931 660th Street, Newell, IA 50568
PHONE: (712)272-3300

EDEN LITERARY AGENCY

Established: 1992 • 84 clients

Romance Agent: Karen Eden

> **SPECIALIZES IN**
> Contemporary Romance, Erotic, Multicultural, New Age, Romantic Horror, Romantic Mystery, Time Travel

Agency is seeking both new and established writers. Offers written contract, binding for 1 year. Author must give 60 days notice to terminate contract. Charges author for postage, copying, envelopes and telephone calls. "It's in our contract and extremely straight forward." Usually obtains clients by reading unsolicited manuscripts. Send full manuscript.

Attends the following conferences/conventions: American Booksellers Association, Romance Writers of America, New York City Street Bookfair, Rocky Mountain Book Festival, SCBWI—National, Sacramento Reads Book Festival.

Advice: "Agents are structured to help authors. Keep in mind if an author knows what an agent is looking for, there is a great chance that things will work. Always, always, always, make sure your material is sent in your most perfect form possible. Never send something you are not proud of. To be given serious attention and reviewed with an advantage, follow the guidelines given by the publishing house."

ADDRESS: P.O. Box 11033 - 1705 14th Street, 321, Boulder, CO 80301
PHONE: (303)441-7877

ETHAN ELLENBERG LITERARY AGENCY

Established: 1984 • 65 clients

Romance Agent: Ethan Ellenberg

> SPECIALIZES IN
> Contemporary Romance, Historical

Agency is seeking both new and established writers. Offers written contract. Author must give 90 days notice to terminate contract.

Recent sales: *Jake's Way* by Angela Benson to Zebra; *A Secret Yearning* by Debra Cowan to Dell; *One Step Away* by Kathleen Kane to St. Martin's Press; *A Margin of Error* by Laura Hayden to Denise Little Presnets/Pinnacle; *The Loves of Ruby Dee* by Curtiss Ann Matlock to Avon; *Breakfast in Bed* by Peggy Moreland to Silhouette Desire.

Charges author for direct cost of submissions only—copying, finished books, and postage. Usually obtains clients upon recommendations from others. Send outline and 3 sample chapters.

Seeks: Manuscripts "having great characters, good plot, and a truly moving romance."

Attends the following conferences/conventions: Novelist, Inc., ABA, RWA National.

Advice: "Create a magical love story and study the genre. There is always room for great storytellers."

ADDRESS: 548 Broadway, #5E, New York, NY 10012
PHONE: (212)431-4554
FAX: (212)941-4652

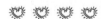

ANN ELMO AGENCY, INC.

Established: 1945 • Member: AAR

Romance Agent: Lettie Lee, Director

> SPECIALIZES IN
> Contemporary romance

Agency prefers to work with established writers, mostly through referrals. Offers written contract. Usually obtains clients upon recommendations from others.

Attends the following conferences/conventions: ABA, RWA conferences.

ADDRESS: 60 E 42nd Street, New York, NY 10165
PHONE: (212)661-2880
FAX: (212)661-2883

FARBER LITERARY AGENCY, INC.

Established: 1991 • Signatory of WGA

Romance Agent: Ann Farber

> SPECIALIZES IN
> Contemporary Romance, Historical, Humorous, Multicultural, Over 45, Romantic Horror, Romantic Suspense, Young Adult

Agency is seeking both new and established writers. Offers written contract, binding for 1 year. Author must give 1 month notice to terminate contract. Usually obtains new clients by word of mouth.

ADDRESS: 14 E. 75th Street, #2E, New York, NY 10021
PHONE: (212)861-7075

JOYCE A. FLAHERTY

Established: 1980 • Member: AAR • 50 clients

Romance Agent: Joyce A. Flaherty

> SPECIALIZES IN
> Contemporary Romance, Fantasy, Ghost, Historical, Regency

Agency prefers to work with established writers, mostly through referrals.

Recent sales: *Everlasting* by Charleen Cross to Pocket Books; *Shawnee Moon* by Judith E. French to Avon. Charges author marketing fee of $50 each book for unpublished book author or if writing in a different field. Usually obtains clients upon recommendations from others, at conventions and conferences and through query letters. Send query and 1 sample chapter.

ADDRESS: 816 Lynda Ct., St. Louis, MO 63122
PHONE: (314)966-3057

FLANNERY, WHITE & STONE

Established: 1987 • 20 clients

Romance Agent: Robin Ann Barrett

> SPECIALIZES IN
> Contemporary Romance, Romantic Horror, Romantic Mystery, Romantic Suspense, Young Adult

Agency is seeking both new and established writers. Offers written contract. Author must give 30 days notice to terminate contract.

Recent sales: *More 6 Minute Mysteries* by Don Wulffson to RGA Lowell House; *Choose Your Own Nightmare* by Don Wulffson to RGA Lowell House; *Waking From the Dream* by Detong Cho Yin to Charles Tuttle, Inc. Charges reading fee. Offers criticism service. A report is prepared, breaking down the manuscript into plot, character, dialogue, style, techniques or any other significant areas that need to be addressed. The analysis, which is done by a staff of editors, lets the author know what works or doesn't work in her manuscript, and also addresses the marketability of the book. 20% of business is derived from reading fees and criticism service. Payment of criticism fee does not guarantee representation of writer. Usually obtains new clients through query letters. Send query and sample chapters.

Seeks: Manuscripts "having well-rounded, believable characters and a plot which, even though the reader will know how it ends, keeps the reader on the edge of her seat."

Attends the following conferences/conventions: ABA, Rocky Mountain Booksellers Convention.

Advice: "It is important to establish which market you are writing for and to adhere to that market's guidelines. Plus, the appearance of the manuscript is very important, try to make it look as professional as possible."

ADDRESS: 1675 Larimer Street, # 410, Denver, CO 80202
PHONE: (303)571-4001
FAX: (303)534-0577

THE FOGELMAN LITERARY AGENCY

Established: 1990 • Member: AAR • Signatory of WGA • 100 clients

Romance Agents: Evan Fogelman/Linda Kruger

> SPECIALIZES IN
> Contemporary Romance, Historical, Romantic Suspense

Agency prefers to work with established writers, mostly through referrals. Offers written contract. Usually obtains clients upon recommendations from others. Query first before submitting manuscript.
Seeks: "Dialogue-driven story."
Attends the following conferences/conventions: RWA national

ADDRESS: 7515 Greenville Avenue, # 712, Dallas, TX 75231
PHONE: (214)361-9956
FAX: (214)361-9553

FORTHWRITE LITERARY AGENCY

Established: 1989 • 50 book clients

Romance Agent: Wendy L. Zhorne

> SPECIALIZES IN
> Historical, Regency, Romantic Horror, Romantic Suspense

Agency prefers to work with established writers, mostly through referrals. Offers written contract, binding for 12 months.

Recent sales: *Larry Wilde, King of Humor* by Larry Wilde to Multimedia Development Corporation; *Self Esteem in the Workplace* by Jack Canfield to McGraw Hill; *101 Ways to Market Yourself* by Raleigh Pinsky to Avon Books. Usually meets new clients at conventions and conferences. Send outline and sample chapters.

Seeks: "Comprehension of genre and a well-read author with impeccable writing skills."

Attends the following conferences/conventions: ABA, ALA, Frankfurt, Win-Win, SCWC, WNB-LA, NSA-GLAC, Learning Annex, CBA.

Advice: "Read in your genre."

ADDRESS: 3579 E. Foothill Blvd, 327, Pasadena, CA 91107
PHONE: (818)798-0793
FAX: (818)798-5653

JAY GARON-BROOKE ASSOC., INC.

Established: 1950 • Member: AAR • Signatory of WGA

Romance Agent: Nancy Coffey

> SPECIALIZES IN
> Contemporary Romance, Fantasy, Futuristic, Ghost, Historical, Humorous, Multicultural, New Age, Over 45, Romantic Mystery, Romantic Horror, Romantic Suspense, Young Adult

Agency is seeking both new and established writers. Offers written contract, binding for 3-5 years. Offers criticism service. "We offer criticism service to our clients only, at no charge. Authors receive monthly reports." 0% of business is derived from criticism service. Usually obtains clients upon recommendations from others. Usually obtains new clients through query letters.

Attends the following conferences/conventions: ABA, Frankfurt Book Fair.

ADDRESS: 101 West 55th Street, Suite 5K, New York, NY 10019
PHONE: (212)581-8300

THE GISLASON AGENCY

Established: 1994 • 12 clients

Romance Agent: Barbara J. Gislason

> SPECIALIZES IN
> Contemporary Romance, Fantasy, Futuristic, Historical, Humorous,
> Regency, Romantic Suspense, Time Travel

Agency is seeking both new and established writers. Offers written contract, binding for 6 months. Charges author for postage and manuscript copying. Usually obtains clients upon recommendations from others, at conventions and conferences and through query letters. Send query and sample chapters. Must send SASE for return of manuscript.

Seeks: "Strong characters, a lively, credible plot and a clear prose style."

Attends the following conferences/conventions: ABA, UMBA, RWA

Advice: "If you love writing and you love stories, you'll make it eventually. Never give up hope."

ADDRESS: 219 S.E. Main St., 506, Minneapolis, MN 55414-2160
PHONE: (612)331-8033
FAX: (612)331-8115

CHARLOTTE GORDON AGENCY

Established: 1983 • 20 clients

Romance Agent: Charlotte Gordon

> SPECIALIZES IN
> Humorous, Over 45, Regency, Romantic Suspense

Offers written contract. Author must give 3 months notice to terminate contract. Charges author for photocopying and overseas calls. Usually obtains clients upon recommendations from others or through query letters.

ADDRESS: 235 E 22nd Street, New York, NY 10010-4633
PHONE: (212)679-5363

THE JEFF HERMAN AGENCY, INC.

Established: 1985 • Member: AAR • 60 clients

Romance Agent: Jamie Forbes

> SPECIALIZES IN
> Contemporary Romance, Futuristic, Historical, Multicultural, New Age,
> Over 45, Romantic Horror, Romantic Mystery, Romantic Suspense

Agency prefers to work with established writers, mostly through referrals. Offers written contract.

Obtains new clients through recommendations from others, at conferences and conventions, and by solicitation. Send query and 3 sample chapters.

ADDRESS: 500 Greenwich Street, #501C, New York, NY 10013
PHONE: (212)941-0540

SUSAN HERNER RIGHTS AGENCY, INC.

Established: 1987 • 30-40 clients

Romance Agent: Sue Yuen

> SPECIALIZES IN
> Contemporary Romance, Erotic, Fantasy, Historical, Humorous, Over 45,
> Paranormal, Regency, Romantic Horror, Romantic Suspense

Agency is seeking both new and established writers. Offers written contract. Author must give 90 days notice to terminate contract.

Recent sales: *Analise* by Libby Sydes to Dell; *Cooking Most Deadly* by Joanne Pence to Harper; *Marian* by Gayle Feyrer to Dell.

Charges author for photocopying, overseas mail, express mail. Usually obtains clients upon recommendations from others. Usually meets new clients at conventions and conferences. Send query and 3 sample chapters.

Seeks: "Good writing—sustained emotionality," strong women's fiction.

Attends the following conferences/conventions: RWA conferences, Romantic Times, regional RWA conferences, ABA, Frankfurt Book Fair.

ADDRESS: P.O. Box 303, Scarsdale, NY 10583
PHONE: (914)725-8967
FAX: (914)725-8969

YVONNE TRUDEAU HUBBS AGENCY

Established: 1983 • 20 clients

Romance Agent: Yvonne Hubbs

> SPECIALIZES IN
> Contemporary Romance, Fantasy, Futuristic, Ghost, Historical, Paranormal, Regency, Romantic Suspense, Time Travel

Agency is seeking both new and established writers. Offers written contract, binding for 1 year. Author must give 30 days notice to terminate contract. Charges reading fee for unpublished writers only. Charges author for travel expenses (if approved first), photocopying and over-seas phone calls. Offers criticism service: $50 for 250 pages; additional pages $10 per 50 pages. "I write the critiques, do light line editing and also outline the flaws in the script. I make suggestions for improvement; it's up to the author to listen." 15% of business is derived from reading fees and criticism service. Payment of criticism fee does not guarantee representation of writer. Usually obtains clients upon recommendations from others, at conventions and conferences and through query letters.

Seeks: "*Sensual tension*, a lively heroine, a remarkable hero and believeable plot."

Attends the following conferences/conventions: RWA and Romantic Times.

Advice: "Always send SASE with a query. Remember to say something about yourself in your query. A clever cute query without personal background is a turn off. Agents need to know the author."

ADDRESS: 32371 Alipaz, #101, San Juan Capistrano, CA 92675
PHONE: (714)496-1970

KIDDE, HOYT & PICARD LITERARY AGENCY

Established: 1980 • Member: AAR • 60 clients

Romance Agent: Laura Langlie

> SPECIALIZES IN
> Contemporary Romance, Historical, Regency, Romantic Mystery, Romantic Suspense

Agency prefers to work with established writers, mostly through referrals, and "whom we feel we will at least eventually place in cloth; we go for good style."
Recent sales: *Love Beyond Time* by Pat Robinson to Avalon.
Charges author for photocopying. Usually obtains clients upon recommendations from others. Query first before submitting manuscript.
Seeks: "Good passion; suspense—at least psychological; flair."

ADDRESS: 335 East 51st Street, New York, NY 10022
PHONE: (212)755-9465

HARVEY KLINGER, INC.

Established: 1977 • Member: AAR • 100 clients

> SPECIALIZES IN
> Contemporary Romance, Historical, Regency, Romantic Horror, Romantic Suspense

Agency prefers to work with established writers, mostly through referrals. Charges author for extra expenses, over and above the norms. Offers criticism service. "Our criticism service is for the clients we represent, done at no charge. We offer verbal and written critiques. The critiques are written by an agent." Usually obtains clients upon recommendations from others. Query first before submitting manuscript.

ADDRESS: 301 W. 53rd Street, New York, NY 10019
PHONE: (212)581-7068

♡ ♡ ♡ ♡

MICHAEL LARSEN/ELIZABETH POMADA LITERARY AGENTS

Established: 1972 • Member: AAR • 100 clients

Romance Agent: Elizabeth Pomada

> SPECIALIZES IN
> Contemporary Romance, Erotic, Fantasy, Ghost, Historical, Humorous, Multicultural, Romantic Horror, Romantic Suspense, Time Travel

Agency is seeking both new and established writers. Offers written contract, binding for 60 days. Author must give 60 days notice to terminate contract.

Recent sales: *A Crack in Forever* by Jeannie Brewer to S&S; *Palace* by Katharine Kerr to Bantam; *Pangaea* by Lisa Mason to Bantam.

Usually obtains clients upon recommendations from others.

Seeks: "A riveting story that is written well about people we want to know and places we want to be in."

Attends the following conferences/conventions: Santa Barbara, Maui, ABA, Writers Connection.

Advice: "Romance is what makes the world go 'round—whether it's literary, commercial, or genre. If you make readers forget where they are, you'll have created a new world for them to enjoy."

ADDRESS: 1029 Jones Street, San Francisco, CA 94109
PHONE: (415)673-0939

RICIA MAINHARDT AGENCY

Established: 1987 • Member: AAR • 20-25 clients

Romance Agent: Ricia Mainhardt

> SPECIALIZES IN
> Contemporary Romance, Fantasy, Futuristic, Ghost, Historical, Humorous, Multicultural, Over 45, Paranormal, Regency, Reincarnation, Romantic Horror, Romantic Mystery, Romantic Suspense, Time Travel, Vampire, Young Adult

Agency is seeking both new and established writers. Author must give 90 days notice to terminate contract. Charges author for photocopy of manuscript. Offers criticism service as needed. Usually obtains clients upon recommendations from others. Send outline and 1 sample chapter.

Seeks: Manuscripts with "good relationship development, with a believable hero or heroine, usually told from the main character's point of view."

Attends the following conferences/conventions: RWA conferences, Romantic Times conference, regional chapter conferences, ABA.

ADDRESS: 612 Argyle Road, #L5, Brooklyn, NY 11230
PHONE: (718)434-1893
FAX: (718)434-2157

MONTGOMERY LITERARY AGENCY

Established: 1984 • Signatory of WGA

Romance Agent: M.E. Olsen

> SPECIALIZES IN
> Contemporary Romance, Historical, Humorous, Multicultural, New Age, Regency, Romantic Horror, Romantic Suspense, Time Travel, Young Adult

Agency is seeking both new and established writers. Offers written contract. Author must give 30 days notice to terminate contract. Send full manuscript or partial, both with a synopsis and SASE.

Seeks: Manuscript "having an interesting plot and likeable, believeable characters—also, a good (and happy) ending."

Advice: "Get some short stories published."

ADDRESS: P.O. Box 8822, Silver Spring, MD 20907-8822

PHONE: (301)230-1807

MULTIMEDIA PRODUCT DEVELOPMENT, INC.

Established: 1971 • Member: AAR • 150 clients

Romance Agent: Jane Jordan Browne

> SPECIALIZES IN
> Contemporary Romance, Historical

Agency prefers to work with established writers, mostly through referrals. Offers written contract, binding for 2 years. Author must give 30 days notice to terminate contract.

Recent sales: *The Scarlet Thread* by Francine Rivers to Tyndale; *Samantha's Secret* by Danice Allen to Avon; *The "Wild" Trilogy* by Lisa Bingham to Pocket.

Charges author for photocopying, foreign fax, postage. Usually obtains clients upon recommendations from others. Query first before submitting manuscript.

Seeks: "Professionalism."

ADDRESS: 410 S. Michigan Avenue, 724, Chicago, IL 60605

PHONE: (312)922-3063

FAX: (312)922-1905

DEE MURA ENTERPRISES, INC.

Signatory of WGA

Romance Agent: Dee Mura

> **SPECIALIZES IN**
> Agency handles all types of romance.

Agency is seeking both new and established writers. Offers written contract. Charges author for postage, photocopying, etc. Usually obtains clients upon recommendations from others or through query letters. Send query and sample chapters.

Seeks: "Unforgettable characters, good structure, thoroughly entertaining and unique story line with lots of surprises."

Advice: "Be unique, accept the challenge, don't be afraid to take risks."

ADDRESS: 269 West Shore Dr., Massapequa, NY 11758
PHONE: (516)795-1616
FAX: (516)798-8797
EMAIL: samurai5@ix.netcom.com (for queries only)

THE NORMA-LEWIS AGENCY

Established: 1980

Romance Agent: Norma Liebert

> **SPECIALIZES IN**
> Contemporary Romance, Historical, Humorous, Over 45, Regency, Romantic Horror, Romantic Mystery, Romantic Suspense, Time Travel, Vampire, Young Adult

Agency is seeking both new and established writers. Offers written contract, binding for 6-12 months. Usually obtains new clients through query letters.

ADDRESS: 360 W. 53rd Street, New York, NY 10019

PHONE: (212)664-0807
FAX: (212)664-0462

ALISON J. PICARD

Established: 1985 • 60 clients

Romance Agent: Alison Picard

> SPECIALIZES IN
> Agency handles all types of romance.

Agency is seeking both new and established writers. Offers written contract, binding for 1 year. Author must give 1 month notice to terminate contract.

Recent sales: *Unsafe Keeping* by Carol Cail to St. Martin's Press; *The Hate Crime* by Phyllis Karas to Avon; *The King's Shadow* by Elizabeth Adler to Farrar, Straus & Giroux

Usually obtains new clients through query letters.

Seeks: "Believable plot and characters, authentic setting and historical details and a likable heroine."

Attends the following conferences/conventions: Cape Cod Writers Conference.

Advice: "Please—no phone or fax queries."

ADDRESS: P.O. Box 2000, Cotuit, MA 02635
PHONE: (508)477-7192

POCONO LITERARY AGENCY, INC.

Established: 1993 • 20 clients

Romance Agent: Carolyn Hopwood Blick, President

> SPECIALIZES IN
> Contemporary Romance, Fantasy, Futuristic, Ghost, Historical, Humorous, Multicultural, Over 45, Regency, Romantic Horror, Romantic Mystery, Romantic Suspense, Time Travel, Young Adult

Agency is seeking both new and established writers. Charges author for office expenses, postage, photocopying, and other reasonable expenses. Usually obtains clients upon recommendations from others. Usually obtains new clients through query letters.

Seeks: Manuscripts "having depth in both plot and characters, creating the right problem, and coming up with the right solution."

Advice: "We do not read material which we have not asked to see. Always remember to enclose SASE. Material sent without SASE will not be read."

ADDRESS: P.O. Box 69, Saylorsburg, PA 18353-0069
PHONE: (610)381-4152

THE DAMARIS ROWLAND AGENCY

Established: 1994 • 31 clients

Romance Agent: Damaris Rowland

> SPECIALIZES IN
> Contemporary Romance, Erotic, Ghost, Historical, Humorous, Multicultural, New Age, Paranormal, Regency, Reincarnation, Romantic Horror, Romantic Suspense, Time Travel

This new agency is actively seeking clients. Offers written contract, binding for 30 days. Author must give 30 days notice to terminate contract.

Recent sales: Cathy Maxwell to Avon, Connie Brockway to Dell. Charges author for fees such as marketing, postage, office expenses, photocopying, etc., only under extraordinary circumstances. Usually obtains clients upon recommendations from others. Send query and 3 sample chapters.

Attends the following conferences/conventions: Romance Writers of America, Novelists Inc., Rocky Mountain Book Festival, local RWA chapter conferences ABA conference.

ADDRESS: R.R. #1, Box 513 A, Wallingford, VT 05773
PHONE: (802)446-3146
FAX: (802)446-3224

PESHA RUBINSTEIN LITERARY AGENCY, INC.

Established: 1990 • Member: AAR • 35 clients

Romance Agent: Pesha Rubinstein

> SPECIALIZES IN
> Contemporary Romance, Historical, Humorous, Multicultural, New Age,
> Romantic Horror, Romantic Suspense

Agency is seeking both new and established writers. Offers written contract.

Recent sales: *Wildwood* by Katharine Kincaid to Zebra; *Kissed* by Tanya Crosby to Avon; *The Rebel and the Redcoat* by Karyn Monk to Bantam. Charges author for photocopying. Usually obtains new clients through query letters.

Seeks: "Un-put-down-ability!"

Attends the following conferences/conventions: Romantic Times conference, RWA

ADDRESS: 1392 Rugby Road, Teaneck, NJ 07666
PHONE: (212)781-7845

RUSSELL-SIMENAUER LITERARY AGENCY, INC.

Established: 1992 • Member: AAR

Romance Agent: Fran Pardi

> SPECIALIZES IN
> Contemporary Romance, Historical, Over 45, Reincarnation

Agency is seeking both new and established writers. Offers written contract, binding for 1 year. Author must give 2 weeks notice to terminate contract. Offers criticism service for $2 per page. A staff of editors and writers write critiques in a report format. 25% of business is derived from criticism service. Usually obtains new clients by word of mouth. Query first before submitting manuscript.

ADDRESS: 957 Cypress Avenue, Brick, NJ 08723
PHONE: (908)262-0783

♡ ♡ ♡ ♡

THE SEYMOUR AGENCY

Established: 1992 • 40 clients

Romance Agent: Mary Sue Seymour

> SPECIALIZES IN
> Contemporary Romance, Fantasy, Futuristic, Ghost, Historical, Humorous, Multicultural, Over 45, Paranormal, Regency, Reincarnation, Romantic Horror, Romantic Mystery, Romantic Suspense, Time Travel, Vampire

Agency is seeking both new and established writers. Offers written contract, binding for 1 year.

Recent sales: *Fools Paradise* by Tori Phillips to Harlequin Historicals; *Whispers of the River* by Tom Hrom to Dutton-Signet; *Saxon Bride* by Tamara Leigh to Bantam. Charges author for postage ($5) which is refundable when/if we sell the book. Offers criticism service. "If we feel an author has a great deal of potential, we edit the first 50 pages of a manuscript for $25. We will only do this for select manuscripts. Mary Sue Seymour, published author/New York State certified teacher, does all critiques." Usually obtains clients upon recommendations from others, through query letters and by reading unsolicited manuscripts.

Seeks: "An author who can paint a picture and bring the characters to life, has an unusual plot, and also a strong command of the English language."

Attends the following conferences/conventions: NYS Outdoor Writers, National Outdoor Writers, RWA conferences.

Advice: "Rejections don't diminish writers as people. There are millions of musicians out of work, but that doesn't diminish the quality of their music."

ADDRESS: 17 Rensselaer Avenue, Heuvelton, NY 13654
PHONE: (315)344-7223
FAX: (315)344-7223

MARY JACK WALD ASSOCIATES, INC.

Established: 1984 • 50 clients

Romance Agent: Danis Sher

> SPECIALIZES IN
> Contemporary Romance, Ghost, Historical, Romantic Horror, Romantic Mystery, Romantic Suspense

Agency prefers to work with established writers, and only takes on new clients through referrals. Offers written contract, binding for 1 year. Usually obtains clients upon recommendations from others. Query first before submitting manuscript.

ADDRESS: 111 E. 14th Street, New York, NY 10003
PHONE: (212)254-7842

CHERRY WEINER LITERARY AGENCY

Established: 1977 • 40-50 clients

> SPECIALIZES IN
> Contemporary Romance, Fantasy, Futuristic, Ghost, Historical, Humorous, Paranormal, Regency, Reincarnation, Romantic Horror, Romantic Mystery, Romantic Suspense, Time Travel, Vampire

Agency prefers to work with established writers, and only takes on new clients through referrals or after one-on-one meetings with authors at conferences. Offers written contract. Author must give written notice to terminate contract. Charges author for photocopying manuscript or large chunks of papers, and for mailing books First Class or Express. Also charges for overseas calls. Usually obtains clients upon recommendations from others.

Attends the following conferences/conventions: RWA and local NY, NJ RWA's

Advice: "Write what you love to read."

ADDRESS: 28 Kipling Way, Manalapan, NJ 07726
PHONE: (908)446-2096

WITHERSPOON ASSOCIATES, INC.

Established: 1991 • 80 clients

Romance Agent: Michele Geminder

> SPECIALIZES IN
> Historical

Agency is seeking both new and established writers. Offers written contract. Usually obtains clients upon recommendations from others. Query first before submitting manuscript.

ADDRESS: 157 West 57th Street, #700, New York, NY 10019
PHONE: (212)757-0567
FAX: (212)757-2982

RUTH WRESCHNER, AUTHORS' REPRESENTATIVE

Established: 1982 • 75 clients

Romance Agent: Ruth Wreschner

> SPECIALIZES IN
> Contemporary Romance, Futuristic, Ghost, Historical, Multicultural, Over 45, Romantic Horror, Romantic Mystery, Romantic Suspense, Young Adult

Agency is seeking both new and established writers. Agency prefers to work with established writers, mostly through referrals. Offers written contract. Author must give 30 days notice to terminate contract. Charges author for postage, copying, long distance phone calls. Usually obtains clients upon recommendations from others, at conventions and conferences and through query letters.

Seeks: Writers "familiar with the genre and writing well enough to hold the reader's interest."

Attends the following conferences/conventions: New Jersey Romance Writers Conference

ADDRESS: 10 West 74th Street, New York, NY 10023
PHONE: (212)877-2605
FAX: (212)595-5843

ANN WRIGHT REPRESENTATIVES

Established: 1961 • Signatory of WGA • 41 clients

Romance Agent: Dan Wright

> SPECIALIZES IN
> Contemporary Romance, Historical, Over 45, Romantic Horror, Romantic Suspense

Agency handling new clients only "if work has strong motion picture potential." Offers written contract, binding for 1-2 years. Author must give 30 days notice to terminate contract. Charges author for postage, photocopying. Offers criticism service. Criticism service available only to signed clients. Usually obtains clients upon recommendations from others. Query first before submitting manuscript.

Seeks: "Style and reader appeal."

Advice: "Will only consider those clients who have some writing experience and who do not tell me how much money we're going to make together."

ADDRESS: 165 West 46 Street, 1105, New York, NY 10036-2105
PHONE: (212)764-6770
FAX: (212)764-5125

Success
Stories

Anatomy of a Sale:
The Warlord

SHAUNA SUMMERS
EDITOR, BANTAM BOOKS

*E*diting and acquiring commercial women's fiction is the perfect job for me because I have been an avid romance reader since I was in the seventh grade. So it seems only right that I would work for Bantam Books, a house where romance is treated with the respect and seriousness it deserves, where an author can have all her professional needs met through editorial guidance, marketing, promotion, and publicity. At Bantam I feel that we are in the business of building authors' careers, helping them grow, helping them reach their full potential.

Because we have so many wonderfully gifted writers already, it isn't easy to break in at Bantam. The market itself is very competitive and our standards are very high. We never have slots that must be filled. Consequently, we must be quite selective with the books we acquire for our list. We receive dozens of query letters and submissions every week. Some are from previously published authors, but most are from unpublished writers. Out of those submissions and query letters, very few are actually bought for publication. In fact, in 1995, we published only four first novels.

I can usually tell quickly if a writer has potential. It is of course easy to rule out those who clearly don't know what we're looking for or even what we publish. When a writer sends a submission for a Loveswept novel (which should run about 55,000 to 60,000 words), telling me her 80,000 word romance is perfect for our line, I immediately know she hasn't done her homework. I cannot emphasize enough to an unpublished writer the importance of targeting a publisher, of knowing their list intimately. This doesn't mean reading a few of their recent titles. This means reading everything you can get your hands on, and then several more. Our list, both for single-title historical and contemporary romances as well as Loveswept, is wonderfully diverse, and only through voracious reading can an aspiring author understand what a publishing house like Bantam wants for its list.

The other submissions that I choose not to pursue have any number of other problems. Often the writing is simply bad. Many new writers struggle with ping-pong point of view (where the point of view switches awkwardly and too often between characters), or overly descriptive writing. Other times the story doesn't captivate me, or the characters are flat, two-dimensional. The story has to keep me turning the pages, and the characters must come to life. Most important, there needs to be that sense of magic, a writer's strong, unique voice that tells me I've found a potential star, a gifted storyteller who has books to write that I must read.

This was definitely the case with Elizabeth Elliott. I think she's a perfect example of cream rising to the top of that infamous slush pile. She was unagented when she first contacted Bantam through a query letter that included a synopsis and the first three chapters (see page 231). Her letter was clever (she discussed her romance novel addiction, confessing that she had no desire to be cured) and to the point. She told me briefly and clearly about the characters and their conflict. Her writing and her story—even in the cover letter and synopsis—spoke for themselves. I got an immediate sense of her voice and style, and that's what prompted me to request the complete manuscript.

The Warlord is a traditional romance about a dark and dangerous warrior and the feisty beauty forced to be his bride. Kenric of Montague, commonly known as the "Butcher of Wales," is the most notorious warlord in all of England. Tess of Remmington is commanded secretly by the king to marry Kenric so that he can reclaim her lands from her evil and abusive stepfather, MacLeith. Tess fears that MacLeith will slaughter her people when Kenric fights him for Remmington. Consequently, she spends much of the story trying to escape to a convent, despite her growing feelings for her husband, in the hope that her lands will then go to the king by default, and that a battle over Remmington will be unnecessary. MacLeith is a constant threat to both Tess and Kenric, attempting to kill them both. She finally realizes that such a battle is inevitable, and that she belongs with Kenric, who needs her as much as she needs him.

Elizabeth includes many traditional romance elements throughout the book, but what set this manuscript apart for me, besides her wonderful writing style, was the characters. I found Kenric to be a particularly compelling hero, a man who is hated for being the king's bastard, and feared for his skills and ruthlessness as a warrior. He is not at all prepared for Tess, who despite her own fear of his reputation, recognizes the good qualities in him that so few have taken the time or the opportunity to see. Kenric is dark, unyielding and at times brutal—an alpha male. Seeing him change and grow as he falls in love with Tess, as he realizes that she loves him unconditionally in return, is perhaps my favorite part of the book.

After my initial reading, I knew *The Warlord*, and more important the author, had tremendous potential, but because of some problems with the manuscript, the book wasn't strong enough for Bantam as it was. I wrote Elizabeth with my concerns, giving her the opportunity to revise the manuscript and re-submit it to me. She did so gladly.

The main problem was with the pacing. Kenric and Tess worked out their emotional conflict too early in the story, which led to a couple of different problems. First, the tension, both sexual and otherwise, dropped too quickly causing the middle of the book to drag. Second, because most of their problems were solved so soon, the characters didn't change and grow enough throughout the book. This was particularly true of Kenric, and because I felt he was one of the book's biggest strengths, I asked Elizabeth to give more of his background—why and how he became so hardened and brutal. The plot also moved slowly in relation to the MacLeith conflict, which was often placed too far on the backburner.

When I received the revised manuscript, I was greatly impressed. Elizabeth had polished and improved the novel beyond my expectations. At that point, I knew I was looking at an opportunity to work with an author who was not only a great storyteller, but also had the skill and desire to enhance and refine her writing, something that is invaluable in building an exceptional and diverse career.

One of the changes to the book that I liked most was the addition of a prologue in which we see Kenric five years before the actual story begins. We see Kenric in his element as a warrior on a Crusade through the Holy Lands. He has just fought a particularly fierce and bloody battle, and now must mete out justice against two men who have been hired by his father to kill him. By the end of the prologue, the reader is given no

1234 Main Street
Anytown, OH 12345

Shauna Summers
Bantam Books
1540 Broadway
New York, NY 10036

*Nice and brief,
Yet gives me a good idea
of the book.*

Dear Ms. Summers:

Is there a 12-step program for Romance Novel Addicts? An advice column for those who promise they'll read "just one" romance this week and end up on an all-night binge? Please, just say "NO." As a confessed RNA (Romance Novel Addict), I don't want to be cured! I will never cancel my Book-of-the-Month membership!!

Like many RNAs, I began churning the stuff out myself one day when the local supply ran short. I sometimes wonder what my friends and family will say, yet that devilish inner voice tells me I've created a "fix" too good to keep to myself. I want all Romance Novel Addicts to experience the "high" of falling in love with Kenric of Montague, a ruthless warlord capable of stealing any woman's heart. Imagine a "trip" to 13th century England. Put yourself in the trembling shoes of Tess Remmington, a feisty heiress destined to marry a man known best as the "Butcher of Wales." Yet think of your relief when you discover the man has been horribly misjudged by others and needs you as much as you need him. The only trouble lies in a nasty stepfather and an illicit connection to the king. Yet there's never a dull moment. THE WARLORD will give no one a "bad trip."

It's true this is the first romance I've brewed up on my own. But one day I would love to join the "king-pins" of the Romance Cartel, authors such as <u>Amanda Quick</u> <u>and Teresa Medeiros</u>. Toward this goal, I've enclosed a sample of THE WARLORD, hoping the first three chapters will whet your appetite for more. There are twenty-six chapters in this completed novel, a total of 125,000 words to satisfy the RNA craving completely. Your response to THE WARLORD would mean a great deal to me.

Most Sincerely,

*Mentions Bantam
authors, which shows
she is knowledgeable
and gives me a
point of reference.*

*Important
information —
how long,
completed, etc.*

Elizabeth Elliott

P.S. Although unrelated to this endeavor, I do have numerous works in publication including marketing promotions, software manuals, and several computer-related articles in trade journals.

*Good to mention other
non-related publications,
but briefly.*

Elliott's Query Letter

231

doubt as to why Kenric is known as the "Butcher of Wales."

Through Elizabeth's changes, the characters and the conflict between them had much more depth. I never once forgot about MacLeith's threat to their marriage, their happiness, or their lives. And the internal conflicts between Tess and Kenric were developed and resolved in a much more satisfying manner. Though few scenes were cut or drastically changed, Elizabeth had added more layers and emotion to the characters, which really beefed up the tension between them, and made me want to keep reading to see how things were going to work out.

At this point I knew the book was ready to go to contract. Though Elizabeth would have to do some minor fine tuning, I felt that the manuscript was strong enough to evoke enthusiasm from others on our editorial staff as well as from our deputy publisher. And I was right. When I made my offer for a two-book contract, Elizabeth was in the process of hiring an agent. So I ultimately negotiated with the agent of her choice. At the time, it had been almost a year since I first read Elizabeth's manuscript.

Elizabeth's career is off to a magnificient start. *The Warlord*, published in July '95, performed even better than we expected. Her second book, *Scoundrel*, which will be published in February '96, confirmed my belief that she has tremendous talent and skill. It is set in the Regency period, and her writing is even better and stronger than in *The Warlord*. To see an author grow and improve with each book is one of the most satisfying parts about being an editor, and I look forward to being a part of that process with Elizabeth. I've just signed her up for three more books. She is currently working on the sequel to *The Warlord*.

The Warlord
ELIZABETH ELLIOTT

PROLOGUE

Very little remained of the ancient city. The work of countless generations was reduced to rubble in a battle that lasted little more than three days. Skeletons of walls and buildings that had stood since the time of Christ rose in a shadow of their former glory, silhouetted against the dawn of a desert sky. Tendrils of smoke snaked upward from the smoldering ashes to join the hazy cloak that shrouded the city.

A lone knight rode through what remained of an archway, over smashed gates that had barred the enemy for a thousand years. Scattered among the tumbled stones and burnt timbers were the people who once lived there, their bodies a mute testimony to the battle that had raged through the city the day before.

With the sights and sounds of battle still fresh in memory, the knight didn't appear disturbed by the carnage that surrounded him. His warhorse picked a careful path through the rubble, the animal alert to his footing even though his head hung low with exhaustion.

Kenric of Montague's dark face remained expressionless, the knight as unmoved by these deaths as the countless others he'd witnessed in the three years he'd been on Crusade in the Holy Lands. The people of Al' Abar had refused to surrender. Their city had been besieged until nothing remained of their defenses and no single structure stood whole that would provide any shelter. They had died. Such events had been repeated too many times over the years for Kenric to feel anything more than the bone-deep fatigue that followed a long battle.

Kenric's armor and that of his horse were covered with ashes, crusty with sweat, the leather stiff with dried blood. Another tunic ruined, he thought idly, gazing down at the once white garment with the scarlet cross emblazoned on his chest. Only the stitches that outlined the cross distinguished the holy emblem from the rest of the mutilated fabric. Luckily, this time none of the blood was his own. With an annoyed sigh, he nudged his horse forward again when the animal ambled to a weary halt.

He saw the shield first, three golden lions on a fiery red field. It lay just outside the ruins of what might have been the home of a prosperous merchant. The half-naked body of a woman lay next to the shield. The soldier Kenric was looking for lay facedown just a pace from the woman, with the body of a young Arab boy sprawled half on top of the soldier.

Kenric considered the scene with the dispassionate logic of one who can no longer be shocked by the atrocities of war. The boy was probably the woman's son or brother. He'd likely saved her from the first knight, but others had finished what the first had begun.

Kenric dismounted and nudged the knight's body with the tip of his boot, rolling the corpse onto its back. He reached inside the soldier's hauberk and removed a gold necklace with an efficient jerk. Next he took a ring from the dead man's hand and placed both items safely inside his hauberk before he remounted and turned the horse toward the edge of the city.

Normally Kenric wouldn't bother with such trinkets, but King Edward would be displeased if his nephew's signet ring or cross fell into the hands of infidels. The personal effects would also prove to the king that his nephew died in battle, rather than meeting an inglorious death from one of the many tortures inflicted on Christians by their Arab captors. He knew the bards would compose sorrowful ballads for the young man, full of brave deeds and glory, with no mention that he'd died attempting rape. Kenric doubted his own ballads would be so generous if he fell in battle. No, there were ballads aplenty about Kenric of Montague, and none could be called flattering.

A small group of knights had gathered near the outskirts of the city and one pointed toward Kenric as he emerged from the ruins. The men turned as a whole to watch the approach of their leader, each trying to guess Kenric's mood as he rode from the city. The king was sure to be upset by his favorite nephew's death, but Kenric had shown no more concern over this death than he would for a common footsoldier's. Some wondered what it would take for any emotion to cross the warlord's face.

A young squire hurried forward to hold Kenric's horse as he dismounted, and a knight named Roger Fitz Alan stepped away from the group to greet his leader. A young priest also hurried toward Kenric, the priest and Fitz Alan noticing each other at the same moment. Both men hastened their steps as they tried to be the first to reach the warrior.

"Sir Kenric," the priest called out, waving a pudgy hand in the air. "A moment of your time."

Kenric ignored the priest and tossed the horse's reins to his squire. "Make sure he has plenty of water, Evard. And a good brushing. Be quick about his care. We leave within the hour."

"Aye, milord," the squire murmured, leading the horse away.

"He found out about the de Gravelle brothers," Fitz Alan said, jerking his head toward the priest.

Kenric acknowledged the warning with a slight nod. "Send Simon to make sure the supply carts are loaded and ready to move. The scouts returned at daybreak with word that Rashid's army is less than two days' march from here. The men are too worn to face that devil right now. With luck, we will encounter little more than skirmishes before we reach the sea."

Fitz Alan bowed slightly, then turned away to find Simon and carry out Kenric's order.

"Sir Kenric," the priest called again, coming to a halt near Kenric's elbow. His face was flushed by the early morning heat, sweat collecting already in the fleshy folds of his pale neck. Father Vachel drew himself up to his full height of five and a half feet, still looking small and insignificant next to the towering figure of the warlord. "You cannot mean to punish the de Gravelles as I have heard, Sir Kenric. No matter their crime, no Christian deserves such a death."

"Begone, priest." Kenric dismissed Father Vachel with a casual wave of his hand, as if to brush the priest away. He strode purposefully toward the group of knights, leaving the priest behind. The knights were gathered around two men who lay side by side in the sand, stripped naked and staked out spread-eagle. Kenric came to a halt at the feet of the staked men, looking slowly from one man to the other. The expressions on the bound men's faces reflected their fear. Kenric crossed his arms across his broad chest and pronounced their judgment.

"Ranulf and Dominic de Gravelle, 'tis known you conspired to murder me, but instead your poisoned wine killed four of my men. For that you will die."

Kenric gave the de Gravelle brothers a moment to come to terms with their fate. He looked toward the horizon at the rapidly rising sun then his gaze swept across the ruins of the city. "Aye, you will die by the heat of the sun, or at the hands of infidels who will be drawn from across the desert by the smoke that still rises from Al' Abar."

Ranulf de Gravelle clenched his jaw bravely, but Dominic broke down and began to sob, his pleas for mercy nearly incomprehensible. Kenric slowly drew his sword, his dark eyes devoid of emotion. "Or you can die a more honorable death than the one you intended for me."

Dominic continued to wail but Ranulf's eyes narrowed, considering his leader.

"You want to know who hired us," Ranulf stated flatly. He levered his shoulders up, struggling against his bonds to look at his brother's tear-streaked face. After a brief glance his head fell back to the sand in defeat. A quick death was the only mercy they could expect. Death from a man who should be dead. Ranulf cursed softly, refusing to reveal the name of the man behind their plot.

"We were approached at court," Dominic blurted out. "We made it known that we were mercenaries and our swords came with a price. My brother and I had no intention of becoming assassins, b-but the reward for your death was too tempting, milord. Gold, a fine keep, and rich lands. Ranulf was also promised the dowry that comes with your sister's hand in marriage."

"My father," Kenric stated quietly, his face expressionless. He'd known without being told that the old warlord was behind this scheme. Yet he'd wanted to be sure.

Dominic nodded uncertainly. "Baron Montague calls you a bastard. A spawn of the Devil. He grows old and sickly, but he is determined that your younger brother, Guy, inherit his lands and title. He hoped that you would die here in the Holy Lands, as so many others have. Indeed, 'tis known the infidels search you out on a battlefield for the glory of your death. Even they have a price on your head. Yet you will not die. When he learned that the king intended to call you home, Baron Montague arranged for us to journey here and join your army."

"Was my brother, Guy, involved in this scheme?"

"I cannot say," Dominic admitted. "The boy was at none of our meetings."

"Was anyone else involved?"

"Nay, just Ranulf and myself. But I would have you know that the plot to poison the wine was Ranulf's, not mine," Dominic confessed. "I beg you, have mercy, milord. I had no wish to involve myself in this blood feud and told Ranulf so."

"But you did not tell me, did you, Dominic?" Kenric asked mildly. "You knew of his plot yet remained silent, thus four men are dead. You will pay the same price for treachery."

"You've wasted your breath, Brother *dear*," Ranulf said sarcastically, though hatred blazed from his eyes toward Kenric of Montague.

"You should have died," Ranulf told Kenric, his voice a harsh, defeated whisper. "What keeps you alive?"

"God's will," Kenric lied. His emotionless gaze moved slowly from Ranulf to Dominic. Dominic's eyes grew round and wide with complete terror as the warlord's sword moved toward his neck. Pinned to the ground, Dominic could do nothing to escape his fate, say nothing more to sway his executioner. Ranulf's shout to face death bravely was drowned out by Dominic's screams.

Kenric turned and stalked away from the de Gravelles, his mood grim. Four men dead by treachery, now another two by his own hand. And the ruins of a city at his back, filled with corpses. Kenric mentally calculated his losses, already planning the knights and soldiers he would move into new positions to replace those who would never leave Al' Abar. His mind conjured images of the dead, men who laughed, drank, and boasted of their skills until they were silenced forever beneath the relentless sun of this hellish place. Yet there were others just like them to take their place. Knights and soldiers, all intent on gold and glory. They would die the same deaths as those who went before them.

And Ranulf de Gravelle wondered how Kenric could survive amidst so much death? The answer was so simple, it was laughable. There was no fear of death left in Kenric. He'd faced the Grim Reaper each day of his life for the past three years and had grown accustomed to the specter's constant presence. It was that acceptance of Death that kept Kenric alive, as much as his skill with a sword. A warrior who fought without fear made few mistakes, his mind intent only on tactics and strategy.

Aye, Kenric knew his worth to king and country. He had all the characteristics of a perfect warrior; a body molded from childhood to the art of combat, a mind educated to the military strategies of a thousand years and countless cultures, and a heart robbed of its soul long ago. Such a warrior left only death and destruction in his path, an instrument of Death itself. There was no thought of glory or honor in this warrior, no gloating or boasts, just calm acceptance. Another battle won. Another would follow soon enough.

Kenric headed toward a blue and white striped tent, the only tent remaining of the battle camp that had stood outside the city for nearly a fortnight. After a quick meal and change of clothes, he would order the army forward, back toward the sea, back to England. And another war.

Aye, Baron Montague was right to fear his return. The old man knew that Kenric's power would only increase when the king sent him to join the war in Wales. As the king's favored henchman, Kenric would not be so easy to murder in England, or even in the mist-shrouded forests of Wales. He just might live long enough to inherit the lands Baron Montague fought so desperately to keep from him.

"Sir Kenric!" the priest shouted. He rushed forward again to tug on Kenric's sleeve, trying to bring the warlord to a halt. Kenric merely shrugged his arm away and continued without breaking stride.

"You begin to annoy me, priest. Best say your blessings over Al' Abar and find your donkey. We do not tarry here."

"You did not give the de Gravelles an opportunity to confess their sins, to meet their Maker with a clear conscience," Father Vachel said defiantly, though he seemed appeased by the justice meted out to the traitors. To leave them here alive would have been the greater sin.

"I heard their confession," Kenric replied, unconcerned.

"You speak blasphemy!"

Kenric shrugged, his attention on his army's preparations to move out. "Take a walk through the streets of the city, priest. Count how many lie dead there, none with benefit of priestly confessions to meet their deaths."

" 'Tis not the same. Those few of your knights who died gave their lives bravely in battle and had no need for confessions," Father Vachel said reasonably. "And the infidels of this city were not entitled to confession. They died by God's will."

"Nay," Kenric said slowly, turning at last to face the priest. Father Vachel backed away from the cold, unblinking gaze. His hand went to his chest, crossing himself against what he saw in those eyes.

"They died by my will."

CHAPTER ONE
FIVE YEARS LATER
NORTHERN ENGLAND

The winter night was not nearly dark enough for Kenric's mission. His gaze swept over the inky silhouette of Langston Keep, scanning the shadows of the battlements for any unusual movement as he silently cursed the cloudless sky. The bright half moon turned the snow-covered ground a silvery shade of blue, making anyone who ventured into the open an easy target for guards posted within the fortress walls.

"This may yet be a trap," Fitz Alan whispered.

Kenric nodded to acknowledge that truth. He could see his breath in the faint moonlight and he stirred restlessly, trying to ward off the frigid night air and his own misgivings. The woods behind them provided little protection. They would be an easy catch, should an ambush be in order. The very fact that their plan depended on one Scotsman betraying another nearly guaranteed a trap. But Kenric was determined to see this through and Fitz Alan wouldn't challenge the decision. Not when the king had a hand in this scheme.

"The plan seems too simple," Fitz Alan warned in a low voice. "We should have brought men to guard our backs."

Kenric didn't reply. He stared intently at a clump of large bushes that filled a gully leading to the keep. The vague outline of two cloaked figures grew more distinct as they emerged from the brush, the soft crunch of snow announcing their approach. Despite the danger they were in, Kenric nearly laughed aloud when he spotted their quarry. One was tall and broad-chested, the other short and amazingly plump. Kenric's soldiers would roll with laughter when they caught sight of this prize. A bear and a butterball were hardly fitting trophies for two of England's fiercest warriors. Five years of war in Wales, suffering every discomfort known to a soldier, and this was to be his reward?

"Perhaps her face will not be as difficult to look upon as her person," Fitz Alan whispered, his smile heard but unseen. " 'Tis the oddest-shaped women I've ever laid eyes on."

The approaching man raised his head, as if he'd caught the scent of danger. Kenric moved silently to the edge of the brush, disappearing into the black shadows of the forest. Fitz Alan crouched low to the ground, watching the two odd shapes as they walked cautiously toward his hiding spot. They halted less than ten paces away.

"This could be a trap, Uncle Ian."

The soft, feminine voice belonged to the butterball. Her words pleased Kenric considerably. It was a good sign that their prey shared their concern. The woman drew her hood back to look around the tiny clearing, attempting to peer into the dark forest as she whispered her plea.

"I say we escape by ourselves while we can. I'll guard your back well enough should we meet with any thieves. 'Tis obvious he is not coming. Let us be gone from here."

The woman gasped at the same instant her uncle swung around with his sword drawn.

"Put your sword on the ground, Laird Duncan. Slowly," Kenric ordered.

Ian Duncan didn't move. The moon provided enough light for Kenric to make out the Scottish laird's shape, but his expression remained obscured by the night's shadows.

"Do as I say," Kenric warned, nudging the woman's bulk with the tip of his sword. "Else she'll take my blade between her ribs."

Ian lowered the weapon to the ground, then pulled his niece to his side, away from the warrior's sword. He looked at Kenric, but nodded toward Fitz Alan. "You were to come alone."

"My man is loyal," he replied with a shrug. "Get the horses, Fitz Alan."

"Lady Remmington will ride with me," Ian said, maintaining a protective hold on the girl. "I left my horse less than a mile from here."

"We have your horse." Kenric picked up Ian's sword then sheathed his own, queerly disappointed that the lady was falling into his hands so easily. He hadn't the slightest desire to get a closer look at his prize. No matter how comely the face, it couldn't possibly make up for the package it came with. She was undoubtedly as homely as his horse or she would have shown herself by now. "The arrangements have been made at Kelso Abbey."

"You are prepared to see this through, to do what is asked of you?" Ian asked. He waited several long, silent moments for an answer.

"Aye." Kenric's reply was firm. "You can stay at Kelso Abbey until the search parties are recalled or make for your fortress immediately after—"

"I ride for Scotland tonight," Ian interrupted.

"Why are we going to Kelso Abbey?" Lady Remmington asked, her whisper nearly muffled by the cloak's heavy hood.

"Hush, Tess," Ian scolded. "Here are the horses. Be a good girl and everything will be fine. Quickly now, we must hurry."

"Yes, Uncle," Tess replied obediently.

Fitz Alan returned with the horses and the two warriors mounted. Ian placed the bulky girl on his horse then swung into the saddle behind her. The animals moved almost silently through the forest, their hooves wrapped with rags to muffle the noise. This late at night they wouldn't have to worry about patrols from Langston Keep, but the woods were home to outcasts; thieves and murderers who controlled the king's highways by preying on unprotected travelers. Kenric knew they could handle that threat, but he didn't have time to deal with such a distraction. The night was half spent already and every hour counted.

Tess Remmington gave little thought to thieves. Her worry centered on the pack of soldiers that could thunder out of the fortress at any moment. Her stepfather was going to be furious when he discovered her escape. Just the thought of Dunmore MacLeith made Tess's blood run cold. In outward appearance there was nothing to dislike about the Scot. Tall and fit, he had two wings of gray at the temples of his dark hair that gave him an air of distinction. But Tess, more than any other, knew a heart capable of coldblooded murder lay beneath the deceptive facade. The beast had married her mother a mere week after her father's suspicious death. Even then the odd set of circumstances that put Dunmore MacLeith inside the fortress had seemed a little too convenient. A month later her mother had also been laid to rest in Remmington's cemetery after a "fall" from the tower steps. Everyone knew the baroness planned to petition the church and King Edward for an annulment. Some, including Dunmore MacLeith, had believed she might get it.

Tess wondered again how King Edward could have turned a blind eye toward MacLeith's evil deeds all these years. Could the war in Wales, problems with the church, and the endless quarrels among his barons keep the king too busy to bother with such a remote barony? Aye, he'd gone and forgotten about her and Tess had no way to bring her cause before him. Dunmore MacLeith sat as lord at Remmington Castle while Tess, the rightful heir, had stayed locked away in remote Langston Keep these five years.

The only good fortune she could claim of late was the recent discovery of a secret passage that led from her bedchamber to the gully outside the walls. Such passages were common in border holdings of Langston's age, built to allow the family a means of escape if the keep fell to an invading army. Now it provided Tess with a different sort of freedom. Freedom from Dunmore MacLeith's plans for her life.

Two hours later, the group dismounted outside Kelso Abbey's main gate.

A small side door swung open and, as if he'd been awaiting their arrival, a cowled monk thrust a lantern through the doorway. Tess watched the taller of the two men they had met in the forest step closer to show his face. The monk nodded, turning without a word to point toward a dark path.

Tess drew her cloak closer, trying to shake a sudden chill. The monk looked like an unholy specter of death with his black robes and long, bony finger pointing them forward. She clutched the back of her uncle's cloak and walked as close behind him as the narrow path would allow.

The path led to the doors of a large chapel and the group stepped inside. Tess pulled her hood aside just enough to get a better look at the structure, but she was careful to keep her face hidden, as Uncle Ian had ordered. Ian had said he wan't sure what kind of men they'd meet with this night and the less they knew of Tess the better. Yet once inside the chapel she couldn't help but gape in wide-eyed wonder at the fine Gothic architecture and Norman workmanship that made Kelso Abbey one of the church's prize jewels. Tess was sure she'd never seen anything so grand. Beautiful religious paintings covered the walls and ceilings, and most statues were leafed with gold. The soft glow from an uncountable number of precious beeswax candles made the place seem more fairy-tale castle than chapel. An old priest stood near the pulpit, garbed in richly embroidered red satin and gold-trimmed robes, his presence lending an air of royalty to the scene. The priest's face was wrinkled with years of wear, but his eyes twinkled with a smile that grew broader as they passed each row of kneelers.

"Greetings, my son." The priest walked stiffly toward Kenric, his gait slowed by age. He grasped Kenric's strong hands with thin, frail ones. " 'Tis been too many years, but you've grown into a fine man."

"Thank you, Father Olwen, 'Tis good to see your familiar face this eve." Kenric smiled grimly at the priest. "I'm sure you remember my friend Roger Fitz Alan. And this is Laird Duncan."

Kenric turned then to get his first good look at the giant Scot. Although Kenric stood well over six feet, Ian Duncan was nearly as tall. The Scottish laird's face was weathered and his blue eyes creased around the edges with the lines of a man who smiled often. Much as he was smiling now at Kenric.

Kenric soon spied the reason for the Scot's humor. Ian's cloak was tossed over his shoulders to reveal not only the Duncan clan's blue and green plaid, but the handle of a massive claymore that was strapped securely to his back. So much for disarming the man. Kenric acknowledged his oversight with a slight nod, then his eyes dropped to Ian's side to inspect Lady Remmington. Her back was turned to Kenric and she seemed absorbed by the doomsday paintings on one wall of the chapel. He tried to imagine a short, fat, female version of Ian Duncan and was immediately glad she had the good grace to keep herself covered. Whoever told King Edward this girl was a pleasure to gaze upon had an odd sense of humor.

The priest interrupted Kenric's thoughts by clearing his throat, a subtle hint that he was waiting for an introduction. Kenric said simply, "Father Olwen, this is Lady Remmington."

The girl's shoulders jerked. She bowed her head, then turned to meet the priest.

"I'm pleased to meet you, my dear." Father Olwen stepped forward and took hold of the girl's hands, giving them a firm squeeze. "These circumstances are a bit unusual, but I'm sure we can make your—"

"Excuse me, Father," Ian interrupted. He ignored the priest's look of surprise and pulled Tess back to his side. "Is there some place I might speak with Lady Remmington in private?"

"Why, I believe there is a—"

"Whatever you need say to the lady can be said right here." This time it was Kenric who interrupted the priest, his expression dark.

"I'm not so sure of that," Ian said uncertainly. "My niece knows very little of this plan. I thought it best to explain the situation once we were safely away from Langston."

"She doesn't know of the marriage?" Kenric questioned sharply.

"Marriage?" the wide bundle croaked.

"Now, lass, don't get all worked up before I have a chance to explain," Ian pleaded turning the girl toward him to take hold of her hands.

"*Marriage!*" she repeated, her voice louder. She jerked her hands away from Ian and tried to rest them on her hips.

The knights and priest stared in amazement when Lady Remmington's wide girth suddenly sank into a lumpy mass around her feet. They continued to watch in stunned silence as she stepped closer to Ian, her cloak dragging forward to reveal two large linen sacks on the floor. It took only a moment for them to realize the sacks had been slung over her shoulders, carried beneath the cloak to keep her arms under the sleeveless garment and protected against the cold.

"You said *nothing* about a marriage!"

The men turned their heads from the floor to Lady Remmington, almost in unison.

"She isn't fat at all," Fitz Alan whispered.

Lady Remmington still had her back to the men, but Kenric smiled when the newly slimmed figure gave Laird Duncan a good poke in the stomach. Her hood fell back onto her shoulders as she glared up at the Scot, providing a pleasing glimpse of honey-blond hair.

"I wasn't sure how you would take the news," Ian began.

"You knew damned well how I would take the news! And now you've made me swear in front of a priest!" She swirled around to face Father Olwen, her hands folded demurely, eyes lowered to the floor. "Forgive me, Father. 'Tis a sinful word I spoke in anger. I will pray God realizes these are trying times for me and can forgive this transgression. It seems my uncle's plans for this evening and my own differ greatly."

Kenric didn't realize he was holding his breath until the woman turned toward her uncle. One look at those flashing violet eyes had actually weakened his knees. Now he was certain the king jested with him. Only a blind man would describe this girl as pretty. Tess of Remmington was magnificient.

"You will explain yourself," Tess ordered, a sharp nod at her uncle emphasizing the point. She unhooked her cloak and shrugged it off, folding the garment carefully over one arm as if she had all day to hear Ian's explanation. "And it had best be good."

"I was going to tell you," Ian said. He spoke in Gaelic, his voice lowered. "But you've had your mind so set on this convent idea that I wasn't sure you would agree to leave, knowing you would be wed to a man you'd never met."

"This plan makes no sense, Uncle." Tess answered in Gaelic as well, with a sidelong glance at the mercenary knights who escorted them here. "A convent can be explained away by a religious calling. But marriage to a man of your acquaintance? Neither your king, nor mine, is like to believe you're not involved. You risk your life with this plan."

"Calm down, lass." Ian placed his big hands on Tess's shoulders. "Now you know I've your best interest at heart. Your own King Edward has named your betrothed."

"What?" Tess looked hopeful for a moment, then her expression turned suspicious. "But the king already approved my stepfather's choice of husband. How can Edward name another when he's given MacLeith his word on the matter?"

"Well now, that's the tricky part," Ian admitted, rubbing his chin. "MacLeith has kept Edward good and worried since the day he took control of Remmington. He's been a loyal subject on the surface these past five years, but Edward knows MacLeith's game well enough to see a snake in his garden. Not one Englishman remains as lord of any Remmington holding and MacLeith plaids litter every battlement. Your stepfather knew it was time to test Edward's patience with this betrothal business. By refusing MacLeith's choice, Edward would have given your stepfather an excuse to defy his overlord and start a war. And everyone knows that any war so close to the border involving the King of England would soon involve the King of Scotland. When he approved the choice, Edward avoided a war, but practically handed Remmington over to MacLeith on a platter."

"So the king doesn't intend to honor his word?" she asked, her brows drawn together in a puzzled frown. "Won't that give MacLeith another excuse to challenge Edward?"

"Not if Edward pretends ignorance of the marriage." Ian smiled over the cleverness of the plan, still amazed that an Englishman could be so shrewd. "Then it becomes a war between your husband and stepfather. Edward can provide your husband with aid, but as long as he avoids direct involvement, King Alexander will have no reason to interfere."

"Who does the king think to pit against MacLeith?"

"Your betrothed is one of the king's finest barons," Ian told her enthusiastically. "You didn't expect a baron, now did you?"

"Nay," Tess said slowly. "Before he approved MacLeith's choice, I thought Edward would pledge my hand to one of the landless knights who vie in his tourneys for just such a favor. 'Tis unusual to offer such a large dower to a man already landed."

"Aye, your betrothed is no pauper. His estates easily match your own. Indeed, he is a man known for protecting what he has made his own. King Edward has pledged your hand to the only warrior capable of tossing Dunmore MacLeith back over the border. Your are to wed Baron Montague," he announced cautiously. "The baron is—"

"The Butcher?" She sounded as if she were being strangled. Her hands flew to her throat, her voice hoarse with fear. "You think to tie me to the Butcher of Wales?"

"Watch your tongue, lass." Ian drew himself up to his full height, the tolerant uncle transforming instantly into the powerful laird. "I'll not listen to you blaspheme the man you're to wed. You've heard one too many wild tales. Baron Montague is a man well respected by those who fight for your country, and well feared by those who do not. I couldn't have made a better choice myself, had I the opportunity. I'll rest easier with Baron Montague on my border than I do with that jackal MacLeith licking his chops over my keeps. Were you expecting MacLeith to give you a fine husband like Montague?"

"You know who I'd get from him."

"Aye, Dunmore MacLeith's own son, Gordon, is the man he chose for you. Though I have my doubts that Gordon MacLeith is much of a man."

"Is this fate any better?" Tess whispered.

She realized her hands were still on her throat and she quickly lowered them to a tight grip at her waist, wondering what she had done to her king to deserve this fate. Why, everyone from Scotland to Normandy knew of Montague's baron. The man had made a name for himself in the tourneys as an undefeatable knight; then later as a fearless warrior in the king's Crusade. His name became a legend in the war against Wales. But the stories of his deeds were never wrapped in gallantry or heroics. Nay, tales concerning the Butcher of Wales were wrapped in blood. Tess thought of Baron Montague as more of a demon than a man who actually walked the earth as a mere human. Even MacLeith's men whispered the name in awe, as if its very mention was reason enough to cross themselves against evil. Tess knew how he'd earned his name and she shuddered over the knowledge. The Butcher of Wales took no prisoners. It was said there were parts of Wales where no one of Welsh blood could be found for as far as the eye could see. He'd slaughtered them all.

Of course, some of the stories were exaggerations, but there must be some shred of truth to the foul tales. Tess had no desire to find out firsthand. She knew from the braced legs and firm tone of voice that her uncle's decision was made and any argument on her part would be a waste of time. She decided to hear Ian out, then appeal to the priest for sanctuary in the church. Surely a man of God wouldn't want to see a gentle maid forced to wed such a monster. By the time the bridegroom arrived she would be under the protection of the church, safely beyond the reach of any man.

"Edward chose Baron Montague some time ago," Ian continued. "Father Olwen here was King Edward's own confessor in his younger days. He's to perform the wedding ceremony, then send a copy of the marriage papers back to London. As for the MacLeiths, they must believe you escaped on your own. They'll be told Baron Montague caught you thinking to collect a reward, but decided to marry you instead."

"MacLeith will go to any lengths to get me back. If I'm recaptured, the marriage could be annulled. Even the English barons would recognize that right. Then where would the king's plan be?"

Ian frowned at her logic, but continued trying to reason with her.

Kenric understood Gaelic well enough to follow the conversation, but he wasn't really listening. He let his eyes wander down the thick blond braid to its tip, past an incredibly small waist and nicely rounded hips. His fingers itched to touch the silky rope, to undo the neatly woven tresses and fill his hands with gold.

That idea held Kenric's attention until he began to wonder if he'd just imagined the color of her eyes. Rich jewels could reflect such a mesmerizing shade of violet-blue, but he'd never seen the like in a woman's eyes. Lady Remmington turned her head slightly as he pondered the unlikely color and he was given another glimpse of her face. Those fascinating eyes were hidden behind the thick fans of lowered lashes, allowing him to examine her features without distraction. Her expression was calm, composed, almost regal. But he noticed the way the corners of her mouth turned down whenever her uncle mentioned the word "marriage." That didn't distract from the lushness of her mouth. Prettily bowed on the top, full and pouting on the bottom, he couldn't wait to feel those luscious lips beneath his. He wanted to touch her, certain her skin would be just as powder-soft as it looked. Her lips parted slightly to reveal the tip of her tongue as she wet her lips. The gesture was so unconsciously innocent yet sweetly seductive, Kenric found himself holding his breath again. It didn't take long to realize the exquisite beauty didn't need bewitching eyes to distract a man's attention. Her delicate profile alone set his groin to aching.

He forced himself to look away, attempting to discipline his wandering imagination. He couldn't remember the last time he'd reacted physically to a woman without even touching her. Hell, he didn't even know her. What was the matter with him? His gaze slid to Fitz Alan, and he was pleased to realize his second-in-command appeared just as dazed by Lady Remmington's appearance. Fitz Alan's mouth hung open quite stupidly.

"You're drooling," Kenric informed him behind one hand. Fitz Alan's mouth snapped shut but his eyes didn't leave the girl.

"You were right after all," Kenric went on, a certain smugness in his voice. "Her face is not *too* difficult to gaze upon."

"She is an angel," Fitz Alan whispered in awe.

Smiling, Kenric looked again to Lady Remmington. She was arguing fiercely with Ian. "Aye, an angel with a temper."

The smile disappeared completely when he heard her next words. "The only solution is to take me to a convent. I'll take the vows."

"The only vows you'll be taking are marriage vows," Kenric growled from his place behind her, his Gaelic almost perfect.

"I have been . . . been . . ."

Her words trailed off the moment Tess spun around and took a good look at the knights, the mercenaries hired to help her escape Dunmore MacLeith. Several unpleasant realizations struck at once.

They weren't mercenaries.

Mercenaries were not known to possess clothing so fine as that worn by the men who stood before her. She also recognized the worth and craftsmanship of their armor. Nay, she wouldn't gain the sanctuary of the church before the bridegroom arrived. He stood before her.

But which one?

Her gaze slid to a man on the right, and she found nothing objectionable in his appearance. In truth, he was downright handsome. He had tawny hair and deep brown eyes that had probably melted many a maid's heart. The knight's roguish grin said he knew of his appeal, but the grin soon faded and became sheepish, as if he'd been caught doing something he shouldn't. Tess felt her heart sink with her hopes. She should have known Baron Montague would not look so nice. Nay, he would look like the other one, the one who looked like the Devil.

The Devil was taller than his friend, taller even than Uncle Ian, and his bulk made him much more imposing. His cloak was thrown back, and her gaze traveled slowly over his body, studying him with open curiosity. He was clad in finely linked chain mail armor covered by a blue and white surcoat. His armor did little to disguise a powerful build and an impossibly broad chest. Her gaze lingered on one of the massive arms crossed against his chest. She wouldn't be able to wrap both hands around those bulging muscles. The man was a giant, although she had to admit there was nothing hulking or clumsy about him. Every part of his body appeared in perfect proportion to his size. He reminded her of the sleek, dangerous panther that Dunmore MacLeith kept as a pet; the coiled power magnificiently fascinating, yet just as deadly.

Her gaze continued upward to his hauberk, which was pulled back to reveal hair as black as his fierce scowl. Even darker eyes glared at her from a face that was marred by a wicked-looking scar that ran the length of one cheek.

Why, his expression was all wrong.

Tess's lips parted slightly in surprise as she realized there was something intensely familiar about this man, a memory that floated just out of reach. Yet there was a difference she couldn't quite name. The eyes were too dark for one thing, Tess decided, her brows drawn together in a frown. And the lines of his face were too sharp, too vivid. She looked him over again from head to foot, trying to recall where she could have seen the man before.

Kenric knew his expression was severe enough to set friends and enemies alike on edge. It was wasted on Lady Remmington. The way she eyed him up and down like a cook inspecting a side of beef was insulting. He was about to redouble his efforts to put the bold wench in her place when their eyes met.

" 'Tis you," she whispered, looking ready to scream.

"Aye, 'tis me," he answered, his voice caustic. For a moment he'd sworn there was a look of recognition in her eyes, the same look a woman would use to greet a cherished friend. Or a lover. But the warmth in her eyes disappeared so quickly that he wondered if he'd only imagined it. The girl's lasting expression of stunned disbelief was more in keeping with a maid's normal reaction. She'd just been introduced to the Butcher of Wales, a man bearing the name mothers used to frighten their children into obedience. At least she hadn't fainted.

"You'll be marrying me whether you like it or not," he said in his own language. He was uncomfortable with the difficult Gaelic burrs and wanted the lady to understand his every word. It didn't matter if she'd rather marry a three-headed goat. The King of England had gifted him with Tess of Remmington, and Kenric had every intention of keeping her. He paused to give her a brief, chilling smile of triumph. "Or do you dare defy our king's command?"

Tess struggled to recover her composure under the baron's icy glare. It was a near impossible task, since she'd been caught so completely off guard. But who wouldn't be startled to see an image from their dreams come to life? It was too eerie. Surely that was the reason her stomach was acting queerly and she suddenly felt light-headed.

Don't be a goose, she scolded herself, shaking her head to brush away the foolish notion. So she'd seen the image of a dark-haired man while she slept, a man whose face haunted her dreams so completely that she thought she knew him. So she'd had the same dream every night for the past week. Coincidence. Aye, pure and simple coincidence.

She risked another glance at the baron's face, just to assure herself on the matter. Chilling, ruthless power emanated from the man who stood before her, a man who could kill without emotion or regret. There wasn't a trace of warmth in the cold black eyes that glared down at her, nor the barest hint of gentleness in that clenched jaw. Their eyes met again and this time she didn't miss the meaning behind his fierce expression. Why, he was trying to intimidate her!

He was succeeding.

She felt a shiver run down her spine and goose bumps prick her arms. She was snared by those eyes as surely as any trapped prey. They held her captive, the power she sensed there absolute, capable of forcing anyone to submit to his will. Surprisingly, the emotions swirling through her were the complete opposite of the fear or horror she should be experiencing. It was the strangest thing, but she had an indescribable urge to stand closer to the warlord. To touch him. To—

"Do you intend to answer, Lady Remmington?" Baron Montague's voice was laced with sarcasm. "Or shall I repeat the question? You do appear confused."

Tess bristled, her temper flaring to life. " 'Tis rude to glare at a gentle lady so evilly."

She turned to Father Olwen, missing the look of disbelief on Kenric's face. "Perhaps you can help these men see reason, Father. I would like to explain the situation, then I am sure you will see the wisdom of my decision and advise everyone accordingly."

"I will do my best," Father Olwen said uncertainly. "You should know that King Edward informed me of the reason for this marriage, Lady Remmington."

Tess nodded, then drew her braid over one shoulder and began to twist the ends.

"Tess . . ." Ian objected, her name long and drawn out, sounding almost like the hiss of a snake. Or a warning.

"I do not wish to marry." Tess saw Ian step forward and she hurried to give the priest her reasons. "My wish is to become a nun. As is customary, my estates can be divided when I take the vows. It will be as though I have died."

"You are hardly dead, Lady."

"Remmington would revert to King Edward," Tess continued, ignoring the baron's interruption. She tried not to think about the deepness of his voice, how it effortlessly filled the room, so penetrating, she could almost feel the sound vibrate through her body. *Dear God, what is happening to me?* she wondered in a panic, struggling to hold on to her argument. "If I enter a convent, Remmington will stay in English hands without bloodshed. My stepfather and King Alexander cannot object because the religious laws are the same in both countries and they would not dare defy the church in such a matter. If I marry anyone, there will be a war."

She ended her small speech by bowing her head, unable to look Father Olwen in the eye another moment. She'd lied outright to a priest! "You do see the wisdom of my plan, Father Olwen?"

The priest pursed his lips, studying the floor as he rocked back and forth on his heels. Tess finally noticed the tattered ends of her braid and smoothed the frayed tassel before letting it drop to her side. She was sure Uncle Ian knew of the lie. He could always see through her fibs. But what of Baron Montague? Did he know the truth as well? Lord help her, she had the most insane urge to marry this savage warlord!

"What say you to the lady's story?" the priest asked Kenric.

" 'Tis the truth as I know it," he agreed amiably. "Except for one part."

Tess felt her heart stop beating. She waited breathlessly for the baron to expose her deceit.

"There will be a war no matter what she does with her life."

She closed her eyes and sighed in relief. Her lie was safe from Baron Montague. She didn't hear him move silently across the room, didn't know he was anywhere near until his warm fingertips lifted her chin. Her eyes flew open in surprise. He looked deep into her eyes, his expression unreadable. Tess was sure time stood still as they stared at each other, nothing spoken, yet a certain message passing between them in that silent exchange. A warning, yes, but perhaps something more.

"She'll marry me," he said arrogantly, his eyes never leaving hers. He lifted his hand and brushed his thumb across her lower lip, sending another strange shiver down her spine. "Surely you suspected this in the woods, Lady Remmington."

He didn't give her a chance to answer. His hand dropped abrubtly to his side, as if he couldn't bear to touch her another moment.

"Do not be difficult, Lady. I am not a man known for his patience with the wiles of women."

Tess frowned over his arrogance but kept silent, not about to explain that she'd thought them mercenaries, hired swords to see her safely to a nunnery. He would surely think her a fool.

"Best we get on with this," Kenric told the priest. He took hold of Tess's hand, dragging her toward the altar. "We have wasted enough time."

That was all Tess needed to spur her into action. She tried to pull her hand away from the baron's, and when that didn't work, she turned to face him.

"I have yet to hear Father Olwen's advice." She took the priest's hand with her free one, her voice pleading. "These are men of war, Father. They think only of fighting. Surely you can see the rightness of my plan and give me sanctuary."

Tess nearly winced from the baron's crushing grip on her fingers but she kept her eyes on the priest, heartened that Father Olwen seemed to consider her words. The priest was her only hope.

"The church is for those with a true calling," Father Olwen said finally. "You must obey the wishes of your king."

"But—" Tess made a strange squeaking sound when Kenric squeezed her hand so hard she thought surely the bones would break.

"The hour grows late," Kenric said in a curt tone. "Your uncle needs to be well on his way when your absence is discovered."

"This is happening so quickly!" Tess looked to her uncle for support, but Ian pushed his hands forward, suggesting she should get on with the business. She bowed her head and softly whispered her misgivings. "I have so little time to think over this new plan."

"Best you think quickly, or your stepfather will be here to witness the ceremony." Kenric sighed impatiently. "You've a choice, Lady. Either me, or MacLeith."

She seriously considered MacLeith, but only for a moment. The

Butcher of Wales was hardly the best choice to her way of thinking, but she was free of her stepfather for the first time in five years and in no hurry to relinquish her freedom. But marriage? To this man? The price of her freedom was too high. Yet, perhaps if she were clever enough, she could escape the baron just as she'd escaped MacLeith. If Tess could somehow reach King Edward and explain her convent plan, he would see the wisdom of her actions and annul this hasty marriage.

Her gaze traveled slowly from the tips of Baron Montague's boots to the powerful arms, again crossed over his chest. She almost smiled at the irony of the situation. Why, Baron Montague was the only man in England whose reputation for wickedness surpassed MacLeith's. No matter how long this marriage lasted, she'd give almost anything to be in the hall when Dunmore MacLeith learned she'd wed the Butcher of Wales.

"I am ready, milord."

Anatomy of a Sale:
Mad About You

MALLE VALLIK
EDITOR, HARLEQUIN TEMPTATION

elighted.

That was how I felt when I read the first chapter of Alyssa Dean's manuscript *Mad About You*. A multipublished author once asked me what an editor hopes for when she picks another tome out of the never-ending slush pile; a slush pile that exists on the floor of my office with its own life force, threatening to someday rule the world. The author was curious: did I want to be able to read a few pages and reject the story, thus having some hope of seeing my office floor again (I believe the carpet is pink); or am I hoping to discover the next great thing?

For anyone who has chosen the daunting, sometimes ridiculous but rewarding career of publishing, the answer, always, is that I begin every story with high hopes. Maybe the writer will have it: voice, style, story and character. The ability to tell her story her way in an entertaining, interesting manner.

Editors love books. I love my monthly delivery of books published by Harlequin. I go to the bookstore two or three times a week to see how "my" books are selling—and to check out the competition. And, of course, to find books to read. Libraries are also great for that reason, although I have a problem with the idea of returning books. Once I've discovered a good author I want to keep him or her with me, or at least in my home.

Finding a new unpublished author creates a peculiar thrilling, emotional and slightly predatory instinct within me. If you are lucky enough to find a good manuscript in the infamous slush pile (at Harlequin we do read *everything* and the odds of being published are about one in a thousand), you feel like yelling, "mine, mine, mine."

But let me return to how I felt "delighted" when I read *Mad About You*. While we editors talk about and write about what makes a manuscript work—voice, character, plot, innovation, pacing, dialogue—what it really boils down to, especially in a romance novel, is emotion. Emotion created in the story, but also the emotion the editor, and eventually the reading public, experiences.

I trust my gut instinct. If the book piques my interest, if I can hear the writer's voice, if the story is intriguing and captivating, if I'm looking forward to turning the pages (even if there are problems), if the butterflies in my stomach start to dance, then I keep reading the story—with hope.

Before I return to Alyssa's story in more detail, I'd like to discuss genre fiction, especially romance. Many people assume that writing a category romance novel means writing to a very specific formula, and I admit there is one very important requirement—a happy ending. Other than that there are as many ways to tell a romance as there are popular songs on the radio (most of which are love songs, I believe). At Harlequin/ Silhouette we publish over 60 romance novels a month and we do have lines: Harlequin Temptation or Superromance, Silhouette Desire or Intimate Moments, etc. Other than the word length, the tone of the story should establish what line you wish to write for. My comparison again must be to another popular medium: whether you want to write for *Seinfield* or *Melrose Place*.

Alyssa Dean had sent her manuscript into Temptation, a contemporary, sexy line of approximately 60,000 words. We publish four Temptation novels every month. While we have a strong author base of regular contributors, we are always on the lookout for new talent (why we read every manuscript we've asked to see). It's never a good time to sell a first novel to a publisher but I can also say we've *never* turned down a good book because we have too much inventory. If it's a good book, I'll buy it. In publishing, things always . . . well, happen.

What Alyssa Dean did so successfully was understand the conventions of the genre—a likable and interesting hero and heroine for whom the reader quickly begins to cheer for their happy ending—and then made them her own.

Mad About You opens on a dramatic moment. The heroine, Faye, is trying to get into the Rinholt building late at night when a stranger confronts her. Good, the writer begins at a point of action and conflict between the hero and heroine.

I was pleasantly surprised and intrigued by Faye. She is clearly out of her element in the big city and she stutters. She doesn't seem to know much about high-security office buildings, or much about where she is. Yet, she has a clear strength and purpose about her.

Interesting. As a Temptation novel we expect a very competent, frequently savvy and sophisticated '90s woman (no frail heroines who are afraid to say what they want). I was curious about Faye. She stuttered, she was clearly out of her element and a little afraid, but she dogged on. I found her appealing.

Especially when the author had the good sense to contrast her with the hero. He seems very much like the standard romance hero: strong, world-weary and charming. Kent MacIntyre takes the stage in full control and then the writer begins to have some fun. And so does the reader.

Out-of-her-element Faye throws completely-in-control Kent—and the editor—for a loop. As we suspected, she has secrets (It turns out she's a pixie determined to save the world from imminent destruction. Seriously.) and the ability to completely befuddle and knock out our gorgeous six foot male.

Then the author segues to Kent's point of view and, while making him more than the cynical private eye, the story is inevitably set in motion. Alyssa Dean has successfully set her characters and plot into motion—and I wanted to know what happened next.

Most importantly Alyssa created strong memorable characters who I knew a lot about without stopping the storyline for the inevitable background narrative. Background is the bane of every editor's and writer's existence. How to clearly define character without endless paragraphs of how he or she got to the beginning of the story.

It is much later in the story that we learn about the heroine's unusual background (at least I consider being a pixie unusual) and the fact that her hero also has some *connection* to this is revealed near the end. But we already have a sense of this by the end of chapter one.

As well, I knew what kind of story this was going to be. Within category romance, the novel can be many things: a drama, an adventure, an intrigue, a paranormal adventure, etc. In Alyssa's writing I heard a sure voice, that her characters were set on the path of a comic paranormal adventure.

Not easy to do. But appealing and intriguing. One of the things that romance editors often state they are looking for is something new. This does not always mean a new and innovative plot, although that doesn't hurt, but new and fresh. Voice. Presentation. Character. Idea.

And Alyssa had all that.

While I had revisions for the author and she had to throw out the last 50 pages of the manuscript and rewrite, I bought the book. Yes, the author had some big work ahead of her, but because so much of the story worked so well—and was new—I was completely confident that she could successfully revise. Which she did.

But back to the first chapter—and a great ending paragraph: "I'll be there, too,' Kent decided. 'I'm looking forward to meeting little Miss Tinker Bell again. When I do, she'll wish she'd stayed in Never-Never Land!"

I was in the sure hands of a confident writer. And the possibilities for the story were endless.

Mad About You

ALYSSA DEAN

"Won't let you in, eh?" asked an amused voice.

Faye whirled around to face a tall, loose-limbed man whose features were obscured by the darkness of the Denver evening. She took a step backward and he held up his hands, palms outward. "I saw you go in," he said, gesturing toward the sixteen-story building across the street. "The way you hot-footed it down the stairs, I figured the security guard had turned you away."

"H-he did," Faye stuttered. She clutched her purse to her chest and wrapped her arms around it. She wasn't used to the city. Its unfamiliarity frightened her. This stranger was no help, either. His brown leather jacket and worn blue jeans suggested he was a creature of the streets—something she'd heard about but had never actually seen before. She had no idea where he'd come from. When she'd stumbled, mortified, across the pavement, she'd been certain there was no one out there. At this time of night all the stores had drawn blinds and Closed signs on the doors, and the bus-stop bench was deserted. Even the neon Café sign was turned off.

"I was in the alley," the man announced, as if reading her thoughts. "Why do you want to go into the Rinholt building?"

"I—I want to see someone." Faye was more than terrified now. The stranger was at least six inches taller than her own five foot three, and there was something sinister about the way the shadows cut across his face, giving her only an impression of darkness. "What were you doing in the alley?"

"Shortcut." He sounded as if he found the situation amusing. "Did you call him?"

"C—call who?"

"The person you're supposed to meet. He—or she—can authorize your admittance."

"I know." Faye moistened her lips with the tip of her tongue. "The se-security guard explained that to me." She shivered, remembering the cold, uncaring voice of that particular gentleman.

"So why not call?" he persisted. "There's a pay phone right over there."

"I tried." Faye hugged her purse tighter. "He didn't answer."

"Had he signed in?"

"N-no. But the security guard said that if he'd been there since before five, they would have a record of it." She swallowed hard, blinking away the threat of tears. She hadn't anticipated an intercom system at the Rinhold building, preventing her from even getting close to the security guard. Now she'd have to try the back, go through the dark abyss of the alley. Her heart pounded frantically at the very idea, but she knew it was the only way. She took a step toward the street, forcing an over-the-shoulder smile. "Well . . . um . . . thanks for your concern."

He slid back into the shadows of the closed buildings. "You shouldn't be out here this late, you know. It's past ten. This isn't the most dangerous city in the world, but it isn't that safe for someone like you."

"I know." She wrapped her arms tighter around herself. "It . . . can't be helped."

"You could come back tomorrow. The building's open during the day."

"During the day," she repeated thoughtfully. She desperately want to grasp onto that idea, for a moment even considered doing it, but it was out of the question. She instructed her trembling legs to take another step toward the street.

"Good Lord," said the stranger in a completely different voice. "You're going to try to break in there, aren't you?"

"D-don't be ridiculous," Fay stammered. "I . . . um . . . Well, it's really none of your business, is it?"

"It might be." He sounded thoughtful. "For all you know, I could own that building."

Faye eyed the tired-looking clothes. "Do you?"

"No." She heard a smile. "I could be an undercover cop."

Her heart took a huge leap. "Are you?"

He chuckled. "Not exactly."

"Well then, um . . . "

"My name's MacIntyre," he announced. He stepped out of the shadows, revealing a long, narrow face, punctuated by the deep vee of a widow's peak. His hair, under the unreal luminescence of the streetlamp, appeared so black it swallowed the beams of the light. His narrowed eyes were a similar color, wolflike, black irises flecked with lines of amber. The entire impression would have been sinister if it wasn't for the amused teasing in his eyes, the smile that hovered around his full lips, and the dimple in his chin. "Call me Kent."

He was now only a couple of feet away, smiling down at her with assessing admiration. Faye found herself returning that smile, as well as the admiration. There was something sensual in his languid movements, and in the way he was standing, his hips thrust slightly forward, his hands hanging loosely by his sides. "Kent MacIntyre," she repeated. Her voice was followed by a faint echo of his name: "Kent MacIntyre . . . MacIntyre . . . MacIntyre."

"That's right." His smile widened, he took a step closer, then seemed to catch himself. "Maybe you should go home. I'm sure your friend will understand."

Home? To her own safe little world? She'd left it only yesterday, but it felt like a lifetime ago. "No." she shook her head. "I can't do that. Home is far away."

"You're not from around here, then?"

"No."

"And you need your friend inside the building to take care of you?"

"Something like that," she said, nodding.

"Which floor is he on?"

"Um . . . I'm not sure. I think it's seven."

His voice took on a tone of suspicion. "What's this friend's name?"

"N-name?" She glanced over at the building, trying to remember the directory at the front. "Andrew. Arthur Andrew."

"The accountant?"

She nodded. "That's right."

Okay." He looked up and down the street, stroking his chin with one hand. "I'll tell you what. You tell me your name, show me some identification, and promise to stick close to me. I'll take you up to Arthur's office. How's that?"

Faye studied him hopefully. Could this be the help her mother's people had promised? "Are you a Wizard?" she whispered.

Kent chuckled and shook his head. "No, babe, I'm not a Wizard."

Faye wasn't convinced. Hadn't her mother told her that Wizards were pretty convincing? "How can you get inside that building, then?"

He took a step closer, his exotic scent surrounding them both. "Without the use of magic. Now, what's your name?"

She hesitated a brief moment, then sighed regretfully. She should have known a Wizard wouldn't be this good-looking. He was just a kind stranger, that's all; perhaps one who could help her. "Anna. Anna . . . Ross."

"Anna, is it? Do you have any identification?"

"Oh, yes." She found the driver's license in her purse and handed it over, not bothering to mention that it wasn't hers.

He squinted at it under the streetlamp. "You're from Rapid City?"

"That's right."

"You sound like you're from Britain."

"Oh?" She forgotten about the accent. "I . . . was."

He handed back the license. "I'm surprised your name isn't Tinker Bell."

"Tinker Bell?"

"As in *Peter Pan*." His long-fingered hands gestured in a movement that encompassed her body. "If you remember, she was pretty tiny." His grin flashed again. "Although very well put-together, I under-stand."

Now Faye's heart was thudding for an entirely different reason. "I'm n-not that sh-short," she stuttered. "Can you really get into that build-ing?"

"Sure." He put a hand around her elbow, his touch sliding through her thin green cotton blouse and up her arm, heating one half of her body. "Come along. Remember, stay with me, okay? I don't want to get into any trouble."

It's too late, Faye thought. She hesitated for a second, not sure she was capable of doing this. He raised an eyebrow, and she nodded. She had no choice.

Kent guided her across the street and spoke into the outside intercom with an air of authority. The security guard rose from behind the desk, strolled toward the wide glass doors and peered at the open wallet Kent pressed against the glass. The uniformed man pushed open the door, flicking a nod in their direction as they entered. "Sign in!"

Kent scribbled his name in a book on the desk, then offered the pen to Faye. Instead she pulled a pen from her purse and wrote "Anna Ross" in nice round letters. "Remember to sign out when you leave," the guard called as they started down the hall.

"You got it." Kent put his hand back on Faye's arm and led her to the elevators. "We're in," he whispered into her ear.

"How did you do that?" she whispered back. "What did you show him?"

"A security pass. I have one for this building." He motioned her to precede him onto the elevator. "Now, which floor did you say?"

She hesitated in front of the panel, then pressed a button. "Seven."

Kent rolled a shoulder against the wall, leaned his head back and studied her. His voice dropped to a suggestive draw. "You really want to see Arthur?"

"I do," she replied. She stared at him, memorizing the dark angles of his face, the lean movements of his fingers against his rib cage.

"Isn't he rather old for you."

Faye had no idea. "He's just a friend," she ventured.

"Good." Kent's lips drew up with wicked suggestiveness. "How long are you in town?"

"N-not that long."

"Well, if Arthur's too busy to show you around, I'll be delighted to fill in for him."

"Would you?" Faye lowered her lashes, resisting the urge to giggle. In this situation it was rather absurd to be flirting with a handsome stranger who, tomorrow morning, would be furious with her. "That's . . . very kind of you."

His grin widened. "*Kind* probably isn't the right word."

Faye struggled against his charm and gave him a huge, grateful smile.

"I really appreciate your help. How did you get a security pass for this building?"

"I work here, sometimes."

"Oh? Who for?"

"Stuart Investigations," he said.

Faye curled her fingers into fists, hoping her face wasn't revealing the horror she felt. "Investigations? Y-you don't look like a detective."

"Don't I?" He sighed dramatically. "And I try so hard. What does a detective look like?"

Faye could hardly breathe. "I'm not sure. I thought you were a street person or something."

"I know." He grinned. "That's what a detective is supposed to do. Blend in." The elevator jarred to a stop on the seventh floor. "Here we are."

Faye stepped out, with Kent a breath behind her. The doors whispered closed. Faye turned her head slowly, checking. The elevator was located in the middle of the building; to her right was a set of glass doors labeled Barkers Insurance, and to the left, matching doors marked Arthur Andrew, Accountant. There was nothing in the hallway, and apparently no one on the floor.

"There's no one here," Kent said in her ear. He crossed his arms over his chest, his eyes clouding into wariness. "How about telling me what you're really after?"

"I just want to . . . to . . . " Her heart slammed so hard against her chest that she thought she'd pass out. She put her right hand in her purse. When she pulled it out, it was filled with fine, white powder. She glanced down at it, forcing herself to breathe. She had to do this. There was no other way. "I'm really sorry about this, Kent MacIntyre. You have no idea how sorry I am." She took one final look at his beautiful dark eyes, held out her palm and, ever so gently, blew into it. The white dust floated into the air. Kent stepped back, swiping it away with his hand, he gave a shuddering moan, then crumpled to the floor.

Faye backed up, shaking with horror at what she'd just done. She scampered down the hall, searching until she found the ladies' room. When she located it she raced back, grabbed Kent's arms, and although it took most of her strength, dragged him down the corridor and into the washroom. Then she knelt beside his unconscious body and struggled to turn him, which allowed her to retrieve his wallet out of his pocket. "I'm so sorry, Kent," she whispered into his ear. "Please forgive me." She pressed a finger against the faint stubble of his jaw, inhaling his scent, fighting the feeling that she'd done something she shouldn't have. Maybe she should have tried to explain, asked for his help. She picked up one of his hands, then dropped it, shivering. No, that wouldn't have been wise. She hugged herself, pulled Kent's security badge out of his wallet. It was too late now to back out. Her self-imposed mission had begun.

"For Pete's sake, can't you talk quieter?" Kent asked through his tensely bunched jaw. "That charming policeman treated me to the same lecture. Now my head really hurts."

Dan Stuart paced across his small, square office, stopping long enough to grace Kent with a look of furious annoyance. "Your head *should* hurt, damn it!"

"It's swell to see you, too," Kent muttered. He watched Dan's usually placid features tighten ominously and winced. There were few people whose opinion of him mattered to Kent, but this sixty-six-year-old man was at the top of the list. Now, because of that pixie woman, his standing with Dan had dropped a notch. He scowled at the thought, and the pounding in his head increased.

Dan took two huge strides to his desk, yanked opened a drawer and pulled out a package of macadamia nuts. "What in hell did you think you were doing?" he snarled as he tossed the package into Kent's lap.

Kent unwrapped the package with slow, painful movements. "Helping a damsel in distress?"

"Maybe you should be a bit more choosy about your lady friends!"

"She's no friend of mine," Kent said bitterly. He nibbled on one nut, and then another. The pain in his head abated a millimeter. "Come on, Dan. It isn't as stupid as you and the police make out. She said she wanted to see someone in the building. I took her up to see him. I'm sure you've done the same sort of thing yourself."

"I may have," Dan allowed. "However, I make sure they follow regular security procedures, such as signing in!"

"She did sign in," Kent insisted. "I saw her do it. So did the guard!"

Dan's voice rose again. "The guard can't remember you coming in, let alone her! As a matter of fact, he doesn't appear to have much recollection of the night at all."

"The police told me that," Kent said glumly. "I get the impression they aren't taking my story very seriously."

"That's not surprising," Dan said, sighing. "Did you have to tell them you were attacked by Tinker Bell?"

"That's what she looked like!" Kent conjured up her image and resisted the urge to smile. "She's short, just over five feet, with silver blond hair, blue-gray eyes. A real cute little thing. She spoke with a slight accent—British, I think."

"You're right," Dan grunted. "You were attacked by Tinker Bell. She won, too." He tossed a laminated square across his desk. "She left this behind."

Kent picked up the square and stared at his own picture. "My security badge?"

"That's right. She used it to break into my offices. I've checked it for fingerprints, but it's been wiped clean."

"Wonderful," Kent said with a groan. "Just wonderful!"

"Oh, it's wonderful, all right. You can't imagine how wonderful it was to have the police call me at—" Dan pushed back the cuff of his striped shirt to reflect on the time—"six in the morning to tell me the security guard had found you, unconscious, in the seventh-floor ladies' room."

Kent shifted uncomfortably.

"What were you doing here last night, anyway?" Dan asked sharply. "I wasn't expecting you until this afternoon."

Kent sighed. "I got into town around ten, and stopped by to see if you were in. I parked my bike in the alley, and saw the woman. I felt sorry for her, Dan. She didn't seem to belong there, and she didn't seem to know what to do. She claimed to be a friend of Arthur's. I volunteered to take her up to his office. When she got off the elevator, she blew some kind of knock-out dust at me and that's the last thing I knew until this morning."

"Next time, let me know where you are!" Dan slammed a fist down onto the desk. "My daughter-in-law phoned. She was worried about you."

Kent dropped his head into his palms. Dan's daughter-in-law was also Kent's sister, Avril. He and Avril had always been able to sense each other's emotion, no matter how great the distance between them.

Although she was hundreds of miles away, Avril had picked up on the fact that he had a problem and, in her usual big-sister fashion, wanted to solve it for him. "Great," he moaned. "The police think I'm crazy, you think I'm incompetent and my sister thinks I need a baby-sitter."

"I don't think you're incompetent," Dan said after a moment. "I think you're too easily fooled by a pretty face, that's all." His voice softened with concern. "You look awful pale, boy. Are you sure you don't want to see a doctor? I have no idea what kind of powder she used. I've never heard of anything that potent."

"Neither have I." Kent took a few breaths and straightened. "I'm okay. Really. It's just that same headache, and the nuts are helping."

Dan's lined face tightened into wrinkled concentration. "Why are the nuts helping? I thought you only got that headache when you—"

"I don't know," Kent interrupted. "I didn't do anything unusual. Go ahead. Tell me what she took."

"She didn't take anything." Dan absently rubbed a shoulder. "Amy's double-checking right now, but nothing seems to be missing. There's no indication that she touched the computer, but Amy will get on it as soon as she finishes going through the paper files. Someone was looking through them. The file cabinet was left slightly open. She must have used your badge to get into the room."

"She could have looked at anything," Kent muttered." Are you working on something special?"

"Not particularly." Dan shrugged. "I'm looking into an insurance claim, and you already found that character who'd joined the motorcycle gang. By the way, his parents are suitably grateful."

Kent grunted a response. He didn't do the sporadic jobs for Dan because he wanted gratitude, or because he had any need for spare cash. Frankly, he was in it for a good time, and a little excitement. This case he'd just wrapped up had been particularly fun. He spent a week riding around on his motorcycle, wearing leather and acting tough while he searched various motorcycle gangs for the kid. As a matter of fact, this last week was the most fun he'd had all year, right up to the point where he'd met a sexy young pixie.

"I might have something," said a deep female voice. Kent carefully turned his head to watch Dan's right-hand woman, Amy Laxton, stride purposefully into the room. Amy was short, squat and middle-aged, and she ran Dan's office with seamless efficiency. "The McAllister file was out of order," she said. "It was in front of McAllaister, instead of behind it." She glared at Dan. "Did you touch my files?"

Dan quickly shook his head. No one, but no one, was that brave.

"Then someone pulled out the McAllister file, or the McAllaister file," Amy continued. "I checked the copier log. Someone made five copies between last night and this morning." She handed a file folder to Dan. "I think it's this one. The other doesn't contain five pieces of paper."

Dan flipped open the file folder as Amy marched out of the room. "Ron McAllister," he said. He did a quick check of the contents, and started swearing.

"Who's Ron McAllister?" Kent asked.

"He's a friend of mine." Dan shook his head, sighing. "Two weeks ago he was made acting head of security for Sharade."

"Sharade. The cosmetic company?"

"That's right. They've got a research facility on the outskirts of town. Ron doesn't know much about security. He was in personnel, but when the chief of security suddenly passed away, Ron took on the acting position."

"Why did he come to you?"

"First off, he wanted me to take the job instead of him. I refused, of course. He knew I would. I don't do that kind of boring junk. I told Ron to study the security plans, and probably leave well enough alone until they find someone with the right qualifications."

"That's it?"

Dan winced and shook his head. "Not quite. As sort of a learning exercise, he and I designed and installed a super-deluxe security system for his house. The plans are in this folder."

Kent rubbed his eyes while he tried to make sense of it. "This Anna Ross sure went to a lot of trouble to get the plans for his house. Does he own something valuable?"

"It's not what he owns. It's what he has there."

"What does he have there?"

"A copy of the security plans for the Sharade Research company building. I know they're there. I was going over them with him last week, just before he left town."

"This gets worse and worse," Kent moaned. "Don't tell me Ron's house is empty?"

"Afraid so. He's out of town this week." Dan shuddered, picked up the phone, and made a quick call. "No alarm was reported at Ron's house last night," he announced when he hung up. "Still, with the plans, it is possible to break in and not trigger the alarms. I bet this Anna Ross character is going to show up at the Sharade Research Lab real soon. Possibly tonight."

I'll be there, too," Kent decided. "I'm looking forward to meeting little Miss Tinker Bell again. When I do, she'll wish she'd stayed in Never-Never Land!"

First Sales

*I*n this section, the six finalists for the 1995 RITA Award in the category of Best First Novel share their stories of how they wrote and published their first romance novel. Each story is different, like the novels themselves, yet they share a few common elements—a love of romance, hard work, rejection, revision, support from the Romance Writers of America and, above all, the determination to never give up.

Each of these writers has gone on to publish more books. No doubt you will see their names on future RITA ballots. But they started out just like everyone else, making mistakes, fighting frustration and pressing on. They made it.

So can you.

DONNA DAVIDSON
Elizabeth's Gift, Signet Regency Romance

"I was an avid reader from the time I was a child," says Donna Davidson. "I read everything from comics to classics, then spies, sci-fi and eventually computer manuals. Then I found romances, and I discovered that they were so much more fun. They had humor, the women were the heroes and there were happy endings. They were simply charming." And that, she says, is basically why she started writing them. "The delightful stories I read conjured up book concepts of my own. Finally, after joining Romance Writers of America, I mustered up enough courage to start putting my stories down on paper. That was the beginning."

One of those stories became *Elizabeth's Gift*, a Signet Regency Romance published in 1994. It won the *Romantic Times* reviewers' award for Best First Regency, *Affair de Coeur's* reviewer's award for Best Regency, and was a finalist for RWA's RITA award for Best First Book.

Elizabeth's Gift is the story of a Regency girl who has dreams and visions warning her of danger to her loved ones. According to Davidson, the premise of the book is based on personal experience. Like her main character, she has warning visions and dreams about her family. "The last time it happened, I dreamed my husband was standing on this high place and he had both of his hands on an electric wire and was being electrocuted. I immediately woke him up to warn him. Then a couple of days later he climbed a ladder going up to our patio cover to clear away a big branch that had fallen off our redwood tree. When he saw that the branch was tangled up in two 220 wires, he remembered the dream and called the electric company. It took two men to disconnect the wires and clear the branch." Had her husband tried to do it himself, she says, he would have been seriously injured or killed.

In addition to drawing on this type of personal experience for the book, Davidson researched the details of Regency era life and medicine for the historical aspects of the novel. "I accumulate probably ten times more research than I ever put in a book. You don't make mistakes," she says. "The average romance reader is a mature woman with a college education. Regency readers especially are very knowledgeable; they know their history." Part of the appeal of historical romances is that readers like learning new details about life in that era. The trick, Davidson says, is to bring something new to the story. "If you can find someone's journals or reports of personal experiences, then weave those facts into the fabric of the story, it makes the book so much more interesting."

How do you get such a volume of research done and still have time to write? One way Davidson has found is to enlist the aid of her spouse. "The main body of my research is done by my husband," she says. "He's a retired engineer and attorney, but his first love has always been historical research. It's worked out perfectly. He goes through libraries and old bookstores digging for good information for me to read. It literally saves me weeks."

Once *Elizabeth's Gift* was written, Davidson entered it in the Orange County RWA's unpublished contest, where it won first place. "After that I was encouraged to take it to Pat Teal, who is an agent in the Orange County area. She loved it and sent it to Jennifer Enderlin at Signet." Enderlin thought enough of Davidson's work to offer her a two-book contract. "In a way, I feel I haven't paid my dues," Davidson says. "It went faster than I could have ever hoped for."

Davidson says that membership in the Romance Writers of America proved extremely valuable to her. "That's where I really gained writing skills. I think all romance writers should belong. RWA offers the practical help of critique groups and the excellent mentor program. And we all need that energy from other writers. Until RWA's network was established, writers were isolated. Now this organization keeps its members informed about what's happening in the publishing world. In addition, RWA—now 8,000 members strong—has crusaded for better contracts and a forum where communication can take place between writers and publishers. Publishers are now listening, and important changes have already taken place."

RWA is just part of the ongoing education that Davidson feels is vital to writers. "A writer should never stop educating herself," she says. "I go to every workshop and conference I can; I'm constantly reading books on the subject; I'm constantly reading to gain more information. The writers whom I admire say that they don't just read about their own subject, but read to broaden their entire scope of understanding." In addition, computer skills and knowledge of English and grammar are important, Davidson says. Once they are ingrained, the story can flow onto the page unencumbered by the technical aspects of writing.

"Writers need time to daydream," Davidson says. "We spend a lot of time in that other world with our characters and their lives. These characters become real to us and, if we are lucky, to our readers as well. One fan thrilled me by saying 'When I finished *Elizabeth's Gift*, I just hugged it.' Another lady asked, 'What are Elizabeth and Hawksley doing now?' And very seriously, I told her."

"Write the book that's burning in your brain," Davidson says finally. "There's no greater high than writing a great story."

MARGOT EARLY
The Third Christmas, Harlequin Superromance

Photo: Rhonda Huffer

It took Margot Early five years to make her first sale. Though editors who saw her early manuscripts acknowledged her talent, her beginning manuscripts contained many of the usual problems of novice writers.

"The first manuscript I submitted was rejected," she says, "but it came back with a personal letter from a senior editor in charge of acquisitions for Harlequin Romance. She said that, although the book was wrong for their line, she thought I had storytelling ability and was interested in seeing more of my work. The second manuscript I submitted to them was what eventually became *The Third Christmas*. I submitted it to the same editor, and she suggested I revise on speculation. She wrote a three-page letter with detailed suggestions and also noted suggested changes in the manuscript."

Over the next few years, Early revised that manuscript twice and also submitted and revised other projects for other lines. The winds of change came at a 1993 Utah RWA conference, where she met the Harlequin editor for whom she had twice revised *The Third Christmas*.

"During that appointment," says Early, "she said she would be acquiring for Harlequin Superromance and that she was still interested in this book I had twice revised for her." Since Superromance published longer books, Early revised the manuscript yet again, "and as though it was always meant to be a longer book, it came together."

All the work paid off, however; *The Third Christmas* was a finalist for the Best First Book RITA Award in 1995 and for the national Award of Excellence from Colorado Romance Writers. It won the regional Heart of Romance Award from the Coeur de Bois chapter of RWA.

In the 18 months since her first sale, Early has sold four more books to Harlequin: *The Keeper* (released November '95), *Waiting for You* (June '96), *Mr. Family* (October '96) and a fifth Superromance to be released in 1997.

Early stresses the importance of knowing the market you're writing for, saying a new writer must read the most current releases. "It's important to know the subtle differences in the particular lines and houses. That means knowing the differences between a Harlequin Intrigue and a Harlequin Superromance, a Bantam Loveswept and a Silhouette Desire, a series romance and a single-title release, a contemporary and a historical."

Early also feels it's important for new writers to be professional. "Sometimes, people who want to write romance don't have a professional background. They're not sure what is expected of them in a professional relationship. It's important to find out that information and act on it. Editors and people in the industry appreciate a professional attitude and the willingness to work together. When you're working with an editor and a publishing house, it is a team relationship. You're trying to produce the best product that you can, and I think that starts when you are unpublished and you are asked for revisions. There is an opportunity to demonstrate that you are a team player, that you are willing to attempt to make these changes."

Early is a team player in more ways than one; she belongs to three writers' groups and RWA. "Belonging to RWA and taking advantage of their services really helped me sell my first book," she says. Early attends a few conferences each year and keeps in frequent contact with her colleagues, both by phone and mail.

"The way to sell a first book," says Early, "is by writing *complete manuscripts*, one after another until you sell. And be willing to change. I think having a writing career means being open to change constantly. Most writers need to undergo significant change in order to sell a book." If you are serious about becoming published, Early says, be realistic. "Live in the real world. Study the market and master the English language. Take advantage of all avenues of knowledge open to you, be professional and pursue writing a book that will sell like you would a Ph.D."

LYN ELLIS
Dear John . . ., Harlequin Temptation

Photo: Sue Ann Kyhn-Smith

"I have found that the essence of telling a story is not what you put in," Lyn Ellis says, "but what you leave out." Her career as a commercial photographer has taught her to tell a complete story with a few pictures. "You can walk out your front door and take a picture of *everything* you see and you'll have an image, but it won't mean anything. However, if you focus on the person walking down the sidewalk, or the old building across the street, or the dog digging up your flower bed, then you have the beginnings of a story."

Like most romance writers, Ellis started writing romance because she loved reading it. "It's my sister's fault," she jokes. "She got me hooked into romance with books by Kathleen Woodiwiss and Rosemary Rogers. I have always been fascinated by the emotional relationships between people, so reading romance was a natural."

Ellis has always been a writer as well, although of a slightly different sort. "I've always been a journaler. For the last twenty years, I've filled a lot of notebooks with my own feelings about events in my life, the adventures of people close to me and, during my college years, my attempts at poetry, short stories and songwriting. I suppose it took all that time for my ambition to evolve into the decision to write a book."

Although *Dear John* ... was the first book she published, it was not the first book Ellis wrote. In fact, it wasn't even the second or the third. "My first three books would be classified as science fiction or fantasy," she says. "Back in the early '80s, I fell in love with the futuristic movies and TV shows; *Star Trek*, *Star Wars*, etc. My only complaint was that they didn't deal with relationships. The stories were based more on technology and different world views. So when I sat down to write, I decided to combine my two loves—sci-fi and romance."

Unfortunately, this was before the popularity of paranormal and futuristic romances. Her first book—a 140,000-word futuristic epic romance—went with Ellis to the Moonlight and Magnolias Conference sponsored by the Georgia Romance Writers. There she met with editors and established writers, and they all gave her the same advice: It won't sell, it's too different and there's no way to market it. Her second book, a time travel romance, met with the same response. In a very nice, handwritten response, one agent said her career would be better served by writing a more traditional book.

"Instead of taking the advice that seemed to be pounding at me from every direction," Ellis says, "I got mad. My next book was a futuristic *romance* with a heroine who was an assassin." At this point, five years had passed since she wrote her first book. Finally, Nicole Jordan, a published friend, "nearly wrestled me to the ground and told me in no uncertain terms what I needed to do. 'No space ships! No barbarians! No trips back in time and *no* assassins! Write a Traditional Book and you will sell it!' "

At the time, Jordan had also talked Ellis into writing to her brother, an Army Infantry captain on the front line in the Gulf War. "I had never met him," Ellis says, "and the idea of corresponding with a man who was a complete stranger intrigued my writer's mind. Also, what could be more 'traditional' than the military? The captain's name was John, and the letters we exchanged became the seed for a book. *Dear John . . .* flowered from that seed."

If the letters were the seed for her story, research was the soil. As part of her research, Ellis traveled to Fort Riley, Kansas, and spent three days following around a captain of the infantry. "My first conclusion was that there aren't too many things about the Army that are romantic.

The long separations are hell on marriages; they are underpaid and are required to live by the rules; they expect to die in a war. What I came out with ultimately is that there are men and women who believe in honor and who would die to preserve this country's freedom, there are men and women who believe in family and commitment, and there is a brotherhood among some soldiers that is a bond worth risking life and limb to uphold. Now that's romance. I used the real and the idealistic and came up with a hero who was everybody's brother and every woman's fantasy."

Ellis entered *Dear John* . . . in the Maggie Award competition when the next Moonlight and Magnolias conference came around. When it won, Ellis sent it to Harlequin Temptation on the advice of Harlequin Superromance Editor Paula Eykelhof. She had no agent and was unsure of how to sell the book.

"Seven months of slowly pulling the hair out of my head one by one followed," Ellis says. "Unable to stand the wait any longer, I went on vacation and left the phone unattended." That's when Temptation Editor Malle Vallik called, reaching Ellis's fiance, who had never read the book. "He proceeded to tell her what a wonderful story it was, and yes, of course I would do revisions and he would certainly have me call her when I got back into town. I can laugh about it now, but at the time I was like, 'Oh God! What did you say to her?' "

But Vallik wasn't put off, writing instead a three-page letter explaining all her concerns with the book. Ellis made the changes and returned the manuscript, and when she met Vallik at the national RWA conference in St. Louis, Vallik told her that Harlequin Temptation wanted to buy the book. "I can't tell you much else about that convention," says Ellis. "I was walking around smiling with one phrase repeating in my head: 'Write a traditional book and they will buy it.' "

Now that she is writing short contemporary romances, Ellis sees the irony in the growing popularity of futuristic romances. "I have two books and a partial sitting in my file cabinet and sketches for three other books I would love to write, and now I don't have time. My plan is to write short contemporary and make a run at getting established as a *romance* writer. I feel Harlequin has given me the opportunity to do that."

CATHY MAXWELL
All Things Beautiful, Harper Monogram

"Right from the very beginning, I was preparing to become published," says Cathy Maxwell. "I didn't play at it."

Maxwell became interested in writing romance after hearing Christine Dorsey speak at a local library. Dorsey told the audience that if they were really interested in writing a book, they should attend a conference the following month sponsored by the local RWA chapter. "I don't pass up good advice, so I called and registered for the conference. I was very fortunate, because Gary Provost was the main speaker. He believed that if you had a writer inside of you, you could learn the mechanics. All you had to do, basically, was sit in a chair and start writing."

That same conference taught her it wasn't quite that easy, however, when she turned in ten pages of work to be critiqued. "I had absolutely no idea what I was doing. I laid out the manuscript completely wrong, with four lines between each paragraph. I had someone nursing someone for all ten pages. We took temperatures, we felt foreheads. It was boring." Nevertheless, the critique panel told her she had talent. "With that and what Gary Provost had to say, I started to educate myself as a writer."

Maxwell joined the local chapter of the RWA, read books on writing and attended as many conferences as possible. She took workshops and talked to writers, paying close attention to what they said. "When a writer said you need to set a goal of how many pages you were going to produce a week, I set a goal of how many pages I was going to produce a week. If they said you need to join a critique group, I joined a critique group. If they said you need to go to these conferences and meet this person, I did it. If they said you need to make presentations to editors, I did it." Sometimes, Maxwell traveled long distances just to meet an editor. "If an editor was invited to a meeting or conference within 100 miles or, in a few cases, 300 miles," she says, "I would make the effort to go to that conference or that meeting, just to meet them." The effort paid off when Maxwell met the Harper Monogram editor who would buy her first book. Having heard the editor was going to be attending a local RWA meeting, Maxwell arranged to be in a group editor appointment with her.

"What often happens," Maxwell says, describing the dynamics of a group appointment, "is that you'll have three to five people in the appointment with you, all sitting around a table. The editor will go from one person to the next, and you get maybe three minutes to pitch your story." Such group appointments are often the only way a writer can meet an editor whose schedule doesn't allow one-on-one meetings. "I ended up being the last interview of the day in a group of five people, and at that point I just introduced myself. I told her who I was represented by and that I had just wanted to take this time to meet her." The editor asked her what she wrote and Maxwell told her she wrote historical romance and that she'd recently submitted a manuscript to Harper Monogram. "She said, 'Fine, I'll look it up.' And that was it. But a month later I sold the book." Maxwell feels that, after a day of hearing one book summary after another, the editor appreciated her succinctness.

For now, Maxwell writes only historicals set in the Regency time period. In addition to *All Things Beautiful*, she has also written *Treasured Vows* (out January '96 from Harper Monogram), *You and No Other* and *This Time, Forever* (due out from Avon). "For every writer, it's important to build a reputation and a name," Maxwell says. "What I opted to do, and what's worked for a number of others, was to take one time period and build a readership in that time period. And then later, I can go into other time periods." It's the same approach Jayne Ann Krentz, writing as Amanda Quick, took. "She wrote one time period for six or seven books until she was very well established, and then she branched out into other time periods."

Although this may seem limiting, Maxwell says the Regency era is a fertile era with many story possibilities. She has shelves of books set in or written about the period, and when those fail to provide the information she needs, she goes to the library. She cautions, however, against letting research get in the way of romance.

"You can research and research, but the emphasis of the book is always on the relationship. And human relationships haven't changed all that much over the years. We still have the same arguments, the same jealousies, the same pettiness, the same things that make us laugh. We're not so much interested in the grand picture—we're interested in what's happening in a particular house on a particular street between a particular two people."

Maxwell shares the Boy Scouts' point-of-view: Be prepared. Investigate agents, keep up on the market and don't be afraid to ask questions. "Writers are extremely candid people," she says. "You ask them a question and they give you a straight answer. I can't recall ever hearing a writer or an editor duck a question." Always keep in mind the next step. "When you sell that first book, it's like jumping over the Grand Canyon with a tricycle; it's a major accomplishment. But then you look up and there's a mountain as high as Everest, and you still have the same tricycle. It's possible to go as high as you want, but you have to learn. You have to teach yourself every step of the way."

JUDITH O'BRIEN
Rhapsody in Time, Pocket Books

Photo: Donal Doherty

A beginning romance writer might stay in safe territory, writing a Regency or a contemporary romance set in a popular era and city. Not so Judith O'Brien. Her first novel, *Rhapsody in Time*, is a time travel romance set in 1920s New York, a time and place not very common in romance fiction.

"Pocket had some concerns with that. Nationally, people don't like New York," says O'Brien, a Brooklyn resident. "Also, the '20s is not considered a really appealing time to write about. I have to give Pocket a lot of credit for letting me do it and not forcing me change it to a different time."

Pocket's decision may have been due to the extensive research O'Brien put into the book. "I became entranced with the 1920s," she says. "It's not a period you read about much in fiction. It's too old to be contemporary, yet too recent to be historical. It sort of exists in this twilight zone of history. There were so many details I wanted to put in that nobody would care about, and I had to force myself to edit down to just what people were interested in and what was important to the story."

As in all romances, the story is the focus and is what led O'Brien to her research. "Seven years ago, I was looking at this book about 1920s composers. When I reached the chapter about George and Ira Gershwin, I found this odd picture of George Gershwin. He never smiled for photographs because he thought his teeth looked too pushed in, yet here he was with this big grin on his face. And there's this woman next to him with her arm around him. She looked as if she stepped out of the late '80s or early '90s. She looked so fresh, without the eyebrows that were plucked to oblivion and the heavy makeup. Her hair was bobbed, but it wasn't Marcelled. And the funny thing was that the seams of her stockings were wrapped around her legs like a barber's pole, as if she didn't know how to deal with seams on stockings." It led O'Brien to ask 'what if?' "All of a sudden I thought, she doesn't look like she came from the 1920s. It looks like this was taken yesterday. And then I thought, wouldn't it be interesting if this *was* taken yesterday, but yesterday was in 1927." From those musings, the story was born.

At the time, O'Brien was researching nonfiction articles at the library. Knowing little of the 1920s, she began spending a little bit each day reading old newspapers. "I was working on some really boring article about vegetarian children or something," she says. "So I allowed half an hour of my library time to research vegetarian children and then I'd look for half an hour in the old *New York Times*. And pretty soon I was spending ten minutes on my articles and three hours reading old magazines and newspapers, watching silent movies."

All that time spent was worth it; *Rhapsody in Time* won the Golden Leaf Award for Best First Book and was nominated for the Best First Book RITA Award, as well.

Along with writing a good book, O'Brien had good contacts. During the year in which she wrote copy for Pocket Books, she often had lunch with a few people who had since moved up in the company. One is now the publisher and the other was Linda Marrow, now senior editor and vice president. "At the time, we were all grunts and used to go to the falafel cart together, because it was about the only thing in Manhattan we could afford," O'Brien says. After having her book rejected at several smaller houses, she got in touch with her old co-worker. "I called her up and I said, 'Linda, you haven't heard from me in a long time, but I have this book that's been rejected all over the place. Would you tell me what I'm doing wrong with it?' " Marrow was very uncomfortable, but agreed, saying she would most likely limit her comments to advice on where to send the book. "I sent it to her on a Friday," O'Brien says, "and she called me on Monday to offer me a two-book contract."

O'Brien negotiated that contract herself, and although she got a fine deal, she says she wished she'd had an agent. "Emotionally, I could have used the support. It was very difficult to call up with an editorial question and then say, 'where's that check?' It blurs the line between creativity and business. I didn't realize how important an agent was, not just for negotiating a contract, but for doing stuff like making sure you get a great cover and being a go-between for all the nastiness, so it doesn't mess up your relationship with your editor. With your editor, you can have a pure relationship that's just based on books. It sounds like a luxury, but it's not. It's a necessity."

Although she worked in the business, O'Brien had never been involved in the entire process, and found it an interesting experience. "I'd worked in editorial. I'd never worked with publicity or contracts or the marketing side. It's very different to see one product go from a manuscript to a viable book." She says the procedure might be intimidating to an unpublished writer, but it's not that bad. "The thing is not to be too frightened of the process. It's not as bad as going to the dentist."

ANGIE RAY
Ghostly Enchantment, Harper Monogram

Photo: debbi de mont

"I've always liked to write, but I never really intended to write a book," says Angie Ray, author of the RITA Award-winning *Ghostly Enchantment*. "It seemed impossible." Ray's attitude changed when a friend talked her into taking a fiction writing class at a local college. "The class was taught by Elizabeth George, who is a mystery writer, and our first assignment was to turn in a ten-page outline of our book. I had to do something, and that's how I started."

Although the class was taught by a mystery writer, it led Ray in another direction. "The teacher told us that we should choose to write something that we love, and for me that was romance. There was no question; I've always loved romance." Ray adds that it was more the *bad* romances that made her want to write than the good ones, because she thought she could write a better book.

She soon discovered that writing a better book was a lot harder than it looked, when she began work on *Ghostly Enchantment*. "I got the idea from a trivia column in the newspaper," Ray says. "There was a small article about how in the 1700s, I believe, a witness was once allowed to testify that a ghost had given him information about a murder.

From that, I started wondering, what if a man were falsely convicted based on such unfair and ridiculous testimony. And wouldn't it be ironic if he was a ghost, and had come back." This provided Ray with her alpha (or "macho") hero, with whom her heroine would become fascinated. Then she added Bernard, the insect-studying beta (or "nice-guy") hero, who is the heroine's fiance. "I used point of view to manipulate the reader," she says, explaining that she switched points of view several times and used it to introduce the main characters. "One of the trickiest things was that I had the heroine falling in love with the ghost and then I had to have her turn around and fall in love with Bernard. And the way I did that was through point of view." Although switching points of view often confuses and alienates readers, Ray's execution worked well. "Most people don't even notice it, but it is something that I did deliberately."

Ghostly Enchantment is set in 1847 England, and Ray spent a lot of time at university libraries researching the period and even visited the country. "There are different levels of research," she says. "There's researching the time period and there's researching insects. I had to do research on clothes and travel and eating and that kind of thing." She writes as much of the story as she can before hitting the books in order to figure out just what she needs to look up.

When she had finished writing the book, Ray sent three chapters and a synopsis to several publishers, noting in her cover letter that it was a multiple submission. Harper asked to see the complete manuscript for their Monogram imprint, so she sent it with a cover letter. "I had won a couple of contests, including the Golden Heart, and I had met an editor from Harper at one of the local romance writer's meetings, so I had something to put in my cover letter to spark their attention." The publisher called within two weeks to buy the book.

While Ray's manuscript sold on its own merits, her story exemplifies the bonuses of networking. Had she not joined that local writer's group, she may not have met the Harper editor. And had she not joined Romance Writers of America, she wouldn't have been able to win the Golden Heart Award, given annually by RWA for the best manuscript by an unpublished writer. In addition, Ray goes to a weekly critique group and participates online in GEnie's Romance Exchange almost every day. "I think it's important for people to realize that writing is not something you study for four years and then you know everything," Ray says. "It's a constant ongoing process of learning. And the business side of it is a whole other aspect that you have to keep up with and try to figure out." It's not easy, she adds, but it's made easier if you join RWA and take advantage of the vast network of romance writers.

"You have to be willing to learn," Ray says. "And you have to finish the book. Someone, I can't recall who, said that if you finish the book, your chances increase 95 percent of getting published. The most important thing is that you have to be willing to really work at it."

CHERYL ST. JOHN
Rain Shadow, Harlequin Historical

When she wrote her first published book, *Rain Shadow*, Cheryl St. John was working 40 or more hours per week as a merchandising artist for a local grocery chain, making all the signs and artwork for the stores. "I wrote whenever I could squeeze in the time—even weekends and holidays," she says. "My husband, bless his heart, would take the two younger kids and go to family events and even out-of-town reunions without me, just to give me time to write."

The sacrifice paid off. Harlequin bought *Rain Shadow* for their Historical line, along with its prequel, *Heaven Can Wait*. "The first book I wrote well and tried to sell was *Heaven Can Wait*. Everyone turned it down—all the publishers, all the agents. But I didn't give up; I kept it on the shelf. When I sent *Rain Shadow*, I got an agent immediately. My agent loved it and sold it to Harlequin within four months. Since the hero of that book is the brother of the hero of *Heaven Can Wait*, we went back and told them we had this other book with some of the same characters in it and asked if they were interested. They said yes, but I had to cut a hundred pages from it. I did, and so basically sold both books right together."

Anton Neubauer, the hero of *Rain Shadow*, is a widower in search of a proper mother for his young son. Rain Shadow, the heroine, is a sharpshooter in Buffalo Bill's Wild West Show. Orphaned as a child when Indians attacked her parents' wagon train, Rain Shadow was raised by the Lakota Sioux and learned to hunt, track and shoot. "I always try to match up my characters with someone they *don't* match up with," St.

John says. "Anton wanted someone prim and demure, and I thought someone who could rope and ride and shoot, a Wild West show performer, was the exact opposite. And that was how I created Rain Shadow."

It worked. *Rain Shadow* was nominated for three major awards in the romance field. *Romantic Times* magazine nominated it for the Reviewer's Choice Award for Best Western Historical; it was an *Affair de Coeur* Reviewer's Choice nominee; and it received a nomination for the Best First Book RITA Award, given out by the RWA at their annual national conference.

Research was relatively easy for St. John, who lives in Nebraska. In addition to her standard library research, she was able to visit the Buffalo Bill Rest Ranch in North Platte. "It's always good to visit a location when you can, but that's not always possible," she says. "Whenever I take a trip, I visit the historic homes and mansions and learn about the furniture and the time period. My passion is the American West, and there are so many places where we live to go to study it." St. John also has an extensive library of books on the subject, uses the local library's resources and watches Western movies or movies related to her subject.

St. John finds other resources in writer's groups and organizations, especially Romance Writers of America and their local chapter, Romance Authors of the Heartland. "I found RWA in 1989, and one of my regrets is that I didn't find them sooner. I belong to a couple of other writer's groups, but RWA is my rock. That's where I do my networking, that's where I learn. Anything you want to find out, you can find out from RWA." St. John goes to as many RWA conferences as she can and has served as a program chairman, vice president and, finally, president of the chapter for two and a half years. She also belongs to a weekly critique group. "It's invaluable help and feedback," she says. "Whenever I'm having a little bit of a problem, I bounce it off of my group. I have all those other brains to work with besides my own and that's the most exciting part. They help me immensely."

Support is another function of critique groups and RWA. "When you're starting out, you always want someone to tell you that you can do this. You need that validation, somebody to tell you you're good, you can do this. But really there isn't anyone that can do that except yourself. You have to believe in yourself." St. John says that the validation comes when the publisher buys your book. "When they are actually willing to take a chance and spend money on you, you know you're good enough.

Until then, you just have to keep believing in yourself and keep writing. There are so many writers who could be published now who just gave up because it took too long; it was too hard and it was too frustrating. I tried for years to sell. When I felt like quitting, I asked myself 'What if my next book is the one that sells?' And so I just kept at it."

Another way to beat feelings of frustration and dejection, St. John says, is to set goals. "Say to yourself, 'By this time next year, I am going to have this book finished and put in the mail,' and then do everything you can to attain that goal. Set short-term goals that are easily achieved, and set long-term goals." Short term-goals give you a feeling of accomplishment, she says, so that the long-term goal is less daunting.

"Don't put it off," St. John says. "One of my regrets is that I didn't get serious about my writing earlier. So many things are learnable, and the only way to find out if you're doing it well is to go ahead and do it and get those rejections. Stack them up and learn from them. It makes you vulnerable to send your work out and let other people look at it. But don't be afraid to do it."

GAYLE WILSON
The Heart's Desire, Harlequin Historical

"I literally could not find the kind of books I like to read," says Gayle Wilson, when asked how she got into romance writing. "And the authors I liked weren't writing fast enough." Like James Fenimore Cooper, Wilson thought she could write a better book than the ones she was seeing in the bookstore, and so she finally sat down to do just that. *The Heart's Desire* was the result.

"I've never had a desire to write 'literature,' " she says. "When you read what's being written today, the so-called 'serious' literary fiction, so much is filled with despair and disillusionment, depravity even. There, the human condition has sunk even lower than it has in the real world. I *read* for pleasure, for escape. I suppose I *write* for the same reasons— to create a world as it should be, where the good guys get what they should and the bad guys do, too. A world where good triumphs over evil and people mean what they say about faithfulness and commitment. I've been married to the same man for 26 years and my parents were married for 56 years before my dad died. That might have something to do with the fact that I still believe in the reality of romance."

Even though she didn't write until recently, Wilson's education in the craft of romance began very early in her life, when she was introduced to the works of Georgette Heyer, the queen of the Regency romance, by her dorm mother. Other early influences were the historical novels of Dorothy Dunnett, Frank Slaughter and Frank Yerby. "If Yerby and Slaughter were published today," Wilson says, "we would say they are writing historical romance."

Wilson sold her first effort to Harlequin by submitting it over the transom. "I didn't write a query letter. I didn't know you were supposed to do that. I just mailed them the whole manuscript." Six months later, the manuscript came back with a letter from Angela Catalano, suggesting changes and saying she would like to see the revised version. Wilson made the changes and sent the book back, at which time Tracy Farrell, the senior editor, called to buy the book. "It should be comforting to somebody out there to know that they do read all those things in the slush pile," Wilson says. "They certainly read mine, and I know that's where it was, on the slush room floor, for part of that six months."

Wilson has since sold five books to Harlequin, two of which are sequels to *The Heart's Desire*—*The Heart's Wager* and *The Gambler's Heart*. Two novels are romantic suspense and the other is another historical, which seems natural for Wilson, who teaches history and English. Most of her research comes from her personal collection of books and the local library, but she also attends any local exhibits or special events that have relevance to her work. "The city of Memphis, Tennessee, had a wonderful exhibit on Napoleon two summers ago. They had uniforms, jewels, dresses. They even had the carriage in which he rode through Russia on the Russian Campaign. I went to that twice, and a lot of that material ended up in *The Heart's Wager*."

Although Wilson has friends now that are writers, she did not when she was starting out. She does belong to RWA, but does not do much networking beyond that. "I'm not online, I don't belong to a critique group. It's wonderful just to have writer friends, because no one understands the ins and outs and frustrations of writing unless they're doing it."

Wilson writes all summer, since that is when school is out. "I write from dawn to dusk. I write best in the morning, so the school year really blows me away." Wilson says she can proof and polish in the evening, but her teaching drains her of any creative energies. "I write on the weekends when I'm teaching, all day Saturday and some on Sunday."

Wilson believes you have to write what you like to read in order to create a great book. "If you're trying to write for a trend, it shows. Your book lacks the emotional depth that it would have if you wrote the kind of book you love to read." Likewise, characterization is important. "The characters have to be real to you before they can be real to anyone else."

But probably the most important advice Wilson ever got was to keep writing. "Write it, send it off and forget about it. Start on the next project. Once you send it off, there's nothing you can do to speed up the process or encourage people to like it. You just have to write the best book you can write, put it out there and get on to the next one."

Resources

Commercial Online Resources

D O N   P R U E S

*W*hile it will be quite some time before dust jackets become a thing of the past, the electronic world grows by a staggering degree every day. It seems you can't turn on the television or pick up a magazine anymore without seeing someone's Internet address, and few are those who haven't heard the term "Information Superhighway." You can send electronic mail ("email") to your friend in Saskatchewan, a major network news show, NASA and even the President of the United States. Universities in New Zealand can instantly exchange information with universities in Brazil. A boy in Paris, France, can pit his video game skills against a girl in Paris, Texas. The uses of this expanding technology are virtually endless.

Writers use the online medium for many reasons: to correspond, conduct research, participate in critique groups, interact with established authors, get acquainted with other romance aficionados, purchase books, express opinions, and just have fun. They take electronic writing courses, receive prompt feedback on manuscripts and talk with writers in various cities through virtual conference calls, or "chat sessions." What's more, they can go online 24 hours a day, every day.

There are, however, some drawbacks to going online. It takes a few hours for new users to acquaint themselves with a particular service to understand how it works. Sometimes they won't know where or how to begin, daunted by the wealth of resources out there. Getting online support can also be difficult, especially if 2 million other users are encountering the same problems at the same time.

Money is another concern. Most online services have a flat monthly fee (about $10) which is billed to your credit card. With this fee you're usually granted 5 or so hours of online time, depending on the service. After you've depleted these given hours, you are charged an hourly rate, usually $3-5 dollars per hour.

The biggest complaint about online services and the Internet, however, is that they are highly addictive. Hours can be quickly sucked away as you peek and poke around the world, reading and responding to debates, chatting with old friends and total strangers or downloading fun new programs and graphics. Much discipline must be used to prevent your online time from encroaching on your writing time.

Assuming you want to take the online plunge, there's still one question you must answer: Which online service is best for me? Sure, you can ask your friends who have an online account if they're happy with their service, but will that same service be the most suitable for you? Unfortunately, the only objective way to ascertain which service suits your fancy is to try them all. If, however, you don't have time to spend testing each service, here's a sampling of what the major online services offer romance writers.

AMERICA ONLINE

America Online is one of the largest commercial online services in the United States, with a very strong romance presence called the Romance Writers Group (RWG). At last count they had over 500 members, including 150 published writers. There's no membership fee or requirements. While they are not associated with the Romance Writers of America, most RWG members are also RWA members, including some top writers: Diana Gabaldon, Stella Cameron, Nora Roberts, Millie Criswell, Rebecca Brandewyne, Ann and Evan Maxwell, Teresa Medeiros and others.

AOL's Romance Writers Group has a very active volunteer staff, consisting of two workshop moderators, a workshop greeter, a newsletter editor and two assistants, four "Cybernauts," a librarian, a World Wide Web expert, and a critique group coordinator. They have weekly workshops and Q & A sessions with editors, agents, publishers, and, of course, published writers. If you feel like socializing, there are 50 folders with over 10,000 messages posted—it's very popular. In the folders you can find information on new releases, author newsletters, and discussions on technique.

Also offered are a monthly newsletter ("Lovelines"), a Cybernauts program, articles and help files. "We solicit files from our members on every aspect of writing and we upload those to the libraries and our romance area," says Carmel Thompson, AOL's romance contact. "We have a librarian who works with memberships and maintains our list.

The list is also posted in the romance area so people can easily find what they need. Our Web/Internet expert finds romance sites, answers questions about the Web, and puts together our Web lists and other interesting sites-lists."

To order AOL software, call 1-800-827-6364. Romance contact is Carmel Thompson (CarmelTh@aol.com).

COMPUSERVE

Like AOL, CompuServe is a major online service that offers vast resources for romance writers. There are two main Forum areas that writers in general will find useful: The Literary Forum and The Writer's Forum. The Literary Forum houses 23 subtopics on issues that most romance writers will find interesting. The two most popular are Section 17, which is devoted solely to romance, and Section 23, a private section for the RWA Online.

Section 17 is dedicated to both readers and writers interested in romance. Included in Section 17 is a Romance Reader's Group that reads one book each month and then discusses it online. There are also numerous published romance writers who frequent Section 17, and they are more than willing to offer advice.

Section 23, the RWA Online's special area, is a full-fledged chapter of the RWA. "We are the first online chapter and offer a unique service within RWA," says Liza Lee Miller, one of its moderators. For various reasons such as geography, time constraints, and family obligations, many writers are unable to interact with members in their regional chapters, so the RWA Online allows them a convenient alternative. "All members of the RWA Online must be members of the RWA national and also subscribe to CompuServe," says Miller. The chapter offers a bimonthly newsletter ("Love Bytes"), critique groups, romance writing classes, and other interesting writing services. All members are writers, both published and unpublished, and there are a few agents and publishers who are members, too.

To order CompuServe software, call 1-800-848-8990. Romance contact is Liza Lee Miller (Lizalee@leland.stanford.edu). Ms. Miller also has a superior Web site with many resources for romance writers, including links to other Web sites and services online.

GENIE

GEnie is extremely popular among romance enthusiasts. One nice aspect of GEnie is that you don't have to be a subscriber to access its Romance and Women's Fiction Exchange (RomEx). "RomEx is a part of GEnie run by authors and fans of romantic fiction for authors and fans of Romantic fiction," says Callie Goble, who moderates the RomEx research discussion area. To get there, contact ROMANCE$@GEnie.com if you are not already using GEnie, or from GEnie type ROMANCE or ROMEX from any menu prompt or move to Page Number 1330 (type m1330 at the menu prompt).

"GEnie allows information to be separated into categories, and then subdivided into topics. Up to 50 categories with 50 topics each are possible within a roundtable. For example, the Craft of Writing category contains separate topics for point of view, description, villains, heros or whatever," says Goble. In addition, there are private categories for discussing sensitive issues and other more public areas to discuss almost anything about writing. Also, some private categories have libraries associated with them, but only members can access the files. These are used by the online critique groups, or to archive messages from a private topic. Other libraries contain archives of messages, or information files uploaded by members or staff. There is also an online newsletter about writing romances called Pen & Mouse.

At last count, there were more than 150 published authors using RomEx. Authors can get feedback on manuscripts in private, basic or advanced critique groups. GEnie provides a review service, online conferences with authors or editors, and regular unmoderated chat sessions and game playing sessions. Authors and editors online include Mary Jo Putney, Susan Elizabeth Phillips, Laura Kinsale, Jo Beverley, Anne Stuart, Susan Wiggs, Roberta Gellis, Jill Barnett, Rebecca Brandewyne, Barbara Samuel, Leslie Waigner, Denise Little, Mary Theresa Hussey and Steve Zacharius.

To order GEnie software, call 1-800-695-4005. Romance contact is PatO@genie.com.

MICROSOFT NETWORK

Because it was created with Windows 95, Microsoft Network is relatively small at the moment. It is predicted that it will grow by leaps and bounds throughout the late 1990s, eventually towering over all other major on-line services. The reason: every IBM-compatible PC with Windows 95 also comes with pre-installed MSN software, so millions of new computer buyers are also getting MSN, and many will be using it. But remember, you must have Windows 95 to access MSN.

Even at the moment, there is a folder devoted to writing of all types. This large umbrella is subdivided into many smaller, more specialized folders and bulletin boards. One is dedicated to romance, and a few published authors have already been cited in this area, providing advice, doing a bit of self-promotion and the like. There is also a folder where you can search for a collaboration/critique partner. This can be quite helpful to beginning writers. And, MSN has chat rooms in which live author interviews take place. By the time you read this, MSN could have quite a bit to offer the romance enthusiast. You might want to check its current status.

To order MSN software, call 1-800-386-5550. Romance contact is Leigh Beckman (Leighab@msn.com).

PEOPLE TOGETHER

Dr. Ken Matsumura created People Together back in 1993. Unlike regular online services, People Together is an affordable online service for "dedicated bulletin bullers." You pay $19.95 a month and you get unlimited access to the service. If you want Internet email, however, you must pay an additional $5.95. There are no hourly or extra charges beyond this, no long distance fees, etc. The service uses an off-line reader, so it doesn't tie up your phone line. The writing host is Alison Hart, who was on Prodigy but changed to People Together two years ago because "both the price and the atmosphere there were not for me—I didn't like the censorship, or the atmosphere of chronic bashing. People Together has none of those disadvantages."

For the romance writer, People Together has a readers' board, and in the writing section, boards dedicated to publishing information, writing techniques, special projects (like critiquing) and a chat board. Because it's small, People Together has room to cater to individual writer's needs. "Our boards contain both genders, all ages, and we have chosen not to separate by fields, but to work together," says Hart. "Our writers' expertise range from contemporary to historical, suspense, fantasy, poetry, and mainstream." While most are romance writers, Hart has found that all writers benefit most (especially when discussing books or writing techniques) when not separated by genre. Active "crew" members include a retired editor, a librarian and a teacher. Consider this a family atmosphere.

To subscribe to People Together, write to One Alin Plaza, 2107 Dwight, Suite 100, Berkeley, CA 94704, or call 510-548-1516 or 1-800-638-9637.

Romance contact is Alison Hart (alisonharttn.com).

PRODIGY

As with America Online and CompuServe, Prodigy has a solid area dedicated to romance writing, the Romance Novels area. To get there, move your cursor to Jump, type in "Books bb" and then select Romance Novels. The Romance bulletin board is very active with a hundred or so subject headings going at once. The abbreviation on subject headings for the writers group is p*rwg (Prodigy Romance Writers Group).

This group offers much to the romance writer: critique sessions, agent news, weekly writing assignments, publisher/editor news, reviews and new releases by authors online. The critique groups are divided by the staff, based on writing level, sub-genre, and whether a member wants to be critiqued. In addition, there are online chat sessions centering on writing techniques and related issues. They have a different topic and speaker each week. Also, they have a monthly newsletter. At last count there were 150 members. In addition to talking about great books, there are subject headings for book swaps, discussions about the appeal of the genre and notices of author signings. Cathie Linz (xgev62brodigy.com) is the Romance bulletin board's "unofficial ambassador." She says, "As ambassador, I make it a point to welcome all newcomers."

To order Prodigy software, call 1-800-822-6922. Romance contact is Carolyn Terril (uddv20arodigy.com).

These commercial online services, like the many smaller services that exist around the world, are wonderful ways for writers to network, exchange critiques, keep informed about the market and conduct research. They also serve as an access to the even larger realms of the Internet and the World Wide Web (see Callie Goble's "Memoirs of a WebMistress" on the next page).

♡   ♡   ♡

Memoirs of a WebMistress

*Or how I ended up with my own Internet domain, fully tangled
in the World Wide Web, speaking HTML like a native, and
why it's all Karen Harbaugh's fault that I'm in this mess*

CALLIE GOBLE

he World Wide Web, usually called the Web, is part of
the Internet (the Net). The Web can transmit text, still
graphics, video clips, and sound from a storage place anywhere in the world to the reader's computer. It started as a way for
scientists to share illustrated technical documents with each other. Now,
you can view clips from the *X-Files*, read all the latest on the Ebola virus
outbreak, or watch live video from the latest hurricane tracking plane.
You can buy chocolates, CDs—or houses!

SOME WEB TERMS

This is technobabble at its best:

Internet Service Provider (ISP). The company you connect to in order
to get to the Net. All the major online services (GEnie, Prodigy,
AOL, CompuServe) connect to the Net.

Server. The computer the ISP uses to send and retrieve things on the
Net. Your computer talks to the server, the server talks to other
servers around the world.

Page. A single Web text file, with its associated graphics, video and
sound.

Browser. The software that lets you see the Web page text, and often
the graphics, video and sound (this varies from ISP to ISP—if you
use GEnie, Prodigy or AOL, you are using their choice, and might
not see all the goodies).

Site. Loosely, a group of servers with a common address. Also a cluster
of related pages, such as the "Jane Austen site."

Home Page. The page that your ISP lets you store on their server.

Hyper Text Markup Language (HTML). Code that Web pages must use.

Addresses. Addresses like http://www.acme.com/more/stuff/and/junk-.htm are usually arcane and bewildering. All you have to remember is to type them in exactly the way you see them and you will go there.

Domain. The top level of an address, such as www.writepage.com (my domain).

FTP—File Transfer Protocol. The Internet way to get non-Web files from one computer to another.

WHAT'S ON THE WEB?

The best description yet of the Web: "It's like the Library of Congress, with the books scattered all over the floor." I'd add: "It's being remodeled constantly, and the janitor moves books without telling anyone, but there are robot librarians that will tell you where the books are if you know what questions to ask."

Technically, what we're dealing with are several interlocking networks, but the boundaries are blurring. From your chair, it all looks like it is happening on your computer. The Net is the world's largest hard drive: millions of files are stashed all over the planet, and moved or deleted without warning. More are added daily, without notification. The Net is the global Bulletin Board Service: you can join discussions (called newsgroups), or mailing lists about any topic you want, and you can receive junk mail. It's the world's party line: if you are logged in through a provider that allows it, you can chat worldwide. And the Net is also the world's emailman: any two persons with connections to the Net can exchange messages. What's more, the Net is the world's public park—everybody hangs out there. Unfortunately the park has its idiots, anarchists, soapbox preachers, hucksters and weirdos. But it's also a great place for authors to promote themselves. The best way to do this is by getting established on a Web site, or home page.

HOME, HOME ON THE WEB

Web sites are usually educational and informative: a way for a university or government to quickly distribute information about their services, make priceless manuscripts available to scholars, or aim you at the place the information is stored. Right now, science and computers predominate, but humanities sites are mushrooming. You can find 14th-century Italian census data, the complete texts of Medieval Latin or Old Norse literature, and even a virtual Louvre.

Although there are commercial shopping mall sites, selling things on the Web isn't booming yet because of security and payment problems. Just how would a buyer in California pay for chocolates from France to be delivered to her mom in Australia? And how safe is her credit card number? More commonly commercial sites give away information about their products in order to influence buyers' decisions. It's low-key advertising because the reader has to deliberately come looking for it. The trick is to have information they want, make it easy to read, easy to find, and make it interesting.

Universities, and some government sites, often allow their staff to create home pages reflecting personal interests. If you can tell a lot about a person by snooping in their bookcase, reading their home page is better. It was love at first pixel when I discovered that Dieter's home page has pointers to godiva.com, the Web-guide to sushi bars of the world, and the jazz sites. Alas, his email address ends in "edu.de" (indicating a German university) so the relationship remains at the cyber-flirt stage.

Personal home pages are multiplying like unwatched coat hangers. Most of them are dull, with scanned photos of the family pet and pointers to the sites the person finds interesting. Others have become world-famous centers for promoting the owner's special interests. While home pages come and go, and therefore addresses change, nonetheless here are some interesting sites related to romance and writing:

http://www.stanford.edu/~lizalee/romance/
http://www.interlog.com/~ohi/www/romance.html
http://www.writepage.com/romance.htm

GETTING YOUR HOME PAGE

How do you get a "Home Page?" Find an ISP that allows customers to create home pages, learn enough HTML to make it look decent, and learn to FTP your page onto their server. If you want graphics, you learn to make GIFs or JPEGs from clip art or scanned images. If you want more than one page, you learn how to construct links. Some ISPs are starting to provide page templates and an easier way than FTP, but it is still a time-consuming task of trial and error. Or, pay a professional "Web Designer" to do the page for you. Rates vary wildly, but $200 or so is a commonly quoted figure.

What will a "Home Page" do for you, as an author, for publicizing your coming books? In truth, a home page on a public ISP won't do much. If 150 writers have 150 individual home pages, advertising the fact that they write romance novels, the user can't easily find them all. If a potential reader asks the librarian robot for "romance novels," the robot would come back with the first 10, then the next 10 . . . and give the reader 150 places to go. Even if each author's home page linked to the other 149 home pages, the logistics are intimidating. Who keeps track of the addresses? What if Pollyanna Pureheart's release date changes? Who's on first?

THE RIGHT SITE, AND THE WRITE PAGE

Here's where it becomes Karen Harbaugh's fault. We were talking about the problems of publicity for authors when I was in Seattle. I had just finished a project involving TCP/IP, HTML, FTP, and the rest of the techno-trivia involved in setting up Web sites for my employer. Somewhere in the course of the conversation she must have slipped something into my sandwich and planted a subliminal suggestion in my brain, because within a couple of weeks I had established a publicity site for authors under my own domain name: http://www.writepage.com, or The Write Page.

At the risk of sounding like a blatant infomercial for my site, I think it's a good idea for authors to use a dedicated publicity site, even if they have an ISP that allows personal home pages. This is why I established my site:

Power. Power on the Net comes from being an information-providing site. It's like an information potlatch. The more you have to give away, the more widespread your reputation, and the more influence you wield. If those 150 writers were linked on a single server, with a single address, they would be a "site"—a place with a lot of related information that is easy to visit in one jump. Everyone attracts more traffic, and everyone gets more publicity.

Author control. There are several publishing house and bookstore sites, but they are run by the publisher or bookstore. They decide who to promote and who to ignore. I want authors to write their own publicity, and have it posted in time to affect sales.

Affordable publicity. There are two ways to get enough money to rent the server space and transmission lines—get a lot of money from a few authors, or get a small amount from a much larger group. A larger group will be more effective because of the concentration of information.

Addressing. http://www.writepage.com is easier to remember than a lengthy path to a personal page—a path that will change if you change providers, or your provider rearranges its files. My domain is on a commercial server, not running off my home computer; that can of worms is too messy to open, even for me. But, because I own the domain name, the address goes with me if I change providers.

Control. Managing updates is easiest if one person maintains the site. With a local ISP, I can test and update pages with a local call. Every author has a single contact for updates. One person knows where all the links go, and has a map of them.

Technical expertise. The Web is easy to use, but a site is not easy to build. You have to know how to register with the search robots, design pages for all browsers, make the site attractive to users, and get the information out there with all the codes correct.

It isn't easy to assimilate all that information, put it into practice, and finish the revisions on your next historical. But it's possible. I get paid to do online books, learned Webmaking on my last job, and am crazy enough to tackle running a genre fiction promotion site. Come on and join me.

Editor's Note:

In addition to romance writers, publishers are now establishing Web pages to promote their books. Avon, Ballantine, Bantam/Doubleday/Dell, Harlequin and Topaz all have Web pages full of information and novel excerpts. Keep your eye on book advertisements—most likely you'll find the Web addresses there.

Organizations, Conferences and Workshops

*N*etworking is important to any writer's career, but it is especially of benefit to the romance writer. Thanks to authors and industry professionals dedicated to improving the genre, information and career-building opportunities are easily accessible to beginning romance writers.

A great part of this is due to the efforts of an organization called **Romance Writers of America** (RWA). With more than 100 chapters around the world, RWA provides its more than 7,600 members with everything from industry news to writing tips, career-building advice to agent and editor information. Unlike similar organizations in other genres, RWA does not require its members to be published; its wealth of information can be yours for the membership fee.

RWA's bimonthly magazine, *Romance Writers' Report (RWR)*, is packed with advice, news, contest and conference listings, articles by romance professionals, and much more. Their widespread chapters provide learning opportunities, editor contact and manuscript critique for writers all over North America and even in Australia. For writers not near a chapter, RWA has the Outreach Committee (see page 329), a correspondence chapter that provides newsletters, manuscript critique by mail and educational opportunities. Outreach also publishes an annual resource directory, available to its members for an additional cost.

RWA sponsors an annual national conference, at which it presents the RITA and Golden Heart awards (see **Contests and Awards**) for both published and unpublished authors. Many RWA chapters also have conferences, awards and contests, and often you do not have to be a member of the chapter to enter.

Another RWA benefit is its Professional Relations Committee, which advises writers about agents and editors, acting somewhat like a "Better Business Bureau" for writers. If members have a grievance with an agent or editor, they can register their complaint with the committee and check to see if other authors have had similar complaints. They can also use the committee to investigate an editor or agent they are unfamiliar with.

Within RWA is a group for published writers called the **Published Authors Network (PAN)**. There is no extra cost to become a member, but to join you must have published "a novel with a romantic theme written for adults (40,000 word minimum) or young adults (30,000 word minimum)" with a "royalty publishing house with national distribution." PAN publishes a bimonthly newsletter, *PANdora's Box*, which is available to all RWA members for $20 per year. PAN also holds members-only conferences and events, and offers Provisional and Associate memberships for writers who have published romantic-themed work other than novels (e.g. novellas, scripts, short stories).

Being active in one of the RWA chapters listed in this section is a good way to begin networking and to further your education as a writer. The information and contacts you will acquire are of a kind you simply can't get anywhere else, and the psychological benefit of other writers' support is itself often worth the membership fee. It behooves you to attend one or two meetings just to "try them out."

NON-RWA ORGANIZATIONS

While RWA is the main organization for romance writers, it is not the only one. Groups such as Novelists, Inc. and Sisters in Crime, while not specifically romance writer's organizations, are also valuable. These groups provide contacts, information, support and education in much the same way as RWA, but with a different emphasis.

Novelists, Inc.

Membership in Novelists, Inc. is open to any author who has published two or more novels, at least one of which was published within the past five years. Annual dues are $50, and include a subscription to the *Novelists' Ink* newsletter. Founded in 1989, the organization has more than 500 members and holds an annual conference each October.

Novelists, Inc. publishes a directory of agents for its members, with information about the listed agents drawn from questionnaires and member feedback. Each listing also includes the names of members who are clients of that agent, for reference purposes. A membership roster is also published to promote networking among members.

If members encounter problems with an agent or editor, Novelists,

Inc. acts as an intermediary in resolving the dispute. The organization is also creating a home page on the World Wide Web.

For more information, contact Novelists, Inc., P.O. Box 1166, Mission, KS 66222-0166.

Sisters in Crime (SinC)

Sisters in Crime was founded in 1987 to address the concerns of women who read, write, buy or sell mystery and crime fiction. With a membership of over 2,200 members, SinC's purpose as defined by their bylaws is "to combat discrimination against women in the mystery field, educate publishers and the general public as to inequalities in the treatment of female authors, and raise the level of awareness of their contribution to the field."

Membership in SinC "is open to all persons worldwide who have a special interest in mystery writing," including writers, readers, editors, agents, booksellers and librarians. SinC seeks to do for the mystery genre what RWA has done for the romance genre—establish a network of authors, educate new writers and assist in the promotion of its members and their books.

Annual dues are $25 in the U.S. and Canada, and $30 for members in other countries. Members receive a membership directory and quarterly newsletter. SinC also sponsors retreats, workshops and conferences. For more information, contact Beth Wasson, SinC Executive Secretary, P.O. Box 442124, Lawrence, KS 66044-8933.

ALABAMA

HEART OF DIXIE

ADDRESS: P.O. Box 2099, Gadsden, AL 35903
PRESIDENT: Linda Winstead Jones
ESTABLISHED: 1988
PROFILE: Meets monthly. 43 members. Meetings held in Cullman, AL. "Our meetings are informal with programs on writing or on a subject of interest to our members." **Dues**: $20. Dues do not include membership to RWA. 25% of members are published. Published members include: Linda Howard, Beverly Barton, Gayle Wilson, Venita Helton

and Kay Cornelius. Usually holds yearly conference in Huntsville or Birmingham on third Saturday in May.

GULF COAST CHAPTER RWA

ADDRESS: P.O. Box 850756, Mobile, AL 36685-0756
PHONE: (334)660-9176
FAX: (334)660-9176
PRESIDENT: Judith G. Bland
ESTABLISHED: 1993
PROFILE: Meets monthly. 80 members. Meetings held at Skyline Country Club, Mobile, AL. "At our meetings we have a social hour followed by lunch and then a speaker or a workshop. Members often stay after meetings to form critique groups." **Dues:** $20. Dues do not include membership to RWA. 20% of members are published. Published members include: Linda Baker, Terryl Boodman, Robert Adams and Cindy Holbrook. Usually holds yearly conference at Gulf Shores, AL in May.
COMMENTS: "Our published writers are THE BEST! They give unselfishly of their time to help others make that first sale."

ARIZONA

PHOENIX DESERT ROSE 60, RWA

ADDRESS: 1482 E. Butler Circle, Chandler, AZ 85225
PHONE: (602)917-8041
FAX: (602)838-6221
EMAIL: p.jennings@genie.geiss.com
PRESIDENT: Dawn Creighton
ESTABLISHED: 1985
PROFILE: Meets monthly. 130 members. Meetings held at Sizzler Scottsdale Pavillions. "Networking and dining begin at 5:00, and the meeting itself begins at 6:45 with RWA business first and then a special program, which varies from grammar checkers to pathology. We have guest speakers from time to time. Our chapter holds several workshops during the year which cater to different levels of writing experience. We also have a mentor program that pairs an unpublished author

with a published author who will critique either a manuscript or a synopsis one-on-one." **Dues:** $20. Dues do not include membership to RWA. 15% of members are published. Published members include: Jacyln Reding, Laurie Campbell, Judith Hill, Sharon Wagner, Pat Warren and Anita Gunnufson. Usually holds annual conference at various locations in second weekend in September.

WRITERS OF THE PURPLE PAGE
ADDRESS: 2340 W. 20th Street, Yuma, AZ 85364
PHONE: (619)572-0876
PRESIDENT: Florence 'Pinkie' Paranya
ESTABLISHED: 1993
PROFILE: Meets biweekly. 14 members. Meetings held at Yuma's Book Gallery, 2340 West 20th Street, Yuma, AZ. "The first meeting of the month is usually devolted to critiques, the second a workshop on craft and technique, or we have a guest speaker. As a group we go to many conferences. We've found these very helpful. We also ask local successful women to speak to us about their careers and how they combine their careers and their personal relationships. This gives us good story ideas." **Dues:** $15. Dues do not include membership to RWA. Published members include: Carrie Peterson.

CALIFORNIA

SAN FRANCISCO CHAPTER, RWA
ADDRESS: % Sonia Simone, P.O. Box 14612, Berkeley, CA 94712
PHONE: (510)649-9618
EMAIL: sonia@well.com
PRESIDENT: Sonia Simone-Rossney
ESTABLISHED: 1988
PROFILE: Meets monthly. 167 members. Meetings held at Berkeley Marina. Meetings consist of "announcements and chapter business, breakfast, speaker. Sometimes an additional speaker gives a brief talk before breakfast." **Dues:** $20. Dues do not include membership to RWA. 35% of members are published. Published members include: Jill Barnett, Susan Krinard and Sonia Simone.

COMMENTS: "Our focus is on professionalism and high-quality speakers. We are a friendly, helpful group and welcome writers at all levels."

IMPERIAL VALLEY RWA

ADDRESS: P.O. Box 395, El Centro, CA 92244
PHONE: (619)352-2853
PRESIDENT: Stacy Madelina Furrer
ESTABLISHED: 1995
PROFILE: Meets monthly. 5 members. "Meetings held at individual members' homes at present, however we are looking for a permanent place. We have a general structure to our meetings, but for the most part we're informal and encourage input from everyone. We meet three times a month for critique sessions. We are willing to help interested romance writers in the area start a new critique group, too." **Dues**: $25 the first year, $20 thereafter. Associate membership is $10. Dues do not include membership to RWA.

INLAND VALLEY RWA

ADDRESS: 2828 W. Via Verde Drive, Rialto, CA 92377
PHONE: (909)823-1477
PRESIDENT: Janelle Denison
ESTABLISHED: 1987
PROFILE: Meets biweekly. 30 members. Meetings held at VCR Extension, Riverside, CA. "We have a business session in the morning and a critique meeting in the early afternoon. We usually spend about three hours in critique sessions." **Dues**: $20. Dues do not include membership to RWA. 25% of members are published. Published members include: Janelle Denison, Brad Koontz, Pamela Scheibe, Linda Carroll-Bradd, Miriam Pace.

SAN DIEGO CHAPTER, RWA

ADDRESS: P.O. Box 22805, San Diego, CA 92192
PHONE: (619)445-4105
FAX: (619)659-6017
PRESIDENTS: Marilyn Forstot, Diana Saenger

ESTABLISHED: 1982

PROFILE: Meets monthly. 150 members. Meetings held at Sports Arena Travel Lodge, 3737 Sports Arena Blvd., San Diego, CA. "Morning workshops on the craft of writing, lunch, a short business meeting and an afternoon program on the business of writing usually with guest speakers or panels. Monthly newsletter "Romantically Speaking" sometimes part of the workshop." **Dues:** $25. Dues do not include membership to RWA. 15% of members are published. Published members include: Dawn Boese, Linda Cajio, Beverlee Covillard, Robin Dieterle, Marian Jones and Jill Limber.

ORANGE COUNTY CHAPTER, RWA

ADDRESS: P.O. Box 395, Yorba Linda, CA 92686-0395

PHONE: (714)498-5619

PRESIDENT: Amy J. Fetzer and Patricia Wright

ESTABLISHED: 1981

PROFILE: Meets monthly. 400 members. Meetings held at Days Inn, 1500 Raymonpave, Fullerton, CA. "Our meetings are from 10:30-3:30. We have workshops for unpublished authors with a published author, book signings, a catered lunch and usually a big-name speaker. We have a mentor program for critiquing with a published author. OCC is the largest chapter in RWA, with over 150 published writers. We offer members an informative 14-page newsletter, and at each meeting we offer speaker tapes, goal-setting challenges, and a lending library. We also have 'how to' book sales four times a year. We keep everyone informed on all romance updates, contests, conferences, editor turnovers, networking news, special events, and anything related to writing and romance." **Dues:** $30. Dues do not include membership to RWA. 33% of members are published.

CONNECTICUT

CONNECTICUT CHAPTER, RWA, INC.

ADDRESS: 80 Hungerford Avenue, Oakville, CT 06779-1711

PHONE: (860)274-3741

PRESIDENT: Sharon M. Schulze

ESTABLISHED: 1986

PROFILE: Meets monthly from September through June. 70 members. Meetings held at Southbury Public Library, Southbury, CT. "After a business meeting, we have a guest speaker(s) who presents programs relating to the fundamentals of writing, or the business of writing." **Dues:** $25. Dues do not include membership to RWA. 23% of members are published. Published members include: Patricia Aust, Nancy Block, Julie Cotler, Mary Jane DeGenaro, Kate Freiman and Christine Healey.

COMMENTS: "Connecticut RWA is a very professional, supportive group of writers. In addition to our meetings, the chapter sponsors an annual writing contest. We also have a Published Author's Forum which meets on a monthly basis to address the specific needs of our published members."

FLORIDA

FIRST COAST ROMANCE WRITERS, INC.

ADDRESS: P.O. Drawer 1680, Fernandina Beach, FL 32035
PHONE: (912)264-2103
FAX: (904)641-3282
PRESIDENT: Sandra Shannon
ESTABLISHED: 1992
PROFILE: Meets monthly. 42 members. Meetings held at Florida Community College of Jacksonville, Jacksonville, FL. "Our business meeting is from 1:00-2:00 followed by a workshop, critiquing or a speaker which lasts until 4:00. Every other meeting is devoted only to critiquing." **Dues:** $15. Dues do not include membership to RWA. 10% of members are published. Published members include: Marguerite Smith, Brenda Jackson, Sandra Davidson, Anne Marie Duquette, Vickie King and Carol Otten.

SOUTHWEST FLORIDA ROMANCE WRITERS, INC. 102

ADDRESS: 16150 Bay Pointe Blvd. N.E. B-307, North Fort Myers, FL 33917
PHONE: (941)731-9449

FAX: (941)731-2691

PRESIDENT: B. Joyce Henderson

ESTABLISHED: 1992

PROFILE: Meets monthly. 35 members. Meetings held at president's and vice-president's homes. "We have informal meetings, with RWA business taking up the first hour or so and then we try to devote the rest of the time to critiques. We welcome female and male writers to attend one meeting to 'look us over' before committing. You must be an RWA member to join SWFRW. We offer a lot of support to budding authors and we turn out in force for book signings in the area for all romance writers if informed of place, time and date." **Dues:** $25. Dues do not include membership to RWA. 15% of members are published. Usually holds annual conference at Naples, FL last weekend in October.

TAMPA AREA ROMANCE AUTHORS (TARA)

ADDRESS: P.O. Box 1465, Valrico, FL 33594

PHONE: (813)681-1946

PRESIDENT: Christy Ruth

ESTABLISHED: 1988

PROFILE: Meets monthly. 80 members. "Our meetings are very organized, covering all aspects of the romance writing industry, from basic writing techniques to the business aspects. There is a guest speaker at every meeting. Our critique sessions last an hour, but we have many critique groups operating autonomously." **Dues:** $25. Dues do not include membership to RWA. 25% of members are published. Usually holds quarterly conference in October, November, January and February.

FLORIDA ROMANCE WRITERS INC.

ADDRESS: % Susan McConnell Koski, President, 2000 N. Congress Ave., #6, West Palm Beach, FL 33409

PHONE: (407)684-3651

PRESIDENT: Susan McConnell Koski

ESTABLISHED: 1986

PROFILE: Meets monthly. 125 members. Meetings held at Ft. Lauderdale Airport Hilton Hotel. "Our meetings generally consist of a pre-meeting workshop for beginning and intermediate writers, which is held from 9:00-11:00. A general meeting with a luncheon and program is then held from 11:00- 2:00.We also have a small critique group that meets outside of the regular, more formal meetings." **Dues:** $25. Dues do not include membership to RWA. 35% of members are published. Published members include: Heather Graham Pozzessere, Marilyn Campbell, Nancy Cane, Raine Cantrell and Garda Parker. Usually holds yearly conference at Ft. Lauderdale in February.

GEORGIA

GEORGIA ROMANCE WRITERS, INC.

ADDRESS: 530 Saddle Creek Circle, Roswell, GA 30076
PHONE: (770)594-1854
FAX: (770)552-2669
PRESIDENT: Ellen Taber
ESTABLISHED: 1981
PROFILE: Meets monthly. 250 members. Meetings held at Piccadilly Restaurant, Holcomb Bridge Road, Norcross, GA. "We have a business meeting followed by a program that includes a Newcomer Forum, chaired by a published author. Also included are business, technical and market updates." **Dues:** $20. $25 late renewal after May 1. Dues do not include membership to RWA. 15% of members are published. Usually holds yearly conference at Doubletree Hotel, Perimeter North, Atlanta, GA in third weekend in September.
COMMENTS: "GRW sponsors the annual published and unpublished Maggie Awards. All unpublished entries are judged by published authors; final judging is done by romance editors. This chapter is one of the largest and oldest of all RWA chapters."

HAWAII

ALOHA CHAPTER, RWA

ADDRESS: P.O. Box 240013, Honolulu, HI 96824-0013
PHONE: (808)373-2994
PRESIDENT: Lynde Lakes

ESTABLISHED: 1987

PROFILE: Meets monthly. 30 members. Meetings held at Aiva Haina Library Conference Room. "We have great guest speakers and 'how to' sessions at our meetings." **Dues:** $15. Dues do not include membership to RWA. Published members include: Laureen Kwock, Terry Gerretsen, Penelope Neri and Jill Marie Landis.

COMMENTS: "We also have tapes, videos and lots of Aloha."

IOWA

HEART OF IOWA ROMANCE WRITERS

ADDRESS: 1885 E Berry Road, Cedar Rapids, IA 52403

PHONE: (319)365-2488

FAX: (319)365-2488

EMAIL: r.rustand@genie.com

PRESIDENT: Roxanne Rustand

ESTABLISHED: 1993

PROFILE: Meets monthly. 18 members. Meetings held at Cedar Rapids, IA. "Our monthly meetings include speakers who are experts in various fields of interest to romance writers, or who are published authors. We welcome new members, whether published or not, and we provide support, educational opportunities, and wonderful networking possibilities with fellow writers." **Dues:** $24. Dues do not include membership to RWA. 50% of members are published. Published members include: Leigh Michaels, Cindy Gerard, Phyllis Volkens, Chelle Cohen and Janet Ramstad.

IDAHO

COEUR DU BOIS CHAPTER, RWA

ADDRESS: P.O. Box 4722, Boise, ID 83711-4722

PHONE: (208)343-4377

FAX: (208)338-1005

EMAIL: Robin4722@aol.com

PRESIDENT: Janis McCurry

ESTABLISHED: 1991

PROFILE: Meets monthly. 31 members. Meetings held at Boise State University. "Meetings cover publishing information, RWA updates, workshops, speakers, and other romance-related issues." **Dues:** $20. Dues do not include membership to RWA. 39% of members are published. Published members include: Brenda Wilson, Deborah Bedford, Vickie Conan, Karen Finnigan and Robin Lee Hatcher.

COMMENTS: "We have small individual critique groups that form on an as-needed basis and meet as often as is desired by those participating."

IDAHO ROMANCE AUTHORS

ADDRESS: 4255 N. Linda Vista, Boise, ID 83704
PHONE: (208)375-4224
PRESIDENT: Sandra Oakes
ESTABLISHED: 1995
PROFILE: Meets monthly. 15 members. Meetings held at Boise Public Library. "Our meetings are relaxed and informal. The main focus is to be a support group for romance writers. One hour is set aside for discussion of problems or critiquing of members' work." **Dues:** $15. Dues do not include membership to RWA. 20% of members are published. Published members include: Marylyle Rogers, StefAnn Holm and Laura Lee Guhrke.

SOUTHERN IDAHO CHAPTER OF ROMANCE WRITERS OF AMERICA

ADDRESS: P.O. Box 304, Gooding, ID 83330-0304
PRESIDENT: Patricia McAllister
ESTABLISHED: 1988
PROFILE: Meets 4 to 6 times a year. 27 members. Meetings held in Twin Falls, ID. "After a general business meeting, we usually have a guest speaker (not always related to romance—we've had police officers, psychics, etc.) or one or more workshops. The critique meetings are held independently of chapter meeting, usually in members' homes. Our chapter offers published and aspiring writers the opportunity to meet like-minds while improving their own work. Every member is encouraged to contribute—whether by conducting a workshop at a meeting, contributing to our newsletter, or participating in a critique

group. Writers from other genres are welcome, too. We've had many positive comments from nonfiction authors who have attended our meetings and joined our chapter. Our purpose is to encourage, enlighten and support those who choose to pursue their love of writing." **Dues:** $15. Dues do not include membership to RWA. 37% of members are published. Published members include: Marilyn Cunningham, Karen Lockwood, Robin Lee Hatcher, Patricia McAllister, Gloria Pedersen, Sherry Roseberry and Pat Tracy. Usually holds conference at Shore Lodge on the Lake, McCall, ID in October.

ILLINOIS

LOVE DESIGNERS WRITERS' CLUB, INC.

ADDRESS: 1507 Burnham Avenue, Calumet City, IL 60409
PHONE: (708)862-9797
PRESIDENT: Nancy McCann
ESTABLISHED: 1983
PROFILE: Meets weekly. 20 members. Meetings held at 1507 Burnam Avenue, Calumet City, IL. "Our meetings are fairly structured. We read the mail first, and then we take care of any other business. If someone has something to be critiqued, we do this, usually at the meeting's end. We also publish, *Rendezvous*, a review magazine." **Dues:** $10 for six months. Dues do not include membership to RWA. 15% of members are published. Published members include: Anne Douglas, Elizabeth Anderson, Beth Stanley and Diane Petit. Usually holds annual conference at Lisle, IL in in October.

HEART & SCROLL - SPRINGFIELD/BLOOMINGTON IL CHAPTER OF RWA

ADDRESS: 2504 Bedford Drive, Champaign, IL 61820
PHONE: (217)398-6844
EMAIL: k.greyle@genie.geis.com
PRESIDENT: Katherine Grill
ESTABLISHED: 1982
PROFILE: Meets monthly. 20 members. Meetings held at Springfield and Bloomington, IL. "We have a business meeting then a critique session.

Eighty percent of the meeting is devoted to critiquing." **Dues:** $10. Dues do not include membership to RWA. 25% of members are published. Published members include: Julie Kistler, Katherine Greyle and Dorothy Ross.

"LOVE ON THE RIVER" RWA CHAPTER 109
ADDRESS: 17580 Rt 5 W. Road, East Dubuque, IL 61025
PHONE: (815)747-6142
PRESIDENT: Rose M. Onufrak
ESTABLISHED: 1992
PROFILE: Meets weekly. 16 members. Meetings held at Johnson Graphics, East Dubuque, IL. "Our meetings begin with RWA business the third Wednesday of each month, and we have weekly readings and critique meetings. We offer constructive suggestions only. We cannot emphasize how important our support is for one another, but we still critique the work honestly, just never cruelly." **Dues:** $20. Dues do not include membership to RWA. 12% of members are published. Published members include: Jane Kidder and JoAnn DeLazzari.

WINDY CITY ROMANCE WRITERS OF AMERICA
ADDRESS: P.O. Box 3523, Lisle, IL 60532
PHONE: (708)495-4731
PRESIDENT: Stacy L. Verden
ESTABLISHED: 1992
PROFILE: Meets biweekly. 45 members. Meetings held at Lisle Public Library. "We meet twice a month, One meeting is our business and presentation meeting; the other is strictly dedicated to critiques. The mission of this group is to share experiences, extend support and elicit advice on the reading, writing, and the publishing of romance novels. Categories represented in this group are contmeporary, historical, mystery, science fiction and time travel." **Dues:** $20. Dues do not include membership to RWA. 16% of members are published. Published members include: Kit Garland, Cathie Linz, Lindsay Longford, Diana Mars, Susan Elizabeth Phillips, Robin Schone and Margaret Watson.

COUP D'ESSAI ROMANCE WRITERS GROUP

ADDRESS: 411 East Roosevelt Road, Wheaton, IL 60187
PHONE: (708)668-3316
FAX: (708)668-3316
PRESIDENT: Susan Leslie Donahue
ESTABLISHED: 1995
PROFILE: Meets weekly. 10 members. Meetings held at College of Du-Page, Lambert Road and 22nd Street, Glen Ellyn, IL. "Our meetings are informal critique groups." 50% of members are published.
COMMENTS: "New members are welcome."

KENTUCKY

KENTUCKY ROMANCE WRITERS, INC.

ADDRESS: P.O. Box 23414, Lexington, KY 40523-3414
PRESIDENT: Deanna Mascle
ESTABLISHED: 1990
PROFILE: Meets monthly. 25 members. Meetings held at public libraries. Meetings are a combination of roundtable discussions with occasional guest speakers. 40% of members are published. Published members include: Elilzabeth Beverly, Marsha Briscoe, Nicole Jordan, Luanne Jones, Natalie Patrick, and Valerie Kane.

LOUISIANA

SOUTHERN LOUISIANA CHAPTER, RWA

ADDRESS: 1021 S. Bayou Road, Kenner, LA 70065
PHONE: (504)469-7349
PRESIDENT: Gina R. Hutcherson
ESTABLISHED: 1987
PROFILE: Meets monthly. 100 members. Meetings held at Tulane University Campus. "Our meeting format consists of a short business meeting followed by a program of speakers—authors, agents, editor, and others in the business. We devote about 45 minutes of each meeting to critique sessions. SOLA is a very successful chapter, growing by leaps,

and each year our conference continues to grow larger as we strive for writing excellence and publication." **Dues:** $15. Dues do not include membership to RWA. 25% of members are published. Published members include: Betsy Stout, Jean Wilson, JoAnn Vest, Linda West, Emily Toth and Deborah Martin. Usually holds annual conference at Embassy Suite Hotel, New Orleans, LA in November.

NORTH LOUISIANA ROMANCE WRITERS, INC.

ADDRESS: P.O. Box 52505, Shreveport, LA 71135
PHONE: (318)797-0188
PRESIDENT: K. Sue Morgan
ESTABLISHED: 1982
PROFILE: Meets monthly. 55 members. Meetings held at El Chico's on Greenwood Road. "We hold a workshop the first Saturday in October. But our regular meetings begin at 9:00 and last through the afternoon. We offer several critique forums to our members." **Dues:** $20 Dues do not include membership to RWA. 25% of members are published. Published members include: Rosalyn Alsobrook, Rosie Buhrer, Suzannah Davis, Patricia Maxwell, Pamela Morsi, Deborah Perkins. Usually holds annual conference at a selected local hotel the first weekend in March.

MASSACHUSETTS

NEW ENGLAND CHAPTER, RWA

ADDRESS: 98 Dartmouth Avenue, Dedham, MA 02026
PHONE: (617)320-9078
PRESIDENT: Betsy Eliot
ESTABLISHED: 1982
PROFILE: Meets monthly. 100 members. Meetings held at Framingham State College, Framingham, MA. "Our meeting structure is a business meeting followed by a workshop or lecture on writing. Our speakers include published authors, editors and agents. We are a warm group of writers who can help you develop your writing." **Dues:** $20. Dues do not include membership to RWA. 20% of members are published. Published members include: Judith Arnold, Mary Burkhardt, Wendy

Sell More of Your Fiction!

The key to selling your work is getting it into the right buyers' hands.

With constant changes in the publishing industry, it's not always easy to know who those buyers are. That's why each year thousands of writers just like you turn to these indispensable market guides. They offer thousands of markets for your work, with every listing updated each year to give you the most current information on the publishing industry.

1996 Writer's Market
Locate the right buyers for your work among the 4,000 publishers listed here. Each listing includes name, address, editorial needs, pay rates and submission requirements—everything you need to successfully sell your work. #10432/$27.99/1008 pages

1996 Novel & Short Story Writer's Market
Get up-to-the-minute market listings of publishers, contests, conferences and writer's colonies. The publisher listings include name, address, pay rates, editorial needs—everything you need to successfully submit your fiction. #10441/$22.99/624 pages

1996 Children's Writer's & Illustrator's Market
Discover hundreds of markets for your fiction, nonfiction, illustrations, and photos for tots to teens. You'll find insight into current trends, plus publisher listings that include vital information to help you target your work to the right buyer. #10442/$22.99/384 pages

1996 Guide to Literary Agents
This one-of-a-kind resource offers information on 500 agents (fee-charging and non-fee-charging) for literature, television, plays and motion pictures. Plus, answers to the most commonly asked questions about finding and working with an agent, to help you find just the right agent to represent you. #10443/$21.99/236 pages

Turn Over for More Great Books to Help You Sell Your Work!

Fine-Tune Your Fiction and Get It Published
with help from Writer's Digest Books

How to Write Romances
Best-selling romance author Phyllis Taylor Pianka guides you through writing and publishing in this lucrative field. She shares advice on choosing a heroine and hero, how to establish conflict, where and how to submit your work, and much more. #10068/$15.99/164 pages

Writer's Digest Sourcebook for Building Believable Characters
Learn how to create vivid characters who think, hope, love, laugh, cry, and cause or feel pain. You'll artfully construct their human characteristics—physical and psychological—to make them so real they'll climb right off the page. #10463/$17.99/288 pages

The Writer's Guide to Everyday Life from Prohibition through World War II
Add color, depth, and a ring of truth to your work using this slice of life reference. You'll get a glimpse of what life was like back then, including popular slang, music and dance, fashion, transportation, and Prohibition and the Depression. #10450/$18.99/272 pages

The Writer's Guide to Everyday Life in the Middle Ages
This time-travel companion will guide you through the medieval world of Northwestern Europe. Discover facts on dining habits, clothing, armor, festivals, religious orders and much more—everything you need to paint an authentic picture of the time. #10423/$17.99/256 pages

The Writer's Guide to Everyday Life in the 1800s
From clothes to food, social customs to furnishings, you'll find everything you need to write an accurate story about this century. Plus, the entries are dated so you don't invent something before its creation. #10353/$18.99/320 pages

Fill out order card on reverse side and mail today!

Leeds and Stobie Piel. Usually holds annual conference at Hyatt Harborside Hotel in April.

MICHIGAN

GREATER DETROIT RWA

ADDRESS: 533 Walnut Avenue, Royal Oak, MI 48073
PHONE: (810)585-4656
PRESIDENT: Marianne Evans
ESTABLISHED: 1982
PROFILE: Meets monthly. 125 members. Meetings held at at varying locations around suburban Detroit. "We hold a business meeting, have a brief intermission, then reconvene for workshops, a speaker or readings. Sometimes half of the meeting can be devoted solely to critiquing." **Dues:** $24 full, $12 associate member. Dues do not include membership to RWA. 30% of members are published. Published members include: Elizabeth Turner, Jeanne Savory and Joan Shapiro. Usually holds a full day conference every other April.

MISSISSIPPI

MAGNOLIA STATE ROMANCE WRITERS

ADDRESS: 253 Magnolia Trail, Brandon, MS 39042
PHONE: (601)992-9831
EMAIL: RRMallory@aol.com
PRESIDENTS: Sherrilyn Kenyon and Rickey Mallory
ESTABLISHED: 1993
PROFILE: Meets monthly. 20 members. Meetings held at Northside Library, Jackson, MS. "Our meetings are decided in advance according to the need of group members. We always spend 50% of our time on critiques. And we love new members." **Dues:** $20. Dues do not include membership to RWA. 20% of members are published. Published members include: Sherrilyn Kenyon, Deborah Cox, Lorraine Caroll and Suzette Vann.

MISSOURI

MID-AMERICA ROMANCE AUTHORS

ADDRESS: P.O. Box 32186, Kansas City, MO 64171

PHONE: (913)856-8521

FAX: (913)856-8521

PRESIDENT: Val Daniels

PROFILE: Meets monthly on fourth Saturday. 110 members. Meetings held at Prairie Village Community Center. "Usually business meeting, followed by short social time, then program/workshop on some aspect of writing." **Dues:** Determined annually, usually $20-$25. Dues do not include membership to RWA. 20% of members are published. Usually holds annual conference at Kansas City, MO second weekend in February.

COMMENTS: "We also sponsor an annual contest, assist in the formation of critique groups, promote our published authors via a Bookseller Newsletter and other special projects."

HEARTLAND ROMANCE AUTHORS (HERA)

ADDRESS: P.O. Box 544, Peculiar, MO 64078-0544

PRESIDENT: Dyann Barr

ESTABLISHED: 1993

PROFILE: Meets monthly. 30 members. Meetings held at Shoney's Restaurant, 301 South M 291, Lee's Summit, MO. "Our meetings begin with a social hour from 12:30-1:30. The business portion of our meeting is from 1:30-2:30. A program pertaining to different aspects of writing follows." **Dues:** $20. Dues do not include membership to RWA. 18% of members are published. Published members include: Lynne Smith, Paula Christopher and Janis Harrison.

COMMENTS: "HERA was founded to provide a positive atmosphere for both published and unpublished authors. Although HERA is a Romance writers group, we welcome persons interested in all genres of literature."

NEBRASKA

CAMEO WRITERS

ADDRESS: 1864 Eldorado Drive, Omaha, NE 68154

PHONE: (402)493-0322

FAX: (402)493-2706

PRESIDENT: Pauline Hetrick

ESTABLISHED: 1989

PROFILE: Meets monthly. 6 members. Meetings held at Denny's at Westroads, 515 North 98th. "We meet from 10:00-10:30 for a business and RWR discussion, from 10:30-11:30 we have a program, from 11:30-12:45 we break for lunch, and then from 1:00-2:00 we critique works in-progress." **Dues:** $15. Dues do not include membership to RWA. 16% of members are published. Published members include: Sally J. Walker.

COMMENTS: "Cameo's primary emphasis is on mutual support, artistic growth and education. Together we learn how to assess the art and craft of writing, thus growing in self-confidence and *getting published*."

NEW JERSEY

NEW JERSEY ROMANCE WRITERS

ADDRESS: P.O. Box 513, Plainsboro, NJ 08536

PHONE: (201)263-8477

EMAIL: elainibonz@aol.com

PRESIDENT: Elaine Charton

ESTABLISHED: 1984

PROFILE: Meets monthly. 165 members. Meetings held at Holiday Inn, Jamesburg, NJ "Our meetings feature a speaker, booksigning techniques, workshops for beginning, intermediate, and advanced writers (three per meeting in different rooms). Our group is a member of the Mid-Atlantic Books Association. We couple our conference with their tradeshow and produce a bookseller giveaway for the attendees. Also, we fund a quarterly bookseller's guide of upcoming published author releases." **Dues:** $45. Dues do not include membership to RWA. 30% of members are published. Published members include: Linda Cajio, Shriley Hailstock, Nora Roberts, Audra Adams, April Kihlstrom and Nancy Hutchinson. Usually holds annual conference at East Brunswick, Jamesburg, NJ end of September.

NEW MEXICO

LAND OF ENCHANTMENT ROMANCE AUTHORS

ADDRESS: P.O. Box 35024, Albuquerque, NM 87176-5024
PHONE: (505)889-0865
PRESIDENT: Michelle Maytorena Thompson
ESTABLISHED: 1992
PROFILE: Meets monthly. 50 members. Meetings held at Fiesta Restaurant. "Our meetings are fun with lots of networking. We have structure but we're very informal—lots of laughter, clapping, and spontaneous chatter." **Dues:** $25. Dues do not include membership to RWA. 10% of members are published.

NEW YORK

THOUSAND ISLANDS - NNY ROMANCE WRITERS

ADDRESS: 35908 NYS Rt. 3, Carthage, NY 13619
PHONE: (315)493-8389
FAX: (315)493-8389
PRESIDENT: Charlene Goldsmith-Bjelke
ESTABLISHED: 1992
PROFILE: Meets weekly. 4 members. Meetings held at Flower Memorial Library, Watertown, NY. "Our meetings are strictly critique sessions." 50% of members are published. Published members include: Charlene Goldsmith-Bjelke and Nancy K. Hardwick.

NYC CHAPTER, INC., RWA

ADDRESS: P.O. Box 3722, Grand Central Station, New York, NY 10163
PHONE: (212)781-0067

PRESIDENT: Rita Madole

ESTABLISHED: 1986

PROFILE: Meets monthly. 100 members. Meetings held at TRS, Inc. Professional Suite 44, East 22nd Street, 11th floor. "At meetings, we usually have a speaker on a particular research topic, a member's roundtable, and a business meeting. Our critique groups are formed outside of the larger meetings. We sponsor an annual reception in honor of editors (a great networking opportunity!). We also organize signings and many members are very active in regional and national RWA activities." **Dues**: $30. Dues do not include membership to RWA. 30% of members are published. Published members include: Sylvia Holliday, Theu Devine, Diana Havilland, Roberta Gellis and Laura Parker. Usually holds annual conference at Melville Marriott Long Island in March.

LAKE COUNTRY ROMANCE WRITERS

ADDRESS: P.O. Box 26207, Rochester, NY 14626

EMAIL: p.ryanio@genie.geis.com

ESTABLISHED: 1992

PROFILE: Meets monthly. 35 members. Meetings held at Gates Town Hall, Rochester, NY. "Our meetings last about four hours (11 a.m.-3 p.m.), and our format is to take care of the business aspects first. Then we have a 'special' program, and we leave room for critiquing." **Dues**: $15. Dues do not include membership to RWA. 15% of members are published. Published members include: Patricia Ryan, Suzanne Barclay, Kathryn Shay, T. Lucien Wright and Pamela Burford.

COMMENTS: "We're a friendly, supportive group, always eager for new members to join at any level. Our members have won the Golden Heart, Maggie, and Emily awards, and three of us have beome published since joining."

NORTH CAROLINA

BLUE RIDGE ROMANCE WRITERS

ADDRESS: P.O. Box 188, Black Mountain, NC 28711

PHONE: (704)669-8421

PRESIDENT: Yvonne Lehman

ESTABLISHED: 1994

PROFILE: Meets monthly. 12 members. Meetings held at Community College and homes. "At our meetings, we have speakers and critique sessions. In fact, probably one third of our meetings are devoted to critiques. Dues do not include membership to RWA. 5% of members are published. Published members include: Yvonne Lehman, Patricia Hagan, Celia Miles, Jill Jones and Joan Medlicott.

COMMENTS: "We are very excited, but we are still becoming organized."

CAROLINA ROMANCE WRITERS

ADDRESS: P.O. Box 470761, Charlotte, NC, 28226

PHONE: (704)332-8214

FAX: (704)332-5968

PRESIDENT: Peg Robarchek

ESTABLISHED: 1984

PROFILE: Meets monthly, with a variety of critique groups meeting throughout the month. 55 members. Meetings held at Ryan's Family Steak House, Tyvola Road, Charlotte. "We have an education meeting program, followed by a dutch-treat lunch for networking, and then a brief business meeting. We have a separate Published Authors Network with members throughout the Carolinas, plus a Published Authors Committee to assist authors with publicity, book signings, etc. We also have a plotting group which meets to brainstorm plot problems." **Dues:** $20. Dues do not include membership to RWA. 20% of members are published. Published members include: Leigh Greenwood, Dixie Browning, Peg Sutherland and Kay Hooper. Usually holds annual conference at various locations in spring.

HEART OF CAROLINA ROMANCE WRITERS

ADDRESS: 2516 Village Grove Road, Raleigh, NC 27613

PHONE: (919)676-4457

PRESIDENT: Christine Hyatt

ESTABLISHED: 1993

PROFILE: Meets monthly. 23 members. Meetings held at various sites, usually in Raleigh. "There is a variety, from speakers (published authors and experts in field of interest), to basics on writing, to field trips (state archives, costuming, etc.) We meet for approximately 2 hours. Very informal. We only do critiquing if the meeting is about critiquing." **Dues:** $20. Dues do not include membership to RWA. 10% of members are published. Published members include: Julie Tetel and Neesa Hart.

OHIO

CENTRAL OHIO FICTION WRITERS
ADDRESS: P.O. Box 292106, Columbus, OH 43229
PHONE: (614)882-3231
PRESIDENT: Linda Miller
ESTABLISHED: 1987
PROFILE: Meets monthly. 64 members. Meetings held at Gahanna Public Library in Gahanna, OH. "We meet at 1:00 p.m.—the business portion is first, followed by a break, and then we have a program. The programs are on various aspects of writing. Our own members are our best resources, but we also bring in outside speakers who have been recommended." The critique group meets 1 hour prior to the business meeting. **Dues:** $15 per year. Dues do not include membership to RWA. 5.8% of members are published. Published members include: Becky Barker, Janet Ciccone, Judie Hershner, Jane Hinchman, Karen Harper, Laurie Miller, Deb Siegenthal, Kathy Stacy, Mel Jacob, Betty Euton and Linda Swink. Usually holds yearly conference at Radisson Hotel in Columbus in late April or early May.
COMMENTS: "We also sponsor a writing contest in conjunction with our spring luncheon/conference. It is called Ignite The Flame."

OHIO VALLEY RWA
ADDRESS: 72 Cherokee Drive, Hamilton, OH 45013
PHONE: (513)863-6053
PRESIDENT: Linda Keller
ESTABLISHED: 1986
PROFILE: Meets monthly. 60 members. Meetings held at Holiday Inn, Route 42 & Interstate 275, Cincinnati, OH. "We begin a 30-45 min-

ute business meeting, then a small break and we're into our program. Our program lasts about two hours and is writing-oriented or aimed at some aspect of the industry. Our chapter has grown by leaps and bounds each year. After our conference, our membership increases yearly by about 15-20%. We make every effort to continually offer support for both the novice and the published author. OVRWA's main goal is to in educate, support, and encourage authors of women's fiction." **Dues:** $20 OVRWA Chapter. Dues do not include membership to RWA. 15% of members are published. Published members include: Leigh Riker, Jennifer Crusie, Beth Daniels, Michele Stegmann, Annie Jones and Lori Foster.

WOMEN'S FICTION WRITERS ASSOCIATION

ADDRESS: 609 South Washington Street, Millersburg, OH 44654
PHONE: (216)674-9413
PRESIDENT: Lorraine Moore
ESTABLISHED: 1988
PROFILE: Meets monthly. 13 members. Meetings held at Portage Lakes Branch of Akron Public Library, 4261 Manchester Road. "Meetings are generally informal discussions on some aspect of fiction writing. We have several speakers come each year. We occasionally devote entire meetings to critiques. Our purpose is to encourage writers and give them a place to gather with others who understand the problems and pitfalls of women who need/want to write. We hold an annual contest called Great Beginnings." **Dues:** $12. Dues do not include membership to RWA. 28% of members are published. Published members include: Leigh Shaheen, Lorraine Moore, Diana Reep and JoAnne Cassity

OREGON

HEART OF THE ROGUE CHAPTER, RWA

ADDRESS: 223 Granite Street, Ashland, OR 97520
PHONE: (503)482-5084
ESTABLISHED: 1993
PROFILE: Meets monthly. 25 members. Meetings held at Francis Ignatius

Room, Providence Hospital, 1111 Crater Lake Avenue, Medford, OR. "The president presides over our meeting. We have a guest speaker each month with periodic workshop formats.We have separate critique groups operating throughout the year." **Dues:** $20. Dues do not include membership to RWA. 25% of members are published. Published members include: Vella Munn, Mary Lou Rich, Wendy Warren, Stephanie Bartlett and Laura Young.

HEART OF OREGON RWA

ADDRESS: 1140 Waverly Street, Eugene, OR 97401-5235
PHONE: (503)345-0540
PRESIDENT: Joyce-Marie Coulson
ESTABLISHED: 1991
PROFILE: Meets monthly. 70 members. Meetings held at McNutt Room, 777 Pearl Street, Eugene, OR. "We have a business meeting that preceeds our monthly program for writers. We sometimes include other non-romance writers, law enforcement personnel, psychologists, accountants, etc. We sponsor an annual writing competition, Magic Moments, which is open to all unpublished writers. The top five finalists advance to Leslie Wainger, Senior Editor at Silhouette Books for final judging." **Dues:** $20. Dues do not include membership to RWA. 20% of members are published. Published members include: Debbie Macomber, Stella Cameron, Lisa Jackson, Laurie Walker, Annie Sims and Carola Dunn. Usually holds annual conference in Eugene during April or May; other times for one-day workshops.

MID-WILLAMETTE VALLEY CHAPTER, RWA

ADDRESS: 490 Lochmoor Place, Eugene, OR 97405
PHONE: (503)687-8879
PRESIDENT: Sharon Anne Morris
ESTABLISHED: 1987
PROFILE: Meets monthly. 17 members. Meetings held at Salem Public Library, Salem, OR. "We meet the third Thursday of each month (except July and December) in the Salem Public Library. Meetings last from 7-9 p.m., with the first hour devoted to general business, and the last hour we either have a speaker or do critiques. Every third

meeting is strictly a critique meeting." **Dues:** $15. Dues do not include membership to RWA. 30% of members are published. Published members include: Sandra James, Vella Munn, Margaret Westhaven and Joyce Beaman. Usually holds yearly conference at Chemeketa Community College in the Spring.

COMMENTS: "We not only have wonderful speakers at our meetings, but we also make sure we put into practice what we learn. New members are always welcome."

PENNSYLVANIA

WESTERN PENNSYLVANIA RWA CHAPTER 140
ADDRESS: 121 East Jefferson Street, Butler, PA 16001-5901
PHONE: (412)283-3346
PRESIDENT: Kathy D. Kline
ESTABLISHED: 1993
PROFILE: Meets monthly. 18 members. Meetings held at Butler Public Library, 218 N. McKean Street. "Meetings are called to order with motions of acceptance for last month's reports. Industry news is discussed, and then progress reports on each person present is shared. Progress reports are done in a round-robin fashion. Length of time devoted to critiques depends on the writer's request." **Dues:** $25. Dues do not include membership to RWA. 16% of members are published. Published members include: Laurel Ames, Marcy Graham-Waldernville and Selina MacPherson.
COMMENTS: "Our group tries to individualize the need of each writer, whether published or unpublished. We strive to help each other become the very best writer he or she can be. We also hold monthly 'RWA Plus' meetings where most serious critiquing is done. It's a fine way to help polish a manuscript for submission."

CENTRAL PENNSYLVANIA ROMANCE WRITERS
ADDRESS: 560 Maywood Road, York, PA 17402
PHONE: (717)755-5893
EMAIL: g.anikienko@genie.com
PRESIDENT: Ginny R. Anikienko

ESTABLISHED: 1990
PROFILE: Meets monthly. 35 members. Meetings held at Community Room at the Camp Hill Mall. "We start the meeting with any business matters pending. Then we usually have a speaker who'll run a workshop.We meet after the official meeting for group critiques four times a year, or more if members want more." **Dues:** $15. Dues do not include membership to RWA. Published members include: Karen Rose Smith, Ginny R. Anikienko, Donna Grove and Valerie Malmont.

SOUTH CAROLINA

GREENVILLE-SPARTANBURG-ANDERSON WRITERS
ADDRESS: 8B Shore Drive, Greenville, SC 29611
PHONE: (803)269-5747
EMAIL: luv2rite@aol.com
PRESIDENT: Jennifer Bayne
ESTABLISHED: 1994
PROFILE: Meets every other month. 10 members. Meetings held at local bookstores. "We hold very informal meetings, discussing the day-to-day stresses of writing, story ideas, contests, new authors and newly published romances." **Dues:** $20.
COMMENTS: "Critique partners are available. We are a budding chapter of RWA, but are not incorporated at this time."

TENNESSEE

RIVER CITY ROMANCE WRITERS
ADDRESS: 1056 Perkins Terrace, Memphis, TN 38117
PHONE: (901)682-7531
FAX: (901)678-3937
PRESIDENT: Martha Shields
ESTABLISHED: 1990
PROFILE: Meets monthly. 60 members. Meetings held at Lovett's Buffet, Eastgate. "Meetings are luncheons, with a business meeting and a critique or some other program following." **Dues:** $36. Dues do not include membership to RWA. 10% of members are published. Pub-

lished members include: Debra Dixon, Patricia Potter, Patricia Keelyn, Carin Rafferty, Virginia Brown and Peggy Webb. Usually holds annual conference at Adam's Mark Hotel in March or April.

TEXAS

RED RIVER ROMANCE WRITERS
ADDRESS: P.O. Box 4822, Wichita Falls, TX 76308
PHONE: (817)696-1586
PRESIDENT: Mary Duncan
ESTABLISHED: 1993
PROFILE: Meets monthly. 18 members. Meetings held at Kemp Public Library, 1300 Lamar Street, Wichita, TX. "Our critique group meets weekly for an hour or more. We also have regular meetings with guest authors as speakers. Our business meeting usually last only 20 minutes. We send out flyers and notices when we have an author speak, so anyone who is interested may join with us in our learning processes. We have members from several outlying towns, and from Oklahoma. Our members range in age from early 30s to mid-70s. Many different walks of life are represented in our chapter." **Dues**: $18. Dues do not include membership to RWA. 1% of members are published. Published members include: Kathy Ishcomer

UTAH

UTAH CHAPTER RWA
ADDRESS: 6678 South Cristobal Street, Salt Lake City, UT 84121
PHONE: (801)944-8277
PRESIDENT: Alice Trego
ESTABLISHED: 1984
PROFILE: Meets monthly. 50 members. Meetings held at Salt Lake Community College Markosian Library. "Meetings consist of a speaker, either a guest speaker or one of our published or unpublished authors. Also, we hold a short business meeting, followed by lunch. We sponsor an annual writing contest, Heart of the West, which is open to unpublished and published writers from around the country. At the same

time, the chapter's own Golden Gate Pen contest (for URWA members only) is conducted. Winners are announced in November. In the Spring, we conduct a chapter one-page contest, called A Great Beginning. We usually have a fall retreat and a summer barbeque, and a Christmas party." **Dues:** $24. Dues do not include membership to RWA. Published members include: Rebecca Winters, Bonnie K. Winn, Danice Allen, Betina Lindsey, Elizabeth Lane, Florence Bowes, Sherry Brown and Charlene Raddon. Usually holds annual conference first Saturday in November.

VIRGINIA

CHESAPEAKE ROMANCE WRITERS
ADDRESS: Box 5345, Hampton, VA 23667
PHONE: (804)867-7547
PRESIDENT: W. Michelle Fronheiser
ESTABLISHED: 1993
PROFILE: Meets monthly. 45 members. Meetings held at Russel Memorial Library, Cheaspeake, VA. "We have a 45-minute business meeting followed by an hour to two hour program. We have a critique partner/group coordinator that helps match members." **Dues:** $25. Dues do not include membership to RWA. 33% of members are published. Usually holds yearly conference at Hampton Roads area in first weekend of October.
COMMENTS: "We also have two contests yearly: the Lastline Contest, which has a deadline in early August, and the First Peake Contest (based on a scene where hero and heroine first meet), which has a deadline of December 1. For more information send a SASE."

VIRGINIA ROMANCE WRITERS
ADDRESS: P.O. Box 35, Midlothian, VA 23113
PHONE: (804)748-0343
FAX: (804)355-8008
PRESIDENT: Vickie Lojek
ESTABLISHED: 1986
PROFILE: Meets monthly. 200 members. Meetings held at Johnston Willis

Hospital in the auditorium. "We devote the first half hour of our meeting to business and then we go into the program." **Dues:** $25. Dues do not include membership to RWA. 47% of members are published. Published members include: Leanne Banks, Patt Bucheister, Christine Dorsey, Carolyn Greene, Nessa Hart and others. Usually holds annual conference at Williamsburg in April.

COMMENTS: "We sponsor the prestigious annual H.O.L.T. medallion (Honoring Outstanding Literary Talent) for published authors. We also sponsor the Fool For Love contest and the First Line contest. We have annual workshops with writing experts. Past instructors have been Gary Provost and Phyllis Whitney."

WISCONSIN

WISCONSIN RWA (MILWAUKEE AREA)

ADDRESS: 400 N. River Rd., Burlington, WI 53105
PHONE: (414)534-3694
PRESIDENT: Kathy Zdanowski
PROFILE: Meets monthly. 60 members. Meetings held at Midway Motor Lodge. "Our meetings are structured like this: business meeting, breakfast, speaker. There are separate critique groups run independent of monthly meetings. Wisconsin RWA has four area groups throughout the state, which are independent of each other." **Dues:** $20. Dues do not include membership to RWA. 10% of members are published. Published members include: Ana Leigh, Mallory Rush, Ann Justice and Kim Hansen. Usually holds conference in spring and workshop in the fall.

WISRWA—GREEN BAY/FOX VALLEY AREA GROUP

ADDRESS: 200 Lake Road, Menasha, WI 54952
PHONE: (414)722-7418
EMAIL: Whiting942@aol.com
PRESIDENT: Barbra Whiting
ESTABLISHED: 1984
PROFILE: Meets monthly. 130 members. Meetings held at various locations. "Our meetings begin with board news and a market update,

followed by a special program and then a critique session. It's all very informal, though, over lunch. We are a state-wide RWA chapter." **Dues:** $20. Dues do not include membership to RWA. 10% of members are published. Usually holds two conferences: one spring conference, usually in May, near Milwaukee; one fall workshop, usually in September, location varies.

VERMONT

LOWER CAPE FEAR CHAPTER RWA
ADDRESS: 921 Hunting Ridge Rd., Wilmington, VT 28412
PHONE: (910)392-3510
PRESIDENT: Deborah E. Daniel
ESTABLISHED: 1992
PROFILE: Meets monthly. 15 members. Meetings held in Southport and Wilmington (alternating months). "Our regular meeting consists of programs with guest speakers, member-generated material, writing exercises, business necessities, and then we adjourn. We hold quarterly full-length business meeting." **Dues:** $15. Dues do not include membership to RWA. 50% of members are published.
COMMENTS: "Although small, we are an enthusiastic and active group. Visitors are always welcome and an information packet is available. Ours is also a diverse group. Members are currently writing in the following areas of romance or other genres: category romance, romantic suspense, time travel, inspirational and mystery."

CORRESPONDENCE CHAPTERS

OUTREACH INTERNATIONAL ROMANCE WRITERS
ADDRESS: 1140 Waverly Street, Eugene, OR 97401-5235
PHONE: (503)485-0583
PRESIDENT: Jan Minter
ESTABLISHED: 1989
PROFILE: This is an international organization that communicates via newsletter. 260 members. "We meet annually at the RWA National Conference. Our structure is informal, but we do conduct business

and have a social hour. We have a newtworking program through the mail which pairs up critique partners. Our bimonthly newsletter is 20 pages of market news, how-to articles, feature, contest and conference information and member news. We also have an annual writing competition for members only. The top five finalists advance to Kate Duffy, senior editor at Zebra/Pinnacle for judging. Our Resource Directory is the first of its kind in RWA. It's available to Outreach members and is a chock full of invaluable resource material." **Dues:** $25. Dues do not include membership to RWA. Published members include: Antoinette Bronson, Roz Fox, Sheila Holland and Lynn Wilding.

FUTURISTIC FANTASY & PARANORMAL CHAPTER OF RWA

ADDRESS: 6047 Elmwood, Philadelphia, PA 19142

PHONE: (215)729-6746

EMAIL: j.dicanio@genie.com

PRESIDENT: Judy Di Canio

ESTABLISHED: 1992

PROFILE: National Chapter corresponds through mail. 120 members. **Dues:** $10. Dues do not include membership to RWA. Usually holds annual conference in July.

CANADA

ONTARIO CHAPTER, RWA

ADDRESS: P.O. Box 69035, 12 St. Clair East, Toronto, Ontario M4T 3A1, Canada

EMAIL: k.freiman1@genie

PRESIDENT: Kate Freiman

ESTABLISHED: 1985

PROFILE: Meets monthly. 100 members. Meetings held at the Brown School, 454 Avenue Road, Toronto. "Our meetings begin with business discussion followed by 'accolades and activities.' We break and then have lectures by authors, editors, agents, and other experts. Our critique workshops are run by member authors, editors, and other experts." **Dues:** $40 for local members; $21 for long-distance members. Dues do not include membership to RWA. 10% of members are published. Published members include: Dawn Stewardson, Kate Frieman, Margaret Moore, Claire Delacroix, Debra Carrol, Naomi Horton, Jill Metcalf, Gail Whitaker

COMMENTS: "RWA Ontario promotes its member authors with free ads, book signings, etc. We also work at bringing new members and beginning writers up to speed with workshops geared toward the nuts-and-bolts of writing commercial fiction. We have an extensive tape library, and our reference library contains books on writing as well as member authors' books and selling synopses. We welcome long-distance members, published and unpublished, and we keep in touch with them through our excellent newsletter."

MARSHLANDS ROMANCE WRITERS

ADDRESS: 2 Mount View Rd., RR#2, Sackville, New Brunswick E0A 3C0, Canada

PHONE: (506)536-3734

EMAIL: torylebl bnet.nb.ca

PRESIDENT: Victoria (Tory) LeBlanc

ESTABLISHED: 1993

PROFILE: Meets monthly. 10 members. Meetings held at Moncton Museum "Our meetings are held on the last Sunday of the month and include information, education and critique sessions. We also have a bimonthly newsletter called 'Bridges.' Half of the meeting time is devoted to critiquing. Separate critique groups, meeting weekly, are also available." **Dues:** $25. Dues do not include membership to RWA.

COMMENTS: "Marshland Romance Writers is the only RWA group in New Brunswick, Canada. Our members come from across the province. In the two years we've been together, we've had three published writers come and talk about writing and publishing."

GREATER VANCOUVER CHAPTER, RWA

ADDRESS: P.O. Box 1152, Whistler, British Columbia, V0N 1B0, Canada

PHONE: (604)932-4512

FAX: (604)938-0499

PRESIDENT: Rhonda Lott

ESTABLISHED: 1987

PROFILE: Meets monthly. 80 members. Meetings held in Vancouver, British Columbia. "Our meetings last three hours starting with a business meeting, a break for lunch and a guest speaker or hands-on workshop. Critique time varies according to our speakers." **Dues:** $25. Dues do not include membership to RWA. 10% of members are published. Usually holds annual conference at Vancouver or Victoria.

AUSTRALIA

AUSTRALIAN CHAPTER, RWA

ADDRESS: 22 Gleneagles Road, Mt. Osmond, Adelaide, South Australia 5064

PHONE: (08)379-0517

FAX: (08)379-0517

PRESIDENT: Diane Beer

ESTABLISHED: 1994

PROFILE: Meets monthly. Meetings held at 22 Glenedgles Road, Mt. Osmond. "Many members are interstate, so therefore our meetings are still informal. We do critiquing by mail." **Dues:** $15, which covers newsletter. Dues do not include membership to RWA.

COMMENTS: "We love to host overseas writers when they visit."

Contests

ere you'll find a list of annual contests geared toward romance writers. These contests are sponsored by Romance Writers of America chapters around the country, and in most cases you must be a member of RWA to enter.

These contests are listed only to make you aware of what opportunities exist. Since contest information changes year to year, you should always write for guidelines before submitting your work. The contact person on the following list may not be the person organizing future contests, but she usually will know who should receive your entry.

Also, since these contests are run by chapters and usually have only one or two people coordinating them, please make sure to send only appropriate submissions; a flood of inappropriate submissions (i.e., sending the finale of your novel to a first chapter contest) only wastes your time and theirs.

NATIONAL RWA

GOLDEN HEART

SPONSOR: Romance Writers of America

DEADLINE: January 10

FEE: $25. Open only to RWA members.

TYPE OF SUBMISSION: Unpublished manuscript

FORMAT: Synopsis and complete manuscript in standard submission format

COMMENTS: Categories are: Contemporary Single Title, Inspirational, Long Contemporary, Long Historical, Paranormal, Regency, Romantic Suspense, Short Contemporary, Short Historical, Traditional Series Romance and Young Adult.

AWARD: Golden Heart pin for winner of each category

CONTACT: RWA - Houston Office, 13700 Veterans Memorial, Suite 315, Houston, TX 77014. Phone: (713)440-6885.

RITA AWARD

SPONSOR: Romance Writers of America

DEADLINE: January 10

FEE: $25. Open only to RWA members.

TYPE OF SUBMISSION: Published book

NUMBER OF COPIES TO SEND: 5

FORMAT: Book must be published in year prior to award year

COMMENTS: All works in this contest are published works, submitted by either the author, editor, agent or any RWA member

AWARD: RITA Award statuette

CONTACT: RWA - Houston Office, 13700 Veterans Memorial, Suite 315, Houston, TX 77014. Phone: (713)440-6885.

REGIONAL RWA

AWARD OF EXCELLENCE COMPETITION

SPONSOR: Colorado RWA

DEADLINE: Early February

FEE: $10

TYPE OF SUBMISSION: Published novel

NUMBER OF COPIES TO SEND: 3

FORMAT: Anyone can submit the work; it doesn't have to be the author. Books are not returned.

AWARD: First place winners in each category receive a plaque; finalists receive a certificate

CONTACT: Colorado Romance Writers, P.O. Box 20271, Boulder, CO 80308-3271.

CHEMISTRY TEST CONTEST

SPONSOR: San Diego RWA

DEADLINE: November 7

FEE: $15. Open only to RWA members.

TYPE OF SUBMISSION: First reaction between hero and heroine

FORMAT: First 10 pages of scene, plus 250-word setup

COMMENTS: Title of contest may change. Please inquire to Jackie Allen.

AWARD: Awards to top 3 submissions at banquet in April

CONTACT: Jackie Allen, 2287 Juan Street, San Diego, CA 92103. Phone: (619)295-0150.

CLOSE ENCOUNTERS OF THE FIRST KIND CONTEST

SPONSOR: Central New York RWA

DEADLINE: April 30

FEE: $12. Open only to RWA members.

TYPE OF SUBMISSION: First touch between hero and heroine

FORMAT: Scene from unpublished contemporary or historical novel

COMMENTS: All work is read by published authors.

AWARD: Finalist and runner-up receive award. Finalist's manuscript is sent to editor in field of category.

CONTACT: P.O. Box 521, Liverpool, NY 13088

DUEL ON THE DELTA CONTEST

SPONSOR: River City Romance Writers

DEADLINE: October 31

FEE: $15

TYPE OF SUBMISSION: First chapter of unpublished work

FORMAT: Include SASE

COMMENTS: Two categories: contemporary and historical.

AWARD: Silver pin for first place in each category; certificates for second and third

CONTACT: Amelia Bomar, 867 Green Acres, Hernando, MS 38632. Phone: (601)429-3459.

EMERALD CITY OPENER CONTEST

SPONSOR: Greater Seattle RWA

DEADLINE: August 15

FEE: $10. Open only to RWA members.

TYPE OF SUBMISSION: Opening of unpublished contemporary, historical or paranormal novel

FORMAT: First 7 pages.

CONTACT: Greater Seattle RWA Chapter 62, P.O. Box 5845, Belleview, WA 98006

FABULOUS FIVE CONTEST

SPONSOR: Wisconsin RWA

DEADLINE: March 1

FEE: $12 for WisRWA members, $14 for nonmembers

TYPE OF SUBMISSION: Opening scene from an unpublished romance novel

NUMBER OF COPIES TO SEND: 3

FORMAT: Up to 10 pages of a contemporary, historical or romantic suspense novel

COMMENTS: Be sure to include SASE with submission.

AWARD: Winners' names published in RWR. Cash awards for First, Second, Third places.

CONTACT: Donna Kay Smith, 5859 Schumann Drive, Madison, WI 53711

FIRST CHAPTER EMILY CONTEST

SPONSOR: West Houston RWA

DEADLINE: December 20

FEE: $25. Open only to RWA members

TYPE OF SUBMISSION: First chapter of non-published work

FORMAT: Label work for either contemporary, historical or other category.

COMMENTS: Deadlines change each year. Submit inquiry to above address. Manuscript should be double-spaced, Courier 10, 1-inch margins, 25 lines/page, with SASE.

AWARD: First place winner in each category receives silver pin and certificate; second and third receive certificates

CONTACT: Anne Dykowski, 1302 Crystal Hills, Houston, TX 77007.

FIRST IMPRESSIONS CONTEST

SPONSOR: Tampa Area Romance Authors (TARA)

DEADLINE: Mid-March

FEE: $20. $25 for non-RWA members.

TYPE OF SUBMISSION: Prologue and first chapter of unpublished work

FORMAT: Entire submission should be 25 pages or under, with SASE

COMMENTS: Categories are historical, long contemporary, short contemporary, time travel/paranormal

AWARD: First place winner in each category receives critique from acquiring editors; 5 finalists receive certificates

CONTACT: TARA, P.O. Box 1465, Valrico, FL 33594

FIRST KISS CONTEST

SPONSOR: New England RWA

DEADLINE: October 31

FEE: $20, $22 foreign entry.

TYPE OF SUBMISSION: First kiss scene from unpublished work

FORMAT: 1-page setup for scene, 10 pages of scene maximum, standard manuscript format, 9×12 SASE

COMMENTS: Judged by Beth de Guzman, editor for Bantam Books.

AWARD: First, Second and Third place winners receive cash prizes; Fourth, Fifth and Sixth receive recognition

CONTACT: Blanche Marriot, Attleboro Woodworks, Inc., 1476 West Street, P.O. Box 3021, S. Attleboro, MA 02703

FIRST LINE CONTEST

SPONSOR: Virginia Romance Writers

DEADLINE: October 16

FEE: $3

TYPE OF SUBMISSION: First line of unpublished work

COMMENTS: VRW also sponsors the "Fool for Love Contest" and the "HOLT Medallion Published Authors Contest"

AWARD: Winner receives cash award and certificate

CONTACT: Virginia Romance Writers, P.O. Box 35, Midlothian, VA 23113. Phone: (804)741-5384.

FIRST 'PEAKE CONTEST

SPONSOR: Chesapeake Romance Writers

DEADLINE: December 1

FEE: $15 for non-RWA members; $10 for CRW members

TYPE OF SUBMISSION: First meeting of hero and heroine in an unpublished work

NUMBER OF COPIES TO SEND: 3 with SASE

FORMAT: Categories: contemporary romance, general fiction, historical romance.

COMMENTS: Judges are encouraged to mark on copies

AWARD: Partial read by editor, plus $25

CONTACT: CRW Contest Coordinator, Box 5345, Hampton, VA 23667

FOOL FOR LOVE CONTEST

SPONSOR: Virginia Romance Writers

DEADLINE: April 1

FEE: $20

TYPE OF SUBMISSION: First chapter of unpublished contemporary or historical romance

AWARD: First, in each category, cash award and certificate; Second and Third, certificate

CONTACT: VRW, P.O. Box 35, Midlothian, VA 23113. Phone: (804)741-5384.

FROM THE HEART CONTEST

SPONSOR: Heartland of Georgia Romance Writers

DEADLINE: October 1

FEE: $15. Open only to RWA members

TYPE OF SUBMISSION: First chapter of an unpublished contemporary, historical or paranormal romance.

NUMBER OF COPIES TO SEND: 3 with SASE

FORMAT: 20 pages maximum

AWARD: Cash awards to First and Second place winners; certificates to Third, Fourth and Fifth place winners

CONTACT: Elaine Manders, 126 Millcreek Way, Warner Robins, GA 31088. Phone: (912)328-0946.

GOLDEN LEAF CONTEST

SPONSOR: New Jersey RWA

DEADLINE: August 1

FEE: None stated. Open only to RWA members

TYPE OF SUBMISSION: Published books by Region I authors only.

FORMAT: Books must be published between October of previous year and September of year of contest to be eligible (i.e. for '97 contest, between 10/96 and 9/97).

COMMENTS: Categories: best first book, historical, regency, short and long contemporary, single title.

AWARD: Plaques to winners, announced at fall conference in early October

CONTACT: Susan Stevenson, 136 Marlton Road, Pilesgrove, NJ 08098. Phone: (609)769-0306.

GREAT BEGINNINGS CONTEST

SPONSOR: Northwest Indiana RWA Chapter 89

DEADLINE: February 14

FEE: $14. Open only to RWA members.

TYPE OF SUBMISSION: First 5 pages of unpublished romance novel (any type)

CONTACT: Ilse Dallmayr, 51888 Old Mill Road, South Bend, IN 46637. Phone: (219)279-5578.

GREAT CONFRONTATIONS CONTEST

SPONSOR: Lake Country Romance Writers

DEADLINE: October 1

FEE: $20.

TYPE OF SUBMISSION: Conflict scene from an unpublished, book-length romance work

NUMBER OF COPIES TO SEND: 4

FORMAT: 10 pages maximum of a scene where the hero and heroine have an argument and/or are in conflict. It can be the first meeting or another appropriate meeting.

COMMENTS: Every entry critiqued by published authors and award winners. Categories are futuristic/fantasy/paranormal (any length), historical/regency (any length), long contemporary (over 70,000 words), short contemporary (under 70,000 words).

AWARD: 5 awards in each category. Finalist judged by editors in genre.

CONTACT: Nancy Vandivert, 1215 Lake Point Drive, Webster, NY 14580-9585

♥ ♥

HEART OF THE ROCKIES CONTEST

SPONSOR: Colorado Romance Writers

DEADLINE: First week of February

FEE: $20; $30 for written critique

TYPE OF SUBMISSION: 20 pages of first chapter, plus synopsis of unpublished romance work; 10 page limit on synopsis

NUMBER OF COPIES TO SEND: 3

FORMAT: Double spaced, standard manuscript preparations

COMMENTS: Categories: historical; long and short contemporary; paranormal/time travel/fantasy

AWARD: First, Second and Third, plaques; Honorable Mention, certificate.

CONTACT: Tanya Moyer, 35381 County Road FF, Wray, CO 80758. Phone: (970)332-3242.

♥ ♥

HEART OF THE WEST CONTEST

SPONSOR: Utah/Salt Lake RWA

DEADLINE: Mid-August

FEE: $20

TYPE OF SUBMISSION: First 20 pages of published or unpublished general romance.

FORMAT: Indicate if published or unpublished. Judged separately.

COMMENTS: Alternate contact is Alice Trego, 6678 S. Cristobal Street, Salt Lake City, UT 84121. Phone: (801)944-8277.

AWARD: Cash award to finalists.

CONTACT: Linda Young, 288 E. 1090 North, Orem, UT 84057. Phone: (801)221-0780 or (901)221-9148.

HEART TO HEART CONTEST

SPONSOR: San Francisco Area RWA

DEADLINE: Unknown for 1996/1997. Inquire to contact address below

FEE: $20. Open only to RWA members.

TYPE OF SUBMISSION: First meeting scene from unpublished work.

COMMENTS: Categories: contemporary, fantasy/paranormal/futuristic, historical.

CONTACT: Sonia Simone-Rossney, P.O. Box 14612, Berkeley, CA 94712. Phone: (510)649-9618.

H.O.L.T. MEDALLION PUBLISHED AUTHORS CONTEST

SPONSOR: Virginia Romance Writers

DEADLINE: January 1

FEE: $25. No entry fee if RWA member.

TYPE OF SUBMISSION: Published, full-length romantic work.

FORMAT: Send copy of published book.

COMMENTS: Categories: best first novel, religious, romantic suspense, short and long contemporary, short and long historical, Southern theme, young adult

AWARD: Medallion to winners of each category; certificates to other finalists

CONTACT: Vivkie Lojek, P.O. Box 35, Midlothian, VA 23113. Phone: (804)741-5384.

HOT PROSPECTS CONTEST

SPONSOR: Valley of the Sun Romance Writers

DEADLINE: February 1

FEE: $30. Open only to RWA members.

TYPE OF SUBMISSION: Unpublished, non-contracted work.

NUMBER OF COPIES TO SEND: 3

FORMAT: Cover page with author name, address, phone number; RWA membership number, title and category. Include synopsis of up to 10 pages (typed, double-spaced) and 15 pages of manuscript. Also include copy of contest waiver.

COMMENTS: Write for more information

AWARD: Registration paid to annual national RWA conference or $150; picture in national conference book ad

CONTACT: Hot Prospects Contest, 3434 West Greenway #26, Suite 335, Phoenix, AZ 85023. Phone: (602)843-9594.

HOT STUFF CONTEST

SPONSOR: Romance Authors of the Heartland

DEADLINE: July 15

FEE: $20. Open only to RWA members.

TYPE OF SUBMISSION: Sexual tension scene

FORMAT: 5 pages of scene, plus 1-page setup, from unpublished work.

COMMENTS: All finalists receive a certificate and their names appear in ad in RWR. Winners announced at annual conference in September. Two categories: A) contemporary romance, mainstream fiction and mystery/suspense/intrigue; and B) historical/regency.

AWARD: Winner of each category receives 1 year's membership in RAH and subscription to chapter newsletter, *Cheering Section*.

CONTACT: Ginny McBlain, 801 Moore Drive, Bellevue, NE 68005

IGNITE THE FLAME CONTEST

SPONSOR: Central Ohio Fiction Writers

DEADLINE: March 31

FEE: $20. Open only to RWA members.

TYPE OF SUBMISSION: First meeting between hero and heroine, scene from unpublished work

FORMAT: Standard manuscript submission format.

COMMENTS: Categories are contemporary, historical and paranormal

AWARD: First, Second, and Third place winners receive certificate and have manuscript read by editor in their category; Fourth and Fifth receive honorable mention.

CONTACT: Christine Stahurski, 13476 Fancher Road, Johnstown, OH 43031-9325. Phone: (614) 967-8766 (days).

A KISS TO BUILD A DREAM ON CONTEST

SPONSOR: Prairie Hearts RWA

DEADLINE: March 14

FEE: $15. Open only to RWA members.

TYPE OF SUBMISSION: Unpublished scene showing first kiss and the day after

NUMBER OF COPIES TO SEND: 6

FORMAT: Title page with name, address and title of book; 1-2 page setup of scene

COMMENTS: Sponsors unsure if contest will run each year and/or will remain the same

AWARD: First, heart-shaped plaque; Second and Third, certificates; Fourth and Fifth, honorable mention.

CONTACT: Nancy Brandt, 17 Rowena Drive, Urbana, IL 61801-1262. Phone: (217)344-5612.

LOVE IN UNIFORM CONTEST

SPONSOR: Red River Romance Writers

DEADLINE: November 11

FEE: $15. Open only to RWA members.

TYPE OF SUBMISSION: Prologue and/or first chapter of any unpublished romance work

FORMAT: Standard manuscript submission format

COMMENTS: No minimum or maximum page counts on submissions

CONTACT: Contest Committee, P.O. Box 4822, Wichita Falls, TX 76308. Phone: (817)723-4864.

THE MAGGIE AWARDS

SPONSOR: Georgia Romance Writers

DEADLINE: Late spring/early summer

FEE: $20 to GRW members; $25 to non-GRW members. Open only to RWA members.

TYPE OF SUBMISSION: Published or unpublished historical, mainstream, short contemporary or long contemporary.

FORMAT: Published category is open only to Region 3 authors, and limited to books published within the calendar year.

COMMENTS: Send for entry form and guidelines before submitting manuscript.

AWARD: Engraved silver pendant

CONTACT: Lillian Richey, 9145 South Point Road, Shawnee, GA 37104-1988

MOTHERLODE CONTEST

SPONSOR: Colorado West Romance Writers

DEADLINE: September 1

FEE: $20

TYPE OF SUBMISSION: First chapter (up to 45 pages) and synopsis (up to 10 pages)

FORMAT: Standard manuscript submission format

COMMENTS: Three categories: unpublished contemporary, unpublished historical, and unpublished work by a published author

CONTACT: D'Ann Linscott-Dunham, 3427-57.25 Road, Olathe, CO 81425. Phone: (303)323-6662.

NOVEL BEGINNINGS CONTEST

SPONSOR: North Louisiana RWA (NOLA)

DEADLINE: Early December

FEE: $15

TYPE OF SUBMISSION: Prologue and/or first chapter

FORMAT: Entry not to exceed 30 pages total

COMMENTS: In final round, top 5 finalists are judged by an editor and/or agent

AWARD: First, $50; Second, $25; Third, $15; Honorable mentions, certificates. Winners announced at annual conference in March.

CONTACT: Jean Walton, P.O. Box 364, Vivian, LA 71082. Phone: (318)375-2939.

NOW AND THEN CONTEST

SPONSOR: Connecticut RWA

DEADLINE: April 30

FEE: $20. Open only to RWA members.

TYPE OF SUBMISSION: First chapter (up to 25 pages) and synopsis (up to 12 pages) of a work by an unpublished writer or a writer not contracted in the past 5 years

COMMENTS: Categories are "Now" (contemporary romance) and "Then" (historical romance)

AWARD: Cash award to First place winner in each category. Finalist in each category judged by an editor. Winner given an additional cash award.

CONTACT: Marianne Zimmitti, 54 Orchard Hill Road, Branford, CT 06405

PUT YOUR BEST HOOK FORWARD CONTEST

SPONSOR: Inland Valley RWA

DEADLINE: April 1

FEE: $15. Open only to RWA members.

TYPE OF SUBMISSION: First 10 pages of unpublished contemporary romance, historical, paranormal or time travel.

COMMENTS: Author must be unpublished in book length

AWARD: Top 3 entries receive cash awards and are judged by editors in their categories

CONTACT: Inland Valley RWA, P.O. Box 1386, Corona, CA 91718-1386

PUT YOUR HEART IN A BOOK

SPONSOR: New Jersey RWA

DEADLINE: Varies. Inquire at address below

FEE: $20 for NJRW members, $25 for nonmembers

TYPE OF SUBMISSION: First chapter and synopsis of unpublished romance work

FORMAT: Send 30 pages maximum.

AWARD: Plaque to finalist. Finalist read by editor.

CONTACT: NJRW, 278 Wychoff Road, Eatontown, NJ 07724

QUERY ME AWAY CONTEST

SPONSOR: Iowa Romance Novelists

DEADLINE: March 15

FEE: $15, $20 for non-RWA members

TYPE OF SUBMISSION: Query letter and synopsis for unpublished romance work

FORMAT: Letter should be 1-2 pages, synopsis up to 10 pages

COMMENTS: Open to all categories of romance

AWARD: Finalist read by editor. First place, book bag with name and year won; Second and Third, certificates.

CONTACT: Roxanne Rene Erb, P.O. Box 145, Minburn, IA 50167. Phone: (515)677-2200.

READING, WRITING AND ROMANCE FIRST CHAPTER CONTEST

SPONSOR: Ohio Valley RWA (OVRWA)

DEADLINE: December 31

FEE: $15. Open only to RWA members.

TYPE OF SUBMISSION: First chapter of unpublished romance novel

FORMAT: No limit to page count. Although only the first chapter should be submitted, entire book should be nearly complete.

COMMENTS: Winners announced at March conference. Editor reads all finalists.

CONTACT: Pamela Heckel, 488 Compton Road, Cincinnati, OH 45215-4115

SILVER HEART CONTEST

SPONSOR: Monterey Bay Chapter

DEADLINE: August 31

FEE: $20. Open only to RWA members

TYPE OF SUBMISSION: First chapter and synopsis of unpublished romance novel

FORMAT: 40 pages maximum

COMMENTS: Categories: historical, series/mainstream contemporary and time travel/paranormal.

No other source offers so much information and instruction...

on writing...

WRITER'S DIGEST is packed with expert advice that can make you a better writer. Whatever your challenge...from generating plot ideas to overcoming writer's block. Whatever your specialty...from writing poetry to children's stories.

and selling what you write!

In every issue you'll learn the secrets of top-dollar free-lancers. Like how to slant your writing for multiple sales. Negotiate contracts with editors and publishers. And how to make (and keep) contacts that help your career. Find out which markets are hot for your work right now, how much they're paying, and how to contact the right people.

Subscribe today and save 47% off the newsstand price!

AWARD: Winners in each category receive critique of partial manuscript from editor

CONTACT: Suzanne Barrett, P.O. Box 806, Capitola, CA 95010. Phone: (408)427-2275.

SOME LIKE IT HOT CONTEST

SPONSOR: Land of Enchantment Romance Authors

DEADLINE: October 15

FEE: $15

TYPE OF SUBMISSION: First 5 pages of an unpublished contemporary or historical romance novel

FORMAT: Requires title, author, address and phone number on separate title page

COMMENTS: Judged by published authors

AWARD: First, $50; Second, $25; Third, $10. All 3 receive certificates.

CONTACT: Contest, P.O. Box 35024, Albuquerque, NM 87176-5024.

SPICE, SIZZLE AND STEAM CONTEST

SPONSOR: First Coast Romance Writers

DEADLINE: Late August

FEE: $20. Open only to RWA members.

TYPE OF SUBMISSION: Hottest love scene of an unpublished romance novel

FORMAT: Up to 10 pages long

COMMENTS: Open to all categories of romance

CONTACT: FCRW, P.O. Drawer 1680, Fernandez Beach, FL 32035

WHEN HEARTS MEET CONTEST

SPONSOR: Southern Idaho Chapter

DEADLINE: April 15

FEE: $15. Open only to RWA members.

TYPE OF SUBMISSION: First contact scene between hero and heroine

FORMAT: 10 pages maximum; include SASE

COMMENTS: Editor or agent reads winners. All entries are edited.

AWARD: Cash awards to First, Second and Third place winners

CONTACT: Sherry Rosebury, P.O. Box 17, Ucon, ID 83330

WHERE DO YOU GO FROM HERE? CONTEST

SPONSOR: Southwest Florida Romance Writers, Inc.

DEADLINE: September 1

FEE: $15. Open only to RWA members.

TYPE OF SUBMISSION: Scene following a prescribed first line

FORMAT: 10 pages maximum, in standard manuscript submission format

COMMENTS: All winners announced at October conference

AWARD: First place, $25 cash award or option to attend October conference free; Second, $15; Third, $10.

CONTACT: SW Florida Romance Writers, 16150 Bay Pointe Blvd. NE B-307, N Fort Meyers, FL 33917

WINNING BEGINNINGS WRITING COMPETITION

SPONSOR: Valley Forge Romance Writers

DEADLINE: First week of December

FEE: $20. Open only to non-RWA members.

TYPE OF SUBMISSION: First chapter and synopsis of unpublished work

COMMENTS: Categories are contemporary, fantasy/paranormal and historical.

CONTACT: Judy Di Canio, 6047 Elmwood Avenue, Philadelphia, PA 19142

THE WRITE TOUCH: READERS AWARD

SPONSOR: Wisconsin RWA

DEADLINE: January 15

FEE: $20. Open to Region II authors only.

TYPE OF SUBMISSION: Published books by Region II authors. Books must have been published within last year.

NUMBER OF COPIES TO SEND: 5, autographed

COMMENTS: Books will not be returned

CONTACT: Peggy Hendricks, N6331 Raven Road, Fall River, WI 53932. Phone: (414)484-3261.

💗 💗

WRITING 101: THE SYNOPSIS CONTEST

SPONSOR: Coeur de Louisiane

DEADLINE: Postmarked by February 1

FEE: $15

TYPE OF SUBMISSION: Synopsis of book by unpublished writer or published author not under contract for 3 years.

FORMAT: 10 pages double-spaced, maximum.

COMMENTS: Finalist read by editor, agent and multi-published author

AWARD: First place, $100; Second place, $50; Third place, $25

CONTACT: Debbie Hancock, 3319 Peach Street, Alexandria, LA 71301

Nonfiction Magazines and Publications of Interest

*H*ere is a list of references for romance writers. Most can be found at your local bookstore or library, but a few might be more difficult to come by outside of actually writing to the publisher. While this is not meant to be a complete list, it will give you a place from which to begin your research and build upon your writing skills.

AFFAIRE DE COEUR

Affaire de Coeur is one of the few trade magazines devoted completely to romance. It publishes short fiction, industry news, reviews, interviews and how-to articles for writers, and has the added bonus of being printed on recycled paper using soy-based inks.

Subscriptions to this monthly magazine are $30 per year in the U.S.; $55 in Canada. For more information, contact Louise Snead, *Affaire de Coeur*, 3976 Oak Hill Drive, Oakland, CA 94605. Phone: (510)569-5675. Fax: (510)632-8868.

THE ART OF ROMANCE WRITING

Subtitled "How to Write, Create and Sell Your Contemporary Romance Novel," this book by Valerie Parv provides the basic information about just that. Parv also includes a Q&A section, sample writer's guidelines and a bibliography. Available at your local bookstore or library, or from IPG Chicago; 130 pages; $11.95 (paperback).

DANGEROUS MEN AND ADVENTUROUS WOMEN

Edited by Jayne Ann Krentz, this book offers romance writers' views on the appeal of romance. Twenty-two writers challenge the stereotypes and myths surrounding their genre, discussing its positive influences and exploring the unique aspects of romantic literature. Readers are charged to abandon their conventional assumptions about the genre and look at it in a new light. The essays explore "the celebration of female power, courage, intelligence, and gentleness; the inversion of the power structure of a patriarchal society; and the integration of male and female."

Available at your local bookstore or library, or from the University of Pennsylvania Press, 418 Service Drive, Philadelphia, PA 19104-9-6097; 186 pages.

THE GILA QUEEN'S GUIDE TO MARKETS

This "mostly monthly" reference source includes complete guidelines for fiction markets. Every issue covers the markets in detail: address changes, dead markets, conferences, contests, editorial changes, anthologies and publishing news in general. They also publish articles on writing topics and review books and software of interest to writers. The February issue is usually devoted to the romance market.

Single copies are $5 and subscriptions are $28 per year for the U.S., $32 for Canada and $45 for overseas. The *Yearly Index of Markets* is available for $3 plus SASE. *Dead Market Listings* is available for $4. Write P.O. Box 97, Newton, NJ 07860-0097 for information.

GOTHIC JOURNAL

Published bimonthly for writers and readers of romantic suspense, romantic mystery, Gothic romance, supernatural romance and woman-in-jeopardy romance, *Gothic Journal* provides reviews, author profiles, market news, upcoming title lists and more. Of special interest are the drawings and floor plans of manors and castles, both real and fictional. Accompanying these are articles and reviews that take an earnest look at the books in these subgenres of romance.

Subscriptions are $18 for one year (6 issues), $24 Canada, $30 foreign. For more information, write to *Gothic Journal*, 19210 Forest Road North, Forest Lake, MN 55025-9766. Phone: (612) 464-1119.

HOW TO WRITE ROMANCES

How to Write Romances, by Phyllis Taylor Pianka, is part of the Genre Writing Series published by Writer's Digest Books. Pianka covers everything from point of view, plot and setting to story research, manuscript format and common pitfalls writers should avoid.

Available at your local bookstore or from Writer's Digest Books, 1507 Dana Avenue, Cincinnati, OH 45207; 164 pages; $15.95 (hardcover).

HOW TO WRITE A ROMANCE AND GET IT PUBLISHED

Edited by Kathryn Falk, the publisher of *Romantic Times* magazine, this guide includes articles from established romance writers, plus romance editors and agents. Falk's contributors cover all aspects of writing romance, with tips on how to break into publication and boost your sales once you're there. Falk also includes reading lists and bibliographies. Available at your local bookstore or library, or from NAL/Dutton; 515 pages; $5.99 (paperback).

THE HOWDUNIT SERIES

Published by Writer's Digest Books, the Howdunit Series is a line of reference books for mystery and romantic suspense writers, explaining the details of various aspects of police work and criminology in laymen's terms. Current titles are:

Armed & Dangerous: A writer's guide to weapons
Cause of Death: A writer's guide to death, murder & forensic medicine
Deadly Doses: A writer's guide to poisons
Malicious Intent: A writer's guide to how murderers, robbers, rapists and other criminals think
Modus Operandi: A writer's guide to how criminals work
Police Procedural: A writer's guide to the police and how they work
Private Eyes: A writer's guide to private investigators

Available at your local bookstore or from Writer's Digest Books, 1507 Dana Avenue, Cincinnati, OH 45207 for $16.99 each (paperback).

I'LL TAKE ROMANCE!

I'll Take Romance! is the newest magazine about romance fiction. Published quarterly, this magazine includes not only romance book reviews and author interviews, but also columns about fashion, travel, home decorating, royal lovers, and the Aspiring Authors Answer Page. *ITR!* also sponsors a Blue Ribbon Fiction Competition.

Subscriptions are $15 for 1 year (4 issues). For more information, contact ITR!, 145 Noble Street, #14, Brooklyn, NY 11222.

THE LAND OF ENCHANTMENT ROMANCE AUTHORS WRITER'S GUIDE

Published by the Land of Enchantment Romance Authors, a chapter of RWA, this guide is stuffed with essays and advice from established romance writers. Its glossary, reference lists and phrase collections are quite extensive and extremely valuable.

To order, contact LERA at P.O. Box 35024, Albuquerque, NM 87176-5024.

MANDERLY

This mail-order catalog for romance readers makes available a wide variety of women's fiction. In addition, *Manderly* offers books for romance writers (including some of the books in this section) and nonfiction books of interest to romance readers.

Put out by Soda Creek Press, the catalog is free and can be ordered by writing to P.O. Box 880, Boonville, CA 95415-0880, or call 1-800-722-0726.

PANDORA'S BOX

PANdora's Box is the newsletter published by RWA's Published Authors Network (PAN). Although membership to PAN is limited to authors that have published a novel, *PANdora's Box* subscriptions are available to all RWA members. The subscription costs the same for both published and unpublished writers—$20 for one year. The newsletter is published bimonthly, and contains "hard-hitting issue-oriented news and opinions by PAN members."

To subscribe, send a check to PAN, RWA Headquarters, 13700 Veterans Memorial Drive, Suite 315, Houston, TX 77014.

PUBLISHERS WEEKLY

PW is the magazine for news about book publishing and bookselling. It tracks trends, reports on book deals, notes editorial staff changes and media company mergers, publishes reviews and offers a myriad of other ways for you to keep informed about the world of books. It does regular market close-ups, focusing on specific areas of the publishing industry (i.e. religious books, audio books, mystery) and examines romance as part of this.

Most libraries carry *PW*, or you can subscribe for $139 per year. Contact *PW*'s subscription department at P.O. Box 6457, Torrance, CA 90504-9806, or call 1-800-278-2991.

ROMANCE WRITERS REPORT (RWR)

Published bimonthly by the Romance Writers of America, RWR is *the* periodical for romance writers. Subscriptions are included as part of RWA membership, and act as one of the major devices for the RWA network to keep its members abreast of changes in the market. RWR also publishes tip articles and essays written by established writers, contest and conference information and articles by romance editors. For membership information, see the **Organizations, Conferences and Workshops** section.

ROMANTIC INTERLUDES

This bimonthly digest is one of the few magazines that buys romantic short fiction and poetry. *Romantic Interludes* also sponsors ongoing writing contests and seeks stories in holiday settings. To submit work, send a cover letter and SASE with your manuscript. Payment ranges from $25 to $100.

Subscriptions are $18 per year (6 issues). Contact *Romantic Interludes* at P.O. Box 760, Germantown, MD 20875.

ROMANTIC TIMES MAGAZINE

This monthly publication is filled with reviews, news and interviews of interest to the romance reader. Published by Katherine Falk, *Romantic Times* is a full-color, glossy magazine—a big change from it's humble, black-and-white pulp beginnings in 1981. Romance reviews are broken down by category and cover science fiction and mystery releases as well. Each issue also has special features such as photo tours of authors' houses, interviews with male cover models and articles on romantic pursuits (teas, salons, etc.).

Subscriptions are $42 for 1 year (4th Class rate in U.S.), $66 Canada. For more information, write to *Romantic Times*, 55 Bergen Street, Brooklyn, NY 11201. Phone: (718) 237-1097.

THE WRITER'S GUIDE TO EVERYDAY LIFE IN THE 1800'S

Written by Marc McCutcheon, this guide details life in America during the 19th century. McCutcheon covers speech and slang, fashion and hygiene, crime and money, and popular pastimes. There are also chronologies of inventions, events, books, periodicals and music.

Available at your local bookstore or from Writer's Digest Books, 1507 Dana Avenue, Cincinnati, OH 45207; 299 pages; $18.95 (hardcover).

About the Contributors

CONTRIBUTORS TO THE INSTRUCTIONAL ARTICLES

Stella Cameron

Stella Cameron is the nationally bestselling, award-winning author of more than 30 romance novels and novellas. Each of her single-title releases has appeared on the Waldenbooks' mass market and romance bestseller lists, and she is a *USA Today* bestseller. Stella has won Waldenbooks and BookRak sales awards.

A sought-after speaker and teacher, Stella has appeared in these capacities throughout the United States and in Canada, and has served as Writer-in-Residence for the University of Montana at Western Montana Summer Writers' program.

Stella is a contributor to *Dangerous Men and Adventurous Women: Romance Writers on the Appeal of the Romance*, edited by Jayne Ann Krentz and published by the University of Pennsylvania Press.

Stella's current fiction titles include the mainstream contemporary romances *Breathless* (also dramatized for audio), *Pure Delights*, and *Sheer Pleasures*. *Fascination*, *Charmed*, and *Bride* are her most recent historical romances.

Robin Gee

Robin Gee is a freelance writer, editor and film reviewer living in Madison, Wisconsin. Prior to her current work, she edited Writer's Digest Books' *Novel & Short Story Writer's Market* for eight years. In addition to writing the marketing article for this edition, Robin interviewed Tracy Farrell at Harlequin.

Stephen Gillen

Steve Gillen is an attorney with the Cincinnati, Ohio, firm of Frost & Jacobs. Steve's practice is concentrated in publishing, licensing, copyrights, trademarks and related matters. Steve is also a published book author and freelance writer with credits in academic and professional journals as well as trade and general circulation magazines. Steve encourages writers to contact his office with contract questions by phone (513-651-6159) or email (Sgillen@aol.com).

Callie Goble

By day, Callie Goble is a technical writer and a senior member of the Society for Technical Communication. She writes and edits books about computer chips, mechanical "doo-dads," software, banks and various other topics.

By night, Callie is one of the staff on GEnie's ROMEX, in charge of the research discussion area. Her technical education and collection of reference books, on almost any topic and from any era, come in handy for the job.

Callie reads historical romances, science fiction, mystery and nonfiction for the fun of it. She is currently at work on a novel.

Kristin Hannah

Kristin Hannah received an undergraduate degree from the University of Washington and a degree in law from the University of Puget Sound. Her first book, *A Handful of Heaven*, became the first debut historical romance to win both the Romance Writers of America's prestigious RITA/Golden Heart award and the Georgia Romance Writers' Maggie award. Her novels, *The Enchantment* and *When Lightning Strikes* were honored by the RWA as among the ten best romance novels of the year, and *If You Believe* was a RITA finalist for Best Historical Romance of 1994. Her most recent novel, *Waiting for the Moon*, was released in November of 1995.

Kristin lives with her husband and young son in the Pacific Northwest.

Denise Marcil

Denise Marcil is the president of Denise Marcil Literary Agency, Inc., which she founded in 1977. Denise represents a wide variety of commercial fiction and nonfiction, from romances to management books, and specializes in commercial women's fiction. Recent examples of books she has agented are *Inside Job: The Looting of America's Savings and Loans*, by Stephen Pizzo, Mary Fricker and Paul Muolo (a *New York*

Times bestseller); *Maiden of Inverness*, by Arnette Lamb; and *How To Want What You Have* by Timothy Miller, Ph. D.

Denise was formerly an editor with Simon and Schuster, and prior to that, Avon Books. She has been featured in many publications, including *The New York Times, The Los Angeles Times,* the *New Yorker, Business Week Home Office Computing* and *Working Woman.* She has been a trustee of Skidmore College, Saratoga Springs, N.Y., and received that college's Outstanding Alumni Service Award in 1989.

Evan Maxwell

Evan Maxwell is co-author, with his wife Ann, of mysteries, thrillers, romantic suspense novels and nonfiction. Ann Maxwell, who began her career writing science fiction novels, is a regular *New York Times* bestseller under the pen name "Elizabeth Lowell."

Evan's latest novel, which is also his first solo work, is *All the Winters That Have Been*, which he describes as "an unabashed romance."

Karen Morrell

Karen Morrell is an accomplished, award-winning author of both fiction and nonfiction for adults and children. She has been an active member of Romance Writers of America since 1986 and has conducted numerous workshops. She received her B.S. in Elementary Education from Ohio State University and has done graduate work in Special Education at the University of Dayton. Her award-winning novels are *For the Love of Laura* (Janet Dailey Award Finalist), *Wish Upon a Star* (Rocky Mountain Fiction Writers' Award), and *Bachelor for Rent* (Colorado Gold Award Winner), all published by Avalon Books.

Karen is a native of Beavercreek, Ohio, and currently lives in Plano, Texas, with her husband and two teenagers.

Don Prues

Don Prues is the editor of Writer's Digest Books' *Guide to Literary Agents* and the assistant editor of *Writer's Market.* Don, who served as the production editor for this book before assuming his current duties, also teaches a Studies in Fiction course at Xavier University in Cincinnati, Ohio.

In addition to writing the online article for this edition, Don interviewed Marcia Markland at Avalon Books; Ellen Edwards at Avon

Books; Birgit Davis-Todd, Harlequin; Carolyn Marino, HarperPaper-backs; Jennifer Weis, St. Martin's Press; Caroline Tolley, Pocket Books; and Isabel Swift, Silhouette Books.

Nora Roberts

New York Times bestselling author Nora Roberts, whose books are published around the world, is a favorite among booksellers and millions of readers who have made her one of America's leading novelists. The first author ever to be inducted into the Romance Writers of America's Hall of Fame, Nora is the recipient of almost every award given in recognition of excellence in the field of romance writing. In addition to her awards from the Romance Writers of America, she has also received a Lifetime Achievement Award from Waldenbooks and has been honored by B. Dalton Booksellers, the romance magazine *Romantic Times*, New Jersey Romance Writers of America and BookRak Distributors.

In all, Nora has written 99 novels, 89 of which are already published. More than 27 million copies of her books are in print, and they are sold in almost every country in the world. In addition to romance, she has written novels of romantic suspense, mystery, adventure and three historical romances.

Nora is a member of the Romance Writers of America and their Washington, D.C. chapter. She is also a member of Mystery Writers of America, Sisters in Crime, The Crime Writers League of America, Novelists Inc. and the Author's Guild.

Suzanne Simmons

Suzanne Simmons is the bestselling author of more than 30 romance novels. She has also contributed to several nonfiction books on the subject of writing, including *Dangerous Men and Adventurous Women*, edited by Jayne Ann Krentz.

Suzanne has a degree in English literature from The Pennsylvania State University. Before pursuing a fulltime writing career, she taught high school English and then went to work in management for AT&T.

Suzanne's historical romances for Penguin USA's Topaz imprint include *Diamond in the Rough*, *Bed of Roses* and the upcoming *You and No Other*. Her latest release from St. Martin's Press is titled *The Paradise Man*.

Jennifer Crusie Smith

Jennifer Crusie Smith began writing romances as part of the research for her doctoral dissertation. A win in the Silhouette Short Reads Contest led to her first sale in 1992, a Stolen Moments novella called *Sizzle*. She has since authored four Harlequin Temptations: *Manhunting, Getting Rid of Bradley* (for which she won the 1995 RWA Rita Award for Best Short Contemporary), *Strange Bedpersons*, *What the Lady Wants*, and *Charlie All Night*. Her seventh book for Harlequin's Love & Laughter line, *Anyone But You*, will be on the stands in August of '96, and she is currently under contract to Bantam.

Her academic publications include an entry on Ngaio Marsh in the *Dictionary of Great Women Mystery Writers*, an essay on fairy tales in romance fiction in the forthcoming *Scholars on Romance*, and a book of literary criticism on the works of Anne Rice for Greenwood Press.

Jenny has a Bachelor's degree from Bowling Green State University in Art Education and a Master's degree from Wright State in both Professional Writing and Women's Literature; her Master's thesis was on women's roles in mystery fiction. She is currently ABD in the PhD program at Ohio State University with concentrations in 19th-century British and American literature and in women's literature, and her dissertation is on the use of humor in 20th-century Western women's popular literature. She taught in the Beavercreek, Ohio, public school system for fifteen years, first as an elementary and junior high art teacher and then as a high school English teacher, and she now teaches literature and composition at Ohio State University. She is a 20-year resident of Alpha, Ohio, where she shares a Victorian bungalow with her daughter Mollie, three dogs, and three cats. Her main ambitions in life are to graduate from college and to learn to plot, not necessarily in that order.

Shauna Summers

Shauna Summers is an editor at Bantam Books, where she acquires and edits books for the general list and the Fanfare and Loveswept lines. Before working on women's fiction, Shauna worked with Senior Editor Beverly Lewis on such authors as Rita Mae Brown, General H. Norman Schwarzkopf, Jonathan Kellerman, Michael Palmer and Robert Ludlum. Shauna has a Bachelor's degree in English from Brigham Young University and a Master's in American Studies from Boston College.

Malle Vallik

Malle Vallik began her publishing career in 1982 as an editorial assistant with Avon Books of Canada—where she first came across the works of writers like Kathleen Woodiwiss and Joanna Lindsey—and has since been through several more publishing companies as editor, publicist and sales rep. It was in the sales area that she *again* noted how well romances sold, how much of the rack space they consumed and decided that it was the field to be in. (It didn't hurt that Malle fondly recalled a summer spent reading all the Mills and Boon doctor/nurse stories.)

For the past six years, she has been with Harlequin as an editor on the Temptation line, and is developing and acquiring Love and Laughter, a new line of romantic comedies. Malle has also had a romance novel, *Tempting Jake*, published by Harlequin Temptation.

CONTRIBUTORS TO THE MARKET PROFILES

Chantelle Bentley

Chantelle Bentley is the production editor for *Poet's Market* and *Novel & Short Story Writer's Market*, published by Writer's Digest Books. She lives in Batavia, Ohio, with her husband and daughter. Chantelle interviewed Barbara Lilland at Bethany House for this edition.

Anne Bowling

Anne Bowling is a Cincinnati-based freelance writer and a frequent contributor to Writer's Digest Books. For this edition, Anne interviewed Melissa Senate and Leslie Wainger at Silhouette, and Paula Eykelhof at Harlequin.

Alice P. Buening

Alice P. Buening is the editor of *Children's Writer's & Illustrator's Market* and assistant editor of *Artist's & Graphic Designer's Market*, published by Writer's Digest Books. She battles an addiction to romance novels and has a secret crush on Fabio. For this edition, Alice interviewed Gwen Montgomery at Avon Flare and Lucia Macro at Silhouette.

Mary Cox

Mary Cox is the editor of *Artist's & Graphic Designer's Market*, published by Writer's Digest Books. She also freelances as a researcher, copywriter and publicist. Mary frequently interviews authors and other creative types for a local community radio station. She interviewed Ann LaFarge at Kensington for this edition.

Cindy Laufenberg

Cindy Laufenberg is the editor of Writer's Digest Books' *Songwriter's Market*, and is also the editor and publisher of the music magazine *The Ledge*. She is a frequent contributor to other Writer's Digest market books, and also plays bass guitar for the Cincinnati- based band 7 Speed Vortex. For this edition, Cindy interviewed Wendy McCurdy at Bantam Books, Stephen Reginald at Barbour & Co., and Tara Gavin at Silhouette. She also was of great help with much of the editorial aspects.

Glossary of Romance Terms

In the following glossary we've included general publishing terms as well as specific romance terms. The romance terms are set in boldface type.

Advance—Payment by a publisher to an author prior to the publication of a book, to be deducted from the author's future royalties.

All rights—The rights contracted to a publisher permitting a manuscript's use anywhere and in any form, including movie and book-club sales, without additional payment to the writer.

Alpha male—Macho male character, usually portrayed as muscular and handsome, sexist, brash and bold. Example: Rhett Butler from *Gone with the Wind*.

Auction—Publishers sometimes bid against each other for the acquisition of a manuscript that has excellent sales prospects.

Backlist—The list of books a publisher has in print, but which were not published within the current season. Backlisted titles usually get little promotion or publicity.

Beta male—Sensitive, caring male character, usually portrayed as respectful and politically correct, with one or two attractive features (warm eyes, great arms). Example: Tom Hanks's character from *Sleepless in Seattle*.

Bodice ripper—A term usually associated with older historical romances featuring lurid covers showing a man tearing away a woman's clothing. Considered a derogatory term for romance fiction.

Book producer/packager—An organization that develops a book for a publisher based upon the publisher's idea, or that plans all elements of a book—from its initial concept to writing and marketing strategies—and then sells the package to a book publisher and/or movie producer.

Category romance—A novel in which the hero and heroine's relationship is the focus and they are monogamous to one another within the story; published as part of a line (e.g., Silhouette Desire, Harlequin Historical).

Cliffhanger—Fictional event in which the reader is left in suspense at the end of a chapter or episode, so that interest in the story's outcome will be sustained.

Clinch—Cover art involving a man and a woman in an embrace.

Contributor's copy—Copy of a magazine or published book sent to an author whose work is included.

Copyright—The legal right to exclusive publication, sale or distribution of a literary work.

Cover art—Artwork on the outside, or cover, of a novel.

Cover letter—A brief letter sent with a complete manuscript submitted to an editor.

Electronic rights—A nebulous term, the definition of which varies from publisher to publisher. Generally, "electronic" rights refers to the right to publish a work on CD-ROM, computer diskette and online sources.

Erotic—Sexually explicit romance, in which the love scenes are very sensual and descriptive.

Fantasy—Romance novels involving elves, witches, sprites and other such mythical creatures, often set in a medieval world. Fantasy romances usually involve magic in some form.

Futuristic—Romance novels set in the future and involving science fiction elements such as space travel, aliens, high technology.

First North American rights—The right to publish material for the first time in the United States or Canada.

Galleys—The first typeset version of a book that has not yet been divided into pages.

Genre fiction—Fiction that belongs to categories including science fiction, western, mystery, horror and romance. Some genres include subgenres; within the broad genre of romance, for example, there is historical romance, romantic suspense, contemporary romance, etc.

Ghost romance—Romance novels in which one or more of the main characters are ghosts. The ghost is usually the hero or heroine, but can also be the villain.

Gothic—A novel with a decidedly dark, brooding tone, often set at an old estate. A Gothic contains elements of romantic suspense and sometimes even supernatural overtones.

Historical romance—A romance novel usually set prior to 1900.

Hook—The first line, paragraph or page that grabs readers and pulls them into the story.

House—A press or publishing company. (Publishing house.)

Imprint—Name applied to a publisher's specific line (e.g., Owl, an imprint of Henry Holt).

Juvenile romance—A novel geared toward children ages 9-12. Often the protagonist and/or narrator manifests characteristics (jealousy of a sibling, parental resentment, etc.) with which kids in this age group can identify.

Lead books—Single-title books placed at the top of a publisher's list. Lead books receive the most publicity and promotion.

Line—Books grouped together by a publisher which are similar in style, length and cover art. Examples: Harlequin Temptation, Silhouette Desire.

Mainstream—A catch-all category that appeals to a wide range of readers. Mainstream romance doesn't abide by some of the rules of category romance; the ending may not always be a happy one, the hero and heroine may not be monogamous to one another within the confines of the story or there may be secondary storylines. Danielle Steele and Ann Tyler are examples of mainstream romance writers.

Mass market paperback—Softcover book on a popular subject, usually measuring around 4×7 inches and directed to a general audience.

Midlist—Titles on a publisher's list that are expected to garner some sales, but not be blockbusters.

Ms(s)—Abbreviation for manuscript(s).

Multi-cultural romance—Romances involving non-white ethnic characters. Kensington/Zebra's Arabesque line is an example of a line of multi-cultural romances.

Multiple submission—Submitting the same manuscript to several publishers or agents at once. Also known as *simultaneous submission*. Few publishers accept multiple submissions.

Net receipts—Royalty payments to author, based on the amount of money a publisher receives on the sale of the author's book after booksellers' discounts, special sales discounts and returns.

New Age romance—Romances involving aspects of holistic health, astrology, spiritual healing, channeling and other forms of modern mysticism and alternative living.

Novella (also novelette)—A short novel or long story, approximately 7,000-15,000 words.

One-time rights—Permission to publish a story in periodical or book form one time only.

Outline—A summary of a book's contents, often in the form of chapter headings with a few sentences under each one describing the action of the story; sometimes part of a book proposal.

Over 45 romance—Romances involving 40- and 50-something heros and heroines. The characters are often divorced or widowed.

Over the transom—Slang for the path of an unsolicited manuscript into the slush pile.

Page rate—A fixed rate paid to an author per published page of fiction.

Paranormal—Romance novels involving metaphysical or occult aspects, such as mind reading, ghosts, UFOs, etc.

Proofs—A typeset version of a manuscript used for correcting errors and making changes, often a photocopy of the galleys.

Proposal—An offer to write a specific work, usually consisting of an outline of the work and one or two completed chapters.

Pseudonym—A false name assumed when the writer does not wish to have her real name connected with her work. Sometimes, publishing houses insist on authors adopting a pseudonym.

Psychological suspense—A story which focuses not so much on physical action but on the workings of the mind, usually told from the antagonist's perspective.

Query—A letter written to an editor to elicit interest in a story the writer wants to submit.

Regency—A subgenre of historical romance, set in England between 1811 and 1820. Characters are often part of the British aristocracy and are governed by the rigid moral code and etiquette of the period.

Reincarnation—A type of paranormal romance in which one or both of the main characters discovers that they lived a previous life.

Reporting time—The number of weeks or months it takes an editor to report to an author about a query or manuscript.

Reprint rights—Permission to print an already published work after one-time rights have been sold to another magazine or book publisher.

Romantic horror—A romance in which the hero and heroine are brought together and fall in love while battling some evil force, such as a monster, a haunted house, etc.

Romantic mystery—A romance novel in which the heroine is involved in solving some mystery or crime, and usually falls in love with the hero during the course of the investigation.

Romantic suspense—A romance novel in which the heroine or someone close to her is in jeopardy. The heroine and hero work together in ending the danger and foiling the villain, usually falling in love as they do so.

Royalties—A percentage of the retail price paid to an author for each copy of the book that is sold.

SASE—Self-addressed stamped envelope.

Second serial rights—Permission for the reprinting of a work in another periodical after its first publication in book or magazine form.

Serial rights—The rights given by an author to a publisher to print a piece in one or more periodicals.

Simultaneous submission—The practice of sending copies of the same manuscript to several editors or publishers at the same time. Some people refuse to consider such submissions.

Single title—Any book that is not published in a line. Most mainstream romances are single title releases.

Slush pile—A stack of unsolicited manuscripts in the editorial offices of a publisher.

Subgenre—A category within a genre. For example, romantic suspense is a subgenre of romance in general.

Subsidiary—An incorporated branch of a company or conglomerate (e.g., Alfred Knopf, Inc., a subsidiary of Random House, Inc.).

Subsidiary rights—All rights, other than book publishing rights included in a book contract, such as paperback, book-club and movie rights.

Subsidy publisher—A book publisher who charges the author to publisher his/her book, rather than paying the author an advance and royalties.

Synopsis—A brief summary of a story, novel or play. As part of a book proposal, it is a comprehensive summary condensed in a page or page and a half.

Tearsheet—Page from a magazine containing a published story or article.

Time travel—A romance in which the heroine and/or hero is transported to another time.

Tip sheets—Guidelines available from a publisher that tell authors specifically what kinds of stories that publisher is looking for.

Trade paperback—A soft bound volume, usually measuring 5×8 inches, published and designed for the general public, available mainly in bookstores.

Unsolicited manuscript—A story or novel manuscript that an editor did not specifically ask to see.

Work-for-hire—Work that another party commissions you to do, generally for a flat fee. The creator does not own the copyright and therefore cannot sell any rights.

World or World English rights—The rights contracted to a publisher permitting a manuscript's sale anywhere in the world, including the right to license it to other publishing companies in other countries. World English rights limit the publisher to use of the manuscript in the English language only, not translation into other languages.

Young adult—The general classification of books written for readers ages 12 to 18.

EDITOR INDEX

Silhouette Special Editions 170

Over 45: Aegina Press and University Editions, Inc. 98; Avalon 99; Avon Books 102; Ballantine 108; Bantam Books 108, 111; Barbour & Co., Inc. 113; Dutton Signet 120; Fine Books/Dutton, A Division of Penguin, USA, Donald I. 122; Silhouette Books 159; Silhouette Intimate Moments 165; Silhouette Special Editions 170

Paranormal: Avon Books 102; Ballantine 108; Bantam Books 108, 111; Berkley Publishing Group 116; Fine Books/Dutton, A Division of Penguin, USA, Donald I. 122; HarperPaperbacks 142; Kensington Publishing 145; Leisure Books/Love Spell 149; Read'n Run Books 155; St. Martin's Press 156; Silhouette Books 159; Silhouette Special Editions 170

Regency: Ballantine 108; Bantam Books 108, 111; Dutton Signet 120; Fine Books/ Dutton, A Division of Penguin, USA, Donald I. 122; Harlequin Mills & Boon, Ltd. 134; Kensington Publishing 145; Silhouette Books 159; Silhouette Intimate Moments 165; Silhouette Special Editions 170

Reincarnation: Avon Books 102; Ballantine 108; Bantam Books 108, 111; Fine Books/Dutton, A Division of Penguin, USA, Donald I. 122; Kensington Publishing 145; Leisure Books/Love Spell 149; Read'n Run Books 155; Silhouette Books 159; Silhouette Intimate Moments 165; Silhouette Special Editions 170

Romantic Horror: Ballantine 108; Bantam Books 108, 111; Fine Books/Dutton, A Division of Penguin, USA, Donald I. 122; Silhouette Books 159; Silhouette Intimate Moments 165; Silhouette Special Editions 170

Romantic Mystery: Aegina Press and University Editions, Inc. 98; Avalon 99; Ballantine 108; Bantam Books 108, 111; Bookcraft, Inc. 119; E. M. Press, Inc. 121; Fine Books/Dutton, A Division of Penguin, USA, Donald I. 122; Harlequin American Romance 123; Harlequin Intrigue 129; PREP Publishing 155; Read'n Run Books 155; St. Martin's Press 156; Silhouette Books 159; Silhouette Desire 162; Silhouette Intimate Moments 165; Silhouette Special Editions 170

Romantic Suspense: Aegina Press and University Editions, Inc. 98; Avalon 99; Ballantine 108; Bantam Books 108, 111; Bookcraft, Inc. 119; Dutton Signet 120; E. M. Press, Inc. 121; Fine Books/Dutton, A Division of Penguin, USA, Donald I. 122; Harlequin American Romance 123; Harlequin Historicals 126; Harlequin Intrigue 129; Harvest House Publishers 144; Read'n Run Books 155; St. Martin's Press 156; Silhouette Books 159; Silhouette Desire 162; Silhouette Intimate Moments 165; Silhouette Special Editions 170

Time Travel: Avon Books 102; Ballantine 108; Bantam Books 108, 111; Berkley Publishing Group 116; Dutton Signet 120; Fine Books/Dutton, A Division of Penguin, USA, Donald I. 122; HarperPaperbacks 142; Kensington Publishing 145; Leisure Books/Love Spell 149; Pocket Books 152; Read'n Run Books 155; St. Martin's Press 156

Vampire: Avon Books 102; Ballantine 108; Bantam Books 108, 111; Berkley Publishing Group 116; Dutton Signet 120; Fine Books/Dutton, A Division of Penguin, USA, Donald I. 122; Kensington Publishing 145; Leisure Books/Love Spell 149; Read'n Run Books 155

Young Adult: Avon Flare 106; Ballantine 108; Bantam Books 108, 111; Fine Books/Dutton, A Division of Penguin, USA, Donald I. 122

Charlotte 212; Herman Agency, Inc., Jeff, The 213; Herner Rights Agency, Susan, Inc. 213; Mainhardt Agency, Ricia 217; Mura Enterprises Inc, Dee 219; Norma-Lewis Agency, The 219; Picard, Alison J. 220; Pocono Literary Agency, Inc. 220; Russell-Simenauer Literary Agency, Inc. 222; Seymour Agency, The 223; Wreschner, Authors' Representative, Ruth 225; Wright Representatives, Ann 226

Paranormal: Ahearn Agency, Inc. 197; Browne, Pema, Ltd 201; Carvainis Agency, Inc. Maria 201; Curtis, Richard Associates, Inc. 204; Diamond Literary Agency, Inc. 205; Herner Rights Agency, Susan, Inc. 213; Hubbs Agency, Yvonne Trudeau 214; Mainhardt Agency, Ricia 217; Mura Enterprises Inc, Dee 219; Picard, Alison J. 220; Rowland, Damaris Agency 221; Seymour Agency, The 223; Weiner Literary Agency, Cherry 224

Regency: Ahearn Agency, Inc. 197; Browne, Pema, Ltd 201; Carvainis Agency, Inc. Maria 201; Ciske & Dietz Literary Agency 202; Cohen, Ruth Inc. 203; Curtis, Richard Associates, Inc. 204; Diamant, Anita 204; Diamond Literary Agency, Inc. 205; Flaherty, Joyce A. 208; ForthWrite Literary Agency 210; Gislason Agency, The 212; Gordon Agency, Charlotte 212; Herner Rights Agency, Susan, Inc. 213; Hubbs Agency, Yvonne Trudeau 214; Kidde, Hoyt & Picard Literary Agency 215; Klinger Inc., Harvey 215; Mainhardt Agency, Ricia 217; Montgomery Literary Agency 217; Mura Enterprises Inc, Dee 219; Norma-Lewis Agency, The 219; Picard, Alison J. 220; Pocono Literary Agency, Inc. 220; Rowland, Damaris Agency 221; Seymour Agency, The 223; Weiner Literary Agency, Cherry 224

Reincarnation: Carvainis Agency, Inc. Maria 201; Collin, Literary Agent, Frances 203; Curtis, Richard Associates, Inc. 204; Mainhardt Agency, Ricia 217; Mura Enterprises Inc, Dee 219; Picard, Alison J. 220; Rowland, Damaris Agency 221; Russell-Simenauer Literary Agency, Inc. 222; Seymour Agency, The 223; Weiner Literary Agency, Cherry 224

Romantic Horror: Ahearn Agency, Inc. 197; Carvainis Agency, Inc. Maria 201; Collin, Literary Agent, Frances 203; Curtis, Richard Associates, Inc. 204; Diamond Literary Agency, Inc. 205; Eden Literary Agency 206; Flannery, White & Stone 209; Garon-Brooke Assoc., Jay, Inc. 211; Herman Agency, Inc., Jeff, The 213; Herner Rights Agency, Susan, Inc. 213; Mainhardt Agency, Ricia 217; Mura Enterprises Inc, Dee 219; Norma-Lewis Agency, The 219; Picard, Alison J. 220; Pocono Literary Agency, Inc. 220; Seymour Agency, The 223; Wald Associates, Mary Jack 224; Weiner Literary Agency, Cherry 224; Wreschner, Authors' Representative, Ruth 225

Romantic Mystery: Ahearn Agency, Inc. 197; Allen, James, Literary Agent 197; Amsterdam, Marcia, Agency 198; Behar Literary Agency, Josh 199; Bova Literary Agency, The Barbara 199; Carvainis Agency, Inc. Maria 201; Ciske & Dietz Literary Agency 202; Cohen, Ruth Inc. 203; Collin, Literary Agent, Frances 203; Curtis, Richard Associates, Inc. 204; Diamant, Anita 204; Diamond Literary Agency, Inc. 205; Eden Literary Agency 206; Farber Literary Agency, Inc. 208; Flannery, White & Stone 209; ForthWrite Literary Agency 210; Garon-Brooke Assoc., Jay, Inc. 211; Gordon Agency, Charlotte 212; Herman Agency, Inc., Jeff, The 213; Kidde, Hoyt & Picard Literary Agency 215; Klinger Inc., Harvey 215; Larsen, Michael/Elizabeth Pomada Literary Agents 216; Mainhardt Agency, Ricia 217; Montgomery Literary Agency 217; Mura Enterprises Inc, Dee 219; Norma-Lewis Agency, The 219; Picard, Alison J. 220; Pocono Literary Agency, Inc. 220; Rowland, Damaris Agency 221; Rubinstein Literary Agency Inc, Pesha 222; Seymour Agency, The 223; Wald Associates, Mary Jack 224; Weiner Literary Agency, Cherry 224; Wreschner, Authors' Representative, Ruth 225; Wright Representatives, Ann 226

Romantic Suspense: Ahearn Agency, Inc. 197; Allen, James, Literary Agent

373